A Critical Essay on Why Blacks Use the "N" Word, and Whites Are Forbidden

A CRITICAL ESSAY ON WHY BLACKS USE THE "N" Word and Whites Are Forbidden

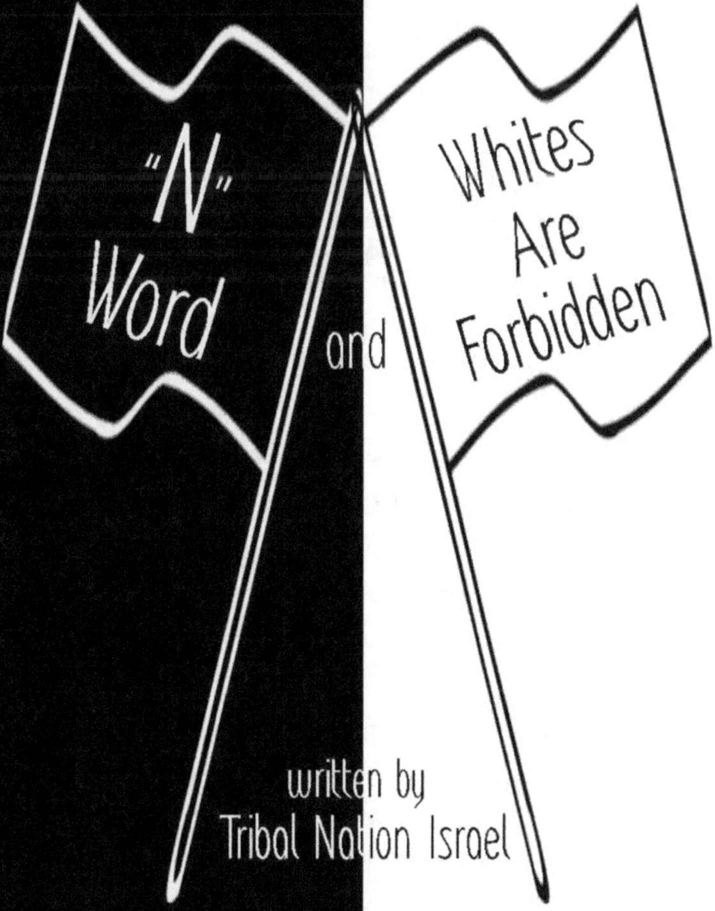

written by

Tribal Nation Israel

Published 2016

Published by

CME Publishings

Milwaukee, WI

Cover Art - The Graphics Lady - TGL

Cover Design - The Graphics Lady - TGL

Typography - CME Publishings

Editing - CME Publishings

Printed Version: ISBN 978-0-9981448-0-1

eBook: ISBN 978-0-9981448-1-8

Manufactured in the United States of America

Table of Contents

Foreword

What's in a name? If that name is *Tribal Nation Israel*, the author of the work herein, there's honesty, candidness, strength, and fortitude. Though the list could go on and on, let's take a moment and examine these few.

Honesty has long since been the missing element in effective communication. People lie for countless reasons - far too many to name. But, the truth of a lie is that it's told to gain the advantage, to sway, to cloud reality in order to get another to believe, act, or feel as the liar does and, in most instances, to then act upon those beliefs and emotions in a manner fitting the liar's purpose.

People lie in groups, individually, consistently, sporadically, subjectively, objectively - motives undisclosed.

How refreshing then, to come across a set of truths told solely for the purpose of moving humanity forward and into a more favorable position for all? To bring out the humanity in the historically inhumane, again, for the betterment of all?

That truth is, "A Critical Essay on Why Blacks Use the "N" Word and Whites Are Forbidden." A freshly penned discussion of one man's take on the reality that is life for so many, himself included. An open letter of sorts for the purpose of moving humanity closer to humane-ness, that key element which separates humans from other species - or at least should.

Candidness has taken a back seat to political correctness. While no human being should be malicious towards another human being, at such a critical time in society as this, correctness for the sake of politics is a luxury we simply cannot afford. If the truth hurts, find out why - the real reason. Then, fix it. Whether it's your psyche, your emotions, or lack of knowledge. Fix it. Then begin to fix others. Make this healing process as contagious as any habit. In fact, make it a habit - something done continuously, religiously, subconsciously.

Strength is not only measured in one's actions at any given moment but over a course of moments - weeks, months, years, decades, lifetimes. It takes discipline to write, to see and research, analyze - write. The craft is difficult enough within itself, but the strength it takes to write in a manner and for the purpose of making better the world of which we live, and the world the next generation and those to come after will live, is writing on a whole other level. It's responsible. One can only hope that it's responded to, and done so in a manner, again, for the betterment of humanity. That moves humanity forward - humanely.

Fortitude is a measure of strength fortified by resilience, grit, endurance, and a number of other like terms. It can be defined as "guts" - having the will to do something unconventional, to talk about the hushed subjects, to bring to light what many would rather keep in the dark. Fortitude. When used in a proper manner and for the right cause, it becomes a most invaluable element of human existence.

No *thing* is all encompassing. But, the truths herein, the revelations, the realities, the historically factual situations that became the circumstances of today, are laid out in such a way to at least begin the conversation of awareness which, prayerfully, will lead to change.

September, 2016

Sista C

Acknowledgments

I give thanks knowing that no matter what race, creed, or color, humanity is better served by us all working together to help shape a better world.

I would like to give my endearing thanks to Sista C. Without her support, expertise, patience, and insightful feedback, writing this essay would have been a very daunting task.

Introduction

I graduated college in 1978 with a Bachelor of Fine Arts degree, just shortly after my twenty-third birthday. Before that time, growing up in the deep, rural south in the state of Mississippi, I was not able to escape the turbulent times of segregation and racial discord between blacks and whites. After I graduated college, I felt inspired to write about it. But, I never envisioned that I'd be writing this essay nearly forty years later, approaching my sixty-second birthday.

First, I would like to point out that in my efforts to explain why blacks use the "N" word and whites are forbidden; it will not be my attempt to uncover the Black Israelite identity and history after the Transatlantic Slave Trade. The true identity of the Black Israelites was lost once our African ancestors became slaves here in America. In this essay, I only make brief mention of our African ancestors as Black Israelite slaves with the hope that those of us who are their descendants will make the commitment to research our historical and biblical roots independent of the subject at hand.

In this essay, one of my main objectives is to focus on how our African ancestors came under the "nigger identity" during slavery. I will also explain my view as to why the nigger word is still so deeply embedded in our culture. My objective is to explain the attitudes and behavior that became shaped under it, and why it is utterly unacceptable and forbidden for whites to call us niggers as they once did during slavery. In doing so, I will make a determined effort to shed further light on the history of slavery and how it still affects us in this country. I will also express my point of view on how racism today affects our social, economic, and political struggle, and how it affects us in the judicial system and law enforcement, as well as how the bias and racist elements within the white news media support it. As proof of this, I have explored some of the events that occurred as I wrote this essay.

However, it would not have been possible for me to conclude this work if I attempted to address each recurring race tragedy that takes place from day to day. Yet, none of them should be swept under the rug of racial conflicts between black America and white America. Within this essay, I have also biographically chronicled some of my personal experiences to reflect that I have dealt with racism up close and not just afar.

The history of slavery and the day-to-day racial conflict between blacks and whites reinforce the theme of this entire essay. But first, there are three areas of conflict of familiarity between blacks and whites that I must set forth as a brief synopsis that will resonate as part of the theme as to why whites are forbidden to use the 'N' word and why it is so deeply rooted in our black expression. These three areas of conflict between blacks and whites exist as the pendulum of our back and forth argument on racial justice and injustice in America. They can be laid out in three words: crime, economics, and politics -- the three critical battlegrounds that exists as the central issues of our racial discord. Under close examination of the racial history between blacks and whites, it shouldn't be difficult for one to conclude why blacks have been cast as the staunchest accusers of racist attacks by whites and why whites have been cast as the staunchest deniers of racist attacks against blacks.

The realm of our struggle to co-exist becomes a vast, unsweep-able terrain to comb for racist landmines, making one of the most difficult conflicts between the two races, defining what makes one a racist and what makes one not a racist. Do blacks simply play the infamous race card when there's no racism to be found, or do whites conveniently accuse blacks of pulling the race card in order to deflect actual racism? It has proven itself to be a very elusive and difficult problem to nail down without finding an emotional, fever pitched objection from both sides.

To examine just how irrational and distorted the race war has made both sides, let's take, for example, a public relations situation where an unfortunate, but all too often hostile dispute occurs between a store clerk and a dissatisfied customer. In this scenario, white vs. white and black vs. black in the clerk and customer dispute. Most likely, the charge between both would be trying to prove who was the biggest jerk. However, if we were to take the same dispute and change it to black vs. white; it quickly becomes a charge of hate and racism. Typically, the pattern in the dispute is that the black individual is charging racism, and the white individual is charging hate.

It's a very flawed position for either side to take because not in every situation of a dispute with whites, can blacks judge it as racism. And, not in every dispute with blacks can whites judge it as hate. It is my belief that the history of slavery is at the root of this generational conflict between the two races.

The point I am trying to uncover is that there are human disputes that have nothing to do with hate and racism. But, do such baseless charges dispel the deep problem of racism that exists between whites and blacks? This is a clear example that demonstrates just how broken race relationships are between the two races.

In spite of this, my position is to approach the problem by defining what racism is in order to define what racism is not. Racism can be defined as a bias and negative attitude against another race of people that displays itself in action, expression, and perception. If one's motive is to do physical harm or discriminate against someone because of race, creed, or skin color, this can be defined as racism. To express hate and dislike for another race, regardless of what medium, can be defined as racism. If someone is of the perception that other races are inferior to their own because of a different racial makeup, this can be defined as racism. And, to add even further to the argument, no one can support racism and racist views against another race and then rationalize that they are not racist.

Anyone who supports racism and racist views against their own race, disqualifies themselves from having any genuine integrity on the issue of human rights and equality. They commit treason against humanity by occupying a self-serving position that only points towards their own narrow minded interest and not those that affect the entirety of their race. When we take an in-depth look at black and white race relations, regardless of blacks as the accusers and whites as the accused, they both have a very difficult time owning the responsibility as to when racism exists and when it does not. And, as I said earlier, the fight mainly takes place on three critical battlegrounds: crime, economics, and politics.

On the crime battle field, racist white leadership in the criminal justice and political system, supported by the racist, white, news media will not take responsibility when blacks are wrongly accused of committing crimes. Their deep fear is that it threatens to weaken their strong, racist indictment of having branded blacks as a race of criminals. It's by far one of the deepest, racist perceptions about blacks that racist whites do not want threatened or overturned.

But, on the other side of the argument, when blacks are the culprit of criminal acts and black civic leaders take a passive approach and not the responsibility of forcibly calling it out, it only reinforces the perception that as a race, we support black criminals or appear to be uncooperative with law enforcement while black criminals go on exploiting it no differently than when they use wrongful convictions that become overturned in the criminal justice system, as a distractor to commit even more crimes.

Because of the brutal history of slavery and the racist laws that still live on after its abolishment, blacks have developed a deep mistrust in how white law enforcement police their community. But, the unfortunate tragedy that too often follows it is that it allows criminals less resistance as they continue preying upon our neighborhoods and communities. Blacks can ill afford to continue allowing our open and raw emotions to blind our sense of reason into total indifference with the law. It only causes further harm by disallowing us any form of protection under the law.

On the economic battlefield, racist whites will not take responsibility for the financial devastation that slavery caused the black race here in America. Racist white's deepest fear is that if they were to take responsibility for the catastrophic, economic loss that slavery cost us, it would weaken their strong, racist indictment of having branded us as a lazy, unproductive, welfare dependent race existing solely off of white taxpayers. However, while they conveniently sweep slavery under the rug, they continue to benefit from the massive, inherited, economic generational wealth that it produced. Racist whites fear that if they admit to this fact, it would further legitimize black's dependence upon government welfare assistance and other social entitlement programs.

This brings us to the battleground of politics where the ultimate, racist attitude is that blacks are solely responsible for having been conquered into slavery and are, therefore, suffering the horrific, economic plight it's caused us. But, on the other hand, they have a very difficult time understanding why blacks are so bent on revolt and wanting to overthrow their racist ass, white system of government.

One of the prime, motivational forces behind it is that blacks have been left to struggle in generational poverty and racist oppression from the time of physical slavery. And now, under this welfare system of poverty, the same racist, white supremacy ideology of hate and discrimination that robbed us of our economic independence under slavery, is still condemning us for welfare dependency while they remain steadfast in holding onto all the financial wealth and power by keeping with the same racist politics that forced us into this catastrophic and destitute condition.

Therefore, the government welfare system for blacks exists like a small, fragile, safety-net, lingering just above a spider web that keeps sinking us closer to becoming totally, economically destroyed and devoured in poverty. For this reason alone, while it might give the masses of poor, struggling, African Americans a very faint life pulse, government welfare dependency will never bring us beyond this point.

Racist whites are such hypocrites. They complain about and cry over welfare dependency by poor, African Americans, knowing they would never receive us with open arms if they were to see us achieving the same level of higher education, economic independence, and political power that they benefit from, but condemn us as a race for not having attained. But, as a race, achieve we must!

We have to set a very high aim at doing it. If the racist ass, white system of power thinks that blacks on government welfare is at their expense, we should be determined with all of our fiber, to find out how they'd react to seeing blacks achieve equality in social, economic, and political power.

Slavery and the residuals of slavery ignited the demise and the destruction of the black family. But, despite the ongoing racism set against us, we cannot continue allowing it to become an escape clause to shed our own family responsibility. We must continue holding onto the strong, family values that we have and the ones that we have lost, we must find them. The ones that we don't have, we must work to build. And, even though we were forced into a devastating, educational, economic, and political disadvantage from the time of slavery, we still have to work with all of our power, and determination to gain the resources to change the poor, educational, economic, and political system that continues failing us while this racist ass, white system continues building more prison systems to incarcerate our youth.

When racist whites finally find themselves having to downsize their own social, economic, and political power as we massively begin building our own, only then will they truly understand what *at their own expense* means when it comes to their racist complaints and criticisms of blacks.

The battlefield of politics is where racist whites have always held their greatest resistance and indifference towards blacks. Their racist white system of government is the designed vehicle that financially powerful, racist whites in the private business sector use to do their bidding in influencing every facet of laws governing the rights of its citizens. The capitalist system of America, in part, being controlled by very powerful racists, plays a vital role in undermining and in tilting the balance of power in government. Let the real truth be told, for both, it's a mutual admiration society with its reoccurring issues of built in racist laws, having no genuine interest in allowing blacks equal rights of participation. Their racist ass, white supremacist attitude is that the slave has no legitimate or intelligible voice on human rights and, therefore, no rights of participation in the political affairs of his master.

To recap, I have initiated the theme that will resonate throughout this entire essay as to why whites are forbidden to call blacks niggers and why it is so deeply rooted and used in our black expression.

As I started my journey on writing this essay, I found myself running into a great deal of uncertainty about which path to take on how the 'N' word should be treated when being applied to the black race here in America. Suddenly, I found myself on a forked road leading in three different directions.

After agonizing over it, I finally had to make a decision. Do I continue straight ahead and just follow the more paved and safe path of the main stream argument to simply reject the "N" word usage altogether because of its deep and painful ties to slavery and racism? Or, do I veer to the left and try and defend its usage within the pop culture of our black, urban youth who possess no definitive answer for their usage of the "N" word? Or, do I veer to my right and make my own, independent decision and not so quickly be influenced by the two other widely held positions without attempting to research the historical root of the "N" word that took hold during our slave captivity in America?

After further agonizing over it, I finally decided to follow the latter route, and then try to explain how the "N" word became connected to our African ancestors, and how it now has a very profound effect on our culture, attitude, and behavior. It will also be my effort to explain how the "N" word is tied to the racist white man's wicked and brutal history of slavery.

I also would like to express that when I speak so profoundly about the racist white man's wicked and brutal history of slavery against African Americans, I am not attempting to indict the entire white race. Regardless of race, all human beings are individuals and should be treated as such and not be wrongly blamed for the unjust acts of others -- it is something the racist ass, white man himself will never acknowledge or practice.

During the abolitionist movement to abolish slavery, there where whites who risked their lives alongside blacks. It happened again during the civil rights movement. Throughout the history of mankind, human beings have had their moral character tested and have unified against the tyranny and inhumanity against mankind. The historic election of Barack Obama as the first African American president with the crucial support of both Hispanic and white liberal voters, and the overwhelming support of the liberal white news media became more than just an attempt at bridging race relations. It became an idea of liberal whites wanting to triumph over the racist filled and discriminatory filled ideology of extreme, right wing conservatism.

Despite the racist opposition President Obama will have faced within the political system, it is my belief that at some point in history, just like the civil rights movement, the white liberal effort to help elect an African American president will stand as one of the long awaited births that was conceived out of the abolitionist movement to end slavery. It will stand as one of white liberal's finest hours in the history of American politics. And, it would be a travesty to Black and white race relations to try and tarnish this historical event because of Black and white racial conflicts which, tragically, will continue in this country mainly because of the ongoing history of racist, white supremacy ideology. America has proven just how great exceptionalism exists in the face of racial conflict. How much longer will it take for these United States of America to transform the ideas of American exceptionalism into an unbroken chain that will, in deeds, live up to civilization's greatest, united melting pot of all races and Nationalities? We've made great strides in electing a person of color as president. And, when a woman becomes elected president, it can only take us further.

Therefore, I feel that we should never allow whites who oppose racism against people of color to become victims of self-guilt because of the history of slavery. In our efforts to justify our position on racism, the one thing we should never want, as black people, is for white supporters against human injustice to fall into biased race traps along with us, created by our own fallibility to misconstrue some issues to be of racist context when the facts don't bare it. It does a great disservice to them and us. We should be strongly opposed to forcing whites into pandering up to us out of race guilt. We should never want them to end up supporting us in the same kind of racist and bias attitudes that we say we oppose.

We do not want whites who support our struggle to be forced into unreasonable obligations or attitudes of support just to prove themselves of not being racist. In this respect, whites shouldn't have to prove themselves any more than the rest of humanity because the potential for hate and racism lurks in the minds of all human beings. So, we need not do anything but be individual human beings in rebuking it because anything other than this would be asking humanity to try and behave as though it is perfect when all human history bares proof that it is not.

For me to deal with this issue, I must attack white, racist, supremacy ideology with a vengeance because, at its core, with any complacency or generational lapse in fighting, it has the potential power and ability to influence all of white America. For centuries, it has been embedded so deeply into the fabric of white culture. Therefore, it is my position that no white person can be totally outside of its grip in some form, no matter how slight. It is also my position that, on the surface, racism by whites is fueled in larger part by their deep, biased, hate and resentment of black people because of our racial makeup and, below the surface, their failed attempt at trying to keep us oppressed under the bondage of physical slavery. Racist whites also deeply despise us because they do not want to relinquish any of the vast wealth they were able to amass by having enslaved us. Abolishing Jim Crow laws was another key issue that helped to rev up their racist hate for us. It is my position that in large part, black's hatred of whites is based not so much on race, but more on our reaction to racist whites hating us because of our race. Our hatred becomes even more compounded only because of the cruel and brutal history of slavery and how we are continuously reminded of it in the way we are still being oppressed.

Our hate is based on the slave experience and the continued racist oppression within this white system of government and society. The racist argument to try and connect blacks to the same kind of race hate and racism as whites only serves further in distorting the historical facts and conflict between the two races. The argument is especially hollow in America seeing how, in the world of racist white theology, blacks, from the beginning of our slave history in America, became whitewashed into submitting ourselves under the worship of a white, blue-eyed, blonde haired Jesus. Even if Jesus Christ could be proven to be a white man, blacks have no religious history that supports them rejecting Jesus Christ based on the color of His skin. But, racist whites have a known history of having replaced black religious figures with white religious figures.

In America, the masses of blacks accepted white skin on the god they serve. But, if Jesus Christ were to appear in this day and age, as a Black man, more whites would have a problem dealing with it than blacks, had he appeared as a white man. I am quite sure that many of us have heard the phrase, "let's have an honest conversation about race." So, as part of my introduction, I will try to provide what I feel to be a small bit of untouched conversation about race.

For the record, if I speak the truth, why should I have to be made to feel guilty or apologetic? Shouldn't it be the other way around for the one who is actually at fault? If I have to lose white friends over socio-economic and political truths regarding the betterment of my own race, all I can say is that it was a great friendship while it lasted.

During the course of my life I have met whites who have befriended me and likewise, I have done the same. What this means is that I have accepted them as not being racist against the Black race. And, hopefully, they have accepted me as not harboring hatred against the white race. But, even when blacks and whites befriend one another, it is very difficult for them not to feel a little guarded in their feelings. Blacks, in the back of their minds, feel a bit guarded in their feelings because of the racism that still exists among whites. And, likewise, I feel that whites, in the back of their minds, feel a bit guarded in their feelings because of the hate that still exists among blacks towards whites.

I have tried to guard myself against racist whites, yet there have been countless times when I have, in the company of other Africans, referred to racist whites in terms that I would not do in the face of whites that I have befriended. I am certain that this is also true for whites when out of the company of blacks that they have befriended. What is there to be said about blacks and whites who declare themselves to be friends, but express themselves differently when they are out of each other's company? Are those same whites actually racist towards blacks? And, are those same blacks actually haters of whites? If so, there's nothing left to debate.

It only takes common sense for someone to be aware of their own prejudices. However, is it possible for some blacks and whites, when out of the presence of one another, to show their disgust for the perpetrators of hate and racism by using words themselves that are racist in context, yet not be racist or haters themselves? The reason I refer to whites as the actual racist and blacks as the actual haters of whites, is because this is what I believe they are by true definition within our racial conflict. It is my belief that much of white racism towards blacks is attributed to whites because of their attitudes towards the racial makeup of blacks.

It is also my belief that much of black's hatred towards whites is attributed to blacks mostly because of white's being racist towards blacks. But, for blacks and whites who might express themselves differently outside of each other's company regarding their relationships with each other, are they being superficial or simply showing a conscious regard to how sensitive the issue of race is between blacks and whites? Even if this is the case, it is my opinion that we should continue to be very mindful to keep such expressions in the company of our own respective races.

It is also my opinion that if we deem ourselves as not being racists or haters when we express ourselves a certain way about race, we should be very careful that the person or persons that we are expressing ourselves to are not actual racists (whites) or haters (blacks) in their practices and beliefs in regard to race. Here, I have tried to give a little untouched perspective on an honest conversation about race. Unfortunately, there will always be gray areas between black and white race relations. But, in many ways, no different than it was during the time of slavery, whites and blacks who have built genuinely, good relationships, still have to find ways to protect them apart from the ones that they have built within their families, as well as those they have built within their respective races.

We have to learn how to trust that we will defend each other against hate and racism within our own respective races and not make ourselves the supreme judges over one another on how we go about achieving it. I would also like for the reader to know that before they begin the journey of reading this material, I made a conscious effort to use the "N" word in such a way as to allow white America to look into the shadows and capture the essence of how we see ourselves seeing racist ass, white America see us as niggers within this deep, historical racial divide that began during our enslavement. I would also like for the reader to be prepared to learn that much of the language that I use in painting this literary picture is extremely brutal and harsh.

With this having been said, I will begin my journey by expressing A Nigga's Prelude.

A Nigga's Prelude

> "Because of the racist ass white man's hate and despise of me as a black man in America and the hate of so many ignorant ass niggas on the street, every day that I awake by the mercy of God, it seems as though I'm always trying to avoid death at the hands of my enemies. Everything I say, everything I do, every place I go, drama is a common theme for me, nigga. Always having to live on the edge of fear of what the next nigga might say or do. Always having to live on the edge of fear of the racist ass white man's system destroying me. So why are there so many other niggas so unwilling to allow another nigga the right to live and die in peace? Instead, nigga, you would rather make drama a common theme for me, nigga.
>
> Against my will, nigga, I have been forced into having

to pick up the sword of violence, nigga. Yet, I still try to do everything within my power to live in peace and not war with other niggas. I have the racist ass white man to deal with for that, nigga. I am always only one swift heartbeat away from trying to end the threat of my enemies, nigga. Drama is a common theme for me, nigga. And you and the racist ass white man would be wise to know it, nigga."

Chapter One

The Beginning of the "N" Word in America

First, allow me to make one thing very clear about the "N" word. Because of its ties to the cruel history of slavery and racism, blacks who use it, as well as those who oppose it altogether, will never accept nor allow it to be used in mainstream society. Otherwise, we cannot take the "nigger" word out of our culture any more than the racist ass, white man is able to wipe away his own evil and perverse history of slavery. We cannot educate the "nigger" word out of our culture. We will not be able to politicize the "nigger" word out of our culture. We will not be able to morally preach the "nigger" word out of our culture. The black race will always remain divided over the usage of the "nigger" word, with a great part of the masses under the influence of its usage. Even though the black race in America came to this position under very tragic circumstances, yet it can never nullify how the "nigger" word is now being used as a part of our black experience and expression. Regardless of how some of us reject the "nigger" word while others embrace its usage, controversy will always exist about the usage of the "nigger" word within our culture.

For the African race that suffered under slavery in America and elsewhere under European rule, the double standard that we have set for ourselves and the white race in the usage of the "nigger" word will always remain a paradox. If there is any ounce of truth that makes rational sense of it, I believe it can be found in the enslavement of the black race by racist ass, white, slave-masters.

One of the most important things that we must understand is that if our history books are accurate, we should have the same integrity of not trying to distort the facts so to fit our own charges or to support our position. And whenever history has been recorded with biased efforts to hide historical facts, it becomes the responsibility of historical scholars to show a moral obligation to uphold the integrity of human history by exposing such corruption. When historical research bares facts to support the information it lays out, then as truth seekers we should move forward with better understanding and enlightenment, even when the facts don't lead us to what we are after. However, in this case, I believe that what I am looking for can be found hidden within all the ill effects that slavery had on our African ancestors in America.

I believe that if we are to get to the real truth about why blacks in America use the "nigger" word, we first must understand how the origin of the "nigger" or "niger" word became a part of the language of the racist ass, white, slave-master. We have to also understand how the initial meaning of the "nigger" word was being applied to African slaves in America. Then we must learn and understand how the "nigger" or "niger" word evolved into the most offensive racist epithet to ever be smeared on a single race of people.

I have included Encyclopedia excerpts on the origin of the "nigger" or "niger" word. Wikipedia, the free encyclopedia states that "nigger" is a noun in the English language. The word originated as a neutral term referring to black people as a variation of the Spanish/Portuguese noun "negro," a descendent of the Latin adjective "niger" (color black). Often used slightingly by the mid-20th century, particularly in the United States, it suggests that the target is extremely unsophisticated. Its usage had become unambiguously pejorative -- a common ethnic slur usually directed at blacks of Sub-Saharan African descent. I will make reference to more of this information later in my text. But for now, there are some very perplexing attitudes among the masses of our race in defense of their usage of the "nigger" word. And, let's just say more specifically among blacks living here in America.

The first thing we do is apply a double standard to its usage. On one hand, we give ourselves a free pass to use it amongst ourselves, while demanding that we not be charged a penalty by those outside the black race. On the other hand, we make our feelings resoundingly known that whites are utterly forbidden to call us niggers. The "N" word also carries ambiguous meaning for blacks. It means that we have created an unexplainable attitude that we have been able to make the "nigger" word into something positive alongside all of its negative representation. We have it in our minds that we are able to use the "nigger" word to lower status or to raise status just by simply changing the spelling and pronunciation from "nigger" to "nigga" or "niggah."

The "nigger" word is a very perplexing contradiction for us. We label the "N" word as being so offensive and explosive with racism when used against us by whites and other races that do not share nor integrate into our black urban experience and expression of street language. Some blacks and Hispanics have forged a relationship among themselves where they will call each other the "nigga" or "niggah" word without any feelings of offense. I believe that it has much to do with the fact that Hispanics have a common thread with blacks whereas racist whites quickly perceive some of them as niggers because of the diversity of their racial makeup. But when the "nigger" word is used against blacks outside of this ethnic circle, it becomes the most derogatory and demoralizing, racist epithet that a white person or any other race can label us with. Yet, by giving ourselves a free pass to use the "nigger" word on ourselves, it places us into a very difficult struggle of trying to explain and justify it. Such attempts have bared no rational answer. In fact, it becomes a contradiction when trying to defend our own moral stance against racism and racial slurs.

Labeling ourselves with the "nigger" word is by far one of the most damaging charges set against our own moral credibility in opposing racism and racial slurs. Our usage of the "N" word in our culture forces our moral scholars and educators back into an inescapable corner of embarrassment. It continues because of the growing usage of the "nigger" word among the urban masses of African Americans, both young and old alike. And now with the birth of gangster rap music, the "nigger" word has taken an even deeper hold within the culture of black America. In other words, the "nigger" word has created its own sub culture. It has left our moral scholars, historical scholars, civic leaders, and educators struggling for answers as to why the "nigger" word is so engrained in our culture.

But, if we are to understand and begin to shed light on this very perplexing and growing conflicting phenomena, we must first begin by pointing out how slavery adversely affected black people in America. When slavery deprived us of our human rights, it meant that we were considered as no more than chattel. As a race of people, we were deprived of education, along with social, economic, and political power. With no human rights, the Declaration of Independence held a "VOID" stamp for black people. And because the Declaration of Independence was being decreed mostly by racist ass, white, slave owning politicians full of racist hypocrisy, only a flawed Constitution would follow it. In fact, when the Constitution was first drafted in 1787, it included Articles that actually promoted the slave trade. For example, Section 9 of Article 1, supported the importation of slavery and did nothing to regulate it for 20 years. Section 2 of Article 4 didn't allow for citizens to help slaves in their efforts to escape from their owners. As chattel property, they had to be returned to their slave-masters.

To add even further quotes from Encyclopedia resources, President James Madison successfully negotiated, under Section 2 of Article 1, slaves being perceived as "others" (persons), was designated to be added to the total of the state's free population at the rate of three fifths of their total number. It was done as a political ploy to establish the state's official population for the purpose of apportionment of congressional representation and federal taxation. It increased the power of southern states in Congress for decades, effecting national policies and legislation. The planner elite (agricultural and political supporters of slavery) dominated the southern congressional delegations and the United States presidency for nearly 50 years. Quoting further from the same sources, the protection of slavery in the Constitution strengthened the political power of southern representatives, and the South's economy had links nationwide. As the historian, James Oliver Horton, noted, "Slaveholders and the commodity of crops of the South had a strong influence on United States politics and economy. New York City's economy was closely tied to the South through shipping and manufacturing. By 1822, half of its exports were related to cotton." Horton said, "in the 72 years between the election of George Washington and the election of Abraham Lincoln, 50 of those years (had) a slave holder as President of the United States, and, for that whole period of time, there was never a person elected to a second term who was not a slave holder."

After reading this information, it should be obvious that owning our African ancestors as "nigger" slaves held very powerful financial and political influence for the racist ass, white, slave-master. Unless these racist ass attitudes change when we address the Declaration of Independence and the Constitution of this country, it will continue to be steeped in racist hypocrisy. The James Madison negotiation under Section 2 of Article 1, is a prime example of the kind of blueprint that the racist ass, white element within this government uses to gerrymander voting districts, along with its continued efforts to destroy a fair voting process.

It's the same now, as it was during the time of President Madison. The mission is, when not exploiting blacks as "niggers," to keep us powerless while attempting to destroy us as "niggers." We have been disenfranchised in this country from the onset of slavery. With our African ancestors not being recognized under the laws of the land, the racist ass, white, slave-master effectively destroyed the foundation and the institution of the black family as our African ancestors arrived as slaves in America and other parts of the world. And to keep us held at the very bottom of this slave system, slavery birthed an attitude of sustained racism and brutal hate towards Black people in America that has not been felt or equaled by any other race living in this country.

Slavery is a product of human exploitation and racism, but, during ancient times, slave owners didn't solely employ racism as the driving force to oppress and enslave other races. In those earliest of times, slavery and human bondage were not always tied directly to the attitudes of racism. Instead, warfare, gender, and class status had much to do with slavery. The oppressors even made people of their own race slaves of indentured servitude.

In ancient times, slavery became more of a violation of human rights and equality, largely based on becoming enslaved from war, and being perceived as inferior because of gender and class status, and ultimately, a demand for human labor. When the enslavement of black people first came to the shores of America, the critical difference of those ancient times was that in some of those societies, the oppressors allowed the indentured servants to work their way out of their slave contracts. But with slavery here in America, such contracts for black slaves were rare to mostly non-existent. Unlike those ancient times when warfare, class status, labor exploitation, and gender were a driving force of slavery, in America racism, itself, rapidly became the driving force to keep slavery intact.

Before racism began to take its deepest foothold of maintaining slavery, the "nigger" word was not being used so much as the battle cry and motivational tool to denote racist hate of black slaves. In the initial stages of slavery in America, the "nigger" word was being used as more of a general term by these racist ass, white, slave-masters to identify all black slaves. Slavery in America was also tied to the long and ancient practice of oppressing people not solely on race, but because of a lower perceived class status of inferiority.

During the 17th and 18th centuries, some historians estimated that nearly half of all white immigrants who made up the English colonies of North America were indentured servants. But, in 1619, about 19 Africans arrived in America near the shores of Jamestown, Virginia, as a result of having been seized by Dutch traders from a captured Spanish slave ship. According to the historical research that I referred to earlier, these 19 or so Africans were treated as indentured servants. The only reason for this was that the Spanish slave traders were said to have had a ritual of baptizing slaves before leaving Africa. Because these slaves were perceived as Christians under English laws, they were exempt from slavery -- a very fortunate occurrence. Yet, this small number of black, indentured servants were pale in comparison to the large colony of whites who were allowed to serve out their contracts of indentured servitude and regain their freedom.

With slave codes pushing to become the law of the land in order to keep blacks enslaved, racist white slave-masters used these same slave codes to deny black slaves indentured contracts. Therefore, they would have to remain under the servitude of slavery for the duration of their lives. By 1640, Virginia had recorded its first case in which a black, indentured servant, John Punch, was sentenced to a life of slavery.

But going back to 1619 when the first African slaves arrived at the Virginia colony, they were said to have been referred to as "negars" by a man named John Rolfe. Later, in English, the spelling was changed and pronounced "negar," or "neggar" in what was called the Northern Colony. The "N" word was said to be pronounced this way in New York under the Dutch in metropolitan Philadelphia's Moravian and Pennsylvania Dutch communities. In New York City, the African burial ground was said to be known by the Dutch name "Begraafplaats van de Negar" (Cemetery of the Negro); the word "Negar" was also said to have had an early occurrence in Rhode Island around the year 1625. The Word "Negar" was being used as an alternative word for African Americans. Among Anglophones, the Word "Nigger" denoted black skinned and was said to not always have had a derogatory intent behind the usage.

The "nigger" word in some nineteenth century English literature was said to have been expressed without racist connotations, such as the Joseph Conrad novel, "The Nigger of the Narcissus" (1897). Great contemporary writers such as Mark Twain and Charles Dickens made reference to the "nigger" word in their works. Dickens distinctly used the word "kaffir" in place of nigger. There also exists other early history that suggested the "N" word was not a term used exclusively for blacks. It has been said that around the early 1800's to the late 1840's in the western United States, the word "nigger" was used among mountain men. During this period, it was said that the "N" word being spelled as "niggur" was used among mountain men to describe their rugged way of life. These groups were said to have included Frenchmen, Indians, Anglos, and also Mexicans.

But, before going any further, just to quickly show how out of perspective something like this would be for niggers of today, niggers think so low of the racist ass, white man that if we inadvertently, in the heat of the moment, have a slip of the tongue, and use the nigger word to attack a racist ass white person in the worse derogatory sense of the word, we will immediately see it as incongruent to their racist ass image, because niggers inherently see the racist ass, white, slave-master and his racist ass descendants, as being even lower than the worst nigger. For niggers, it would be like saying something favorable about the racist ass, white man. Therefore, we penalize ourselves with a sense of regret for having said it.

Getting back to the issue at hand, according to the same historical research, George Fredrich Ruxton regularly used the word “niggur” as part of the “mountain man” lexicon and did not appear to have had a pejorative intent. The words “travler,” “marm,” and “this niggur’s no travler,” are from a passage from Ruxton’s “Life in the Far West,” and the writer was said to be referring to himself.

Other historical examples can be seen in the works of Victorian writer Rudyard Kipling in “How the Leopard Got His Spots,” and, “A Counting Out Song.” Another writer of the time, P.G. Wodehouse, used the “N” word in his works, “Nigger Minstrels,” and “Thank You Jeeves,” and as late as 1980’s Agatha Christie book, “Ten Little Niggers,” first published in London, 1939, and continued to be printed under the original title. The title was later changed to read as “Ten Little Indians.” This popular children’s book of its time goes, “Ten little nigger boys went out to dine, one choked his little self and then there were nine. Nine little nigger boys sat up very late, one overslept himself and then there were eight. Eight little nigger boys traveling in Devon, one said he’d stay there and then there were seven. Seven little nigger boys chopping up sticks, one chopped himself in halves and then there were six. Six little nigger boys playing with a hive, a bumblebee stung one and then there were five. Five little nigger boys going in for law, one got in Chancery and then there were four. Four little nigger boys going out to sea, a red herring swallowed one and then there were three. Three little nigger boys walking in the zoo, a big bear hugged one and then there were two. Two little nigger boys sitting in the sun, one got frizzled and then there was one. One little nigger boy living all alone, he got married and then there was none.” The obvious use of the “nigger” word in satirical form to describe how black people were to be portrayed is clearly unmistaken.

Even though the “nigger” word was adopted in some of George Ruxton’s literary works to describe a kind of pioneer spirit, it would be blacks alone who would not be able to escape the “nigger” word tied to all the hate of the racist ass, white man as well as the other races who have adopted the same racist attitude towards African Americans and black Africans, elsewhere.

Mark Twain wrote about the black persona which had been mostly made up of the slave culture. It was said to not have been as a pejorative, but used the “nigger” word in his literary work to depict the black experience. Twain’s usage of the “nigger” word gets right at the heart of his own fascination with the slave culture and its effect on his own literary expression.

I have used these literary writers as an example of how the "nigger" word was used to depict blacks and the culture of slavery. It is my goal to try and help the reader understand how the "nigger" word became so easily adopted within the slave culture, and how it has been passed on from generation to generation. Within the slave owners' society, using the "nigger" word as a single name for all African slaves was a common expression among whites, and African slaves became very submissive and obedient in their acceptance of their "nigger" name. I believe my claim is strongly supported by the fact that the "nigger" word is still so deeply rooted in our modern day, African culture.

Chapter Two

Nat Turner & John Brown

Racism toward blacks as "niggers" in America started to take its deepest root during the beginning of the slave revolts of the 1600's, and all the way up to the American Civil War of 1861. According to the same historical research, it was estimated that at least two hundred separate slave revolts and conspiracies took place from the 1600's to the end of the Civil War in 1865. It was during these slave revolts that the "nigger" word became the racist outcry for lynching and the constant spilling of the blood of black slaves.

Slave uprisings had become a serious threat to the enforcement of slavery. There could have been no greater notoriety placed on the "nigger" word than the violent and bloody slave revolt of 1831. A black man by the name of Nat Turner, a literate slave who believed that he had been given the power of spiritual visions carried out what he might have felt to be a divine plan. In South Hampton County, Virginia, he organized a rebellion in which he and his followers went on a violent killing spree. By the time it was over, about 60 white people were dead, with most of the slain being women and children.

Nat Turner and his followers were eventually caught and killed. Nat Turner was hanged, beheaded, skinned, and dismembered by the racist white militia. In the aftermath of the revolt, many innocent slaves were also beheaded, and their heads jammed onto stakes and placed along crossroads as an act of revenge and to strike fear and send a clear message that a new reign of terror had now replaced the old. These racist ass, white, wicked bastards were the Isis of slavery in this country - a truth which should not be allowed to go glossed over.

The white racist militia ended up murdering over a hundred other, innocent, black slaves who had no involvement in the slave uprising. The retaliation was also said to have included the whipping and beating of hundreds more innocent slaves in a violent effort to strike such fear that it would dissuade future attempts of insurrection. But, in that county and throughout the country, Nat Turner had forever made the "nigger" word the most hated and despised name to be used by racist ass, whites in their efforts to see all Black slaves exploited, brutalized, and destroyed. And, nearly three decades later, arose a white abolitionist by the name of John Brown.

Nat Turner and John Brown could well be seen as two interchangeable forces in the violent revolt against slavery. Both men existed so parallel to each other in the sense that they felt they were given divine intervention from God in their fight against the evil deeds of slavery.

Brown's conviction that the only way to overthrow slavery was with armed insurrection could well be seen as a fulfilled prophecy. In 1856 Brown, with his followers, led an attack at the Battle of Black Jack and then at the Battle of Osawatomie. Brown and his followers killed five slave supporters at Potawatomi. In 1859, he organized a liberation movement made up of some of his white followers, three of them his own sons, and several African slaves, and then led a bold attack upon a federal armory in Harpers Ferry, Virginia, in an effort to seize weapons to help arm slaves in their revolt. But, the attempt failed. One of Brown's sons escaped. Two were killed, and Brown was captured, tried, and hanged for treason against the Commonwealth of Virginia.

Brown was a Northerner and some historians support the position that Brown's attack at Harper's Ferry was a key turning point in the fight to end slavery, and played a critical role in igniting the final spark that caused the South's succession from the union the following year, which was the beginning of the civil war. Regardless of what racist, white America thought of Brown during his generation, or even now, for enslaved niggers, Brown had to be God sent to have had the courage to stand up against the powerful and evil forces of slavery. If there is any such thing as a white man with the spirit of a rebellious nigger inside of them, then John Brown was it. And, if the country was in search of a white man who had repented for all of the evil deeds of slavery, John Brown represented this as well. Even though Abraham Lincoln's place in history is the Emancipation President, John Brown's place should be the bold, white martyr who signed the declaration of civil war against the south by being the first white man to fire the union's shot against slavery.

Brown, in my opinion, was the greatest white radical liberator of his time. And to try and label him as the first American terrorist as some racist, white historians have attempted, would be the same as labeling the entire Union army's efforts to end slavery as an act of terrorism. Brown was not some backwoods, self-absorbed, fanatic, zealous, pious preacher looking to bring attention to himself as some racist ass, white historians would have us to believe. Brown was not some misfit outside of the intellectual and aristocratic order of his time. President Ulysses S. Grant's father was an apprentice under Brown's father.

Nearly the entire country was steep in violent hate and racism against enslaved Africans, but John Brown was one of the rarest kinds of shining lights, trying to sustain a conscious for white America against slavery. John Brown is owed a tremendous debt that racist, white historical scholars are very unwilling to pay because of his bold and defiant stance against the status quo of a slavery supported government. If there is any white man that should be honored alongside Black historical leaders at any time in this country, blacks owe John Brown a tremendous, freedom felt debt of honor and gratitude.

During Brown's time in history, there existed other exceptional, white, anti-slavery abolitionists such as Elijah Lovejoy and Charles Turner Torrey. It was as though many slaves feared receiving freedom more than these men feared giving up their lives at the hands of racist violence by showing the courage to help deliver their freedom to them. But, in the end, it would be Brown alone who would find himself front and center to face the brute forces of hate and racism coming from all the slavery supported states of the country.

Brown was tried and hanged just over a year before the attempt at succession began and the start of the civil war. At the time, the United States was still a union held government but did nothing to pardon Brown from his death sentence. Racist, white historians, would like to have Brown portrayed as a political terrorist, but I see him as one of the true, authentic, great American heroes of the abolitionist movement to end slavery. If President Andrew Johnson's 1865 declaration was a signature point of the ending of the civil war, then I believe that it was by divine fate that it occurred in the same month and day that John Brown was born.

If I were ever to have a statue built alongside a white man, I would want it built alongside a white man such as John Brown. We were both born in May. Brown was born May 9, 1800, and I was born May 6, 1954. I take it to be a sign to follow the path of those who fight against racist oppression. The day of our births can be divided equally by three. And, just as Jesus Christ rose on the third day, men like Brown will rise up in the world and have their voices heard against the evil injustice of mankind. Not through any well-conceived and hidden vanity in life, but because of the light of truth shining on human vanity that brings men to humility.

Malcolm X, another Black, radical leader of his time, was born May 19, 1925. The date of his birth can be divided equally by three, which I take as having been another sign regarding the arrival of a defiant, radical, rebellious leader set against the racist order within this system of government.

During the abolitionist movement, Brown strategized and collaborated with Black leaders such as Frederick Douglas and Harriett Tubman. He stood up against the notorious, Fugitive Slave Act passed by the united, racist, white government mandating that free states assist in the return of escaped slaves. The Fugitive Slave Act also penalized anyone aiding and abetting in their escape. Brown in his effort to fight this act, founded a militant group called The League of Gileadites to prevent slave capture. The organization was founded in Springfield, MA, and it was said that no escape slaves were returned to slavery from Springfield.

Brown was once quoted as saying, "Nothing so charms the American people as personal bravery. Blacks would have ten times the number [of white friends than] they now have were they but half as much in earnest to secure their dearest rights as they are to ape the follies and extravagancies of their white neighbors and to indulge in idol show, in ease, and in luxury." Is it not prophecy that Brown's words still utters true 'til this very day?

One should not misunderstand Brown's criticism. It was not his assertion that blacks didn't deserve the same material and financial wealth as whites in this country. What Brown was saying is that slavery had psychologically conditioned niggers into thinking inferior of themselves. Instead of niggers defining their own identity under liberty and freedom, they were more intent on mimicking and seeking after the material status of whites while thinking it would somehow make them more accepted in the same image of whites. Niggers were psychologically brainwashed into wanting to be seen as white. It's the very reason we had so many, "I wanna be seen as a white man," house niggers during slavery. And, it's the same reason we still have so many, "I wanna be seen as a white man," house niggers this very day.

I believe that Brown had to be an extraordinary visionary because blacks as a race had to finally come to the realization that we had to begin rediscovering our roots to regain our identity. We had to start appreciating our proud and rich African history and legacy instead of continually living with the racist, white, slave-master, conditioned minded, complex of wanting to be White.

I ask you, "Where are the John Browns of the white race in this day and age?" There is a very high probability that they are not in a racist ass led, conservative, Republican Party carrying the torch and leading the way to liberty and justice for all citizens of this country regardless of race. .

Chapter Three

The Great Divide -- Democrats vs. Republicans

As the bitter tides of slavery pushed onward in most of the southern parts of the country, and as the western part of the county was said to become more expansive, a political effort to maintain a balance between the number of slave and free states became an important political issue. The south didn't want to face threats to end slavery because of the wealth being attained from its rich cotton growing industry. By 1850, the political language of the south was to secede from the Union. When Abraham Lincoln won the 1860 presidential election, he did so by campaigning on the promise of not allowing any more slave states to be formed. Along with Brown's insurrection at Harpers Ferry, VA, according to some historical scholars, it became the final political straw that caused the south to break away from the Union and form its confederacy. The hateful and stubborn will of the South to maintain its slave states forced the start of the Civil War era. It was also the beginning of the end of physical slavery, and would bring an even deeper racial hatred towards niggers.

In the eyes of white racists, black slaves had now become a race of vile and rebellious niggers being aided and unshackled by the Northern war machine. The "nigger" word would now carry the full brutal force of white racism and despise towards black slaves in America, and for all of their generations to follow.

Even with the North's willingness to finally make efforts to abolish slavery, Lincoln's decision had not altogether been a purely humanitarian one. It was also in part a political strategy because of the northern leadership opposing any efforts of a southern nation taking control over the Mississippi River and western territories. Lincoln had to choose politically, between the lesser or greater of two evils, though it can be strongly argued that he did possess a moral conscience against the indignation and continued enslavement of our African ancestors. Quoting again from Encyclopedia resources, "in 1861, Lincoln expressed the fear that premature attempts at emancipation would mean the loss of the Border States." He believed that "to lose Kentucky would be the same as losing the entire war efforts." At first, Lincoln reversed attempts at emancipation by Secretary of War Simon Cameron and General John C. Fremont (in Missouri), and David Hunter (in South Carolina, Georgia, and Florida), to keep the loyalty of the Border States, and war Democrats.

By no means am I trying to discredit Lincoln for helping to change the landscape of the South by ending slavery. According to the historical position on slavery, it was Lincoln's Republican Party who were more anti-slavery while the old Democratic Party was more pro slavery. But as this country started to move into the 20th century, both parties began to flip flop their ideologies in the aftermath of slavery. Initially, the flip flopping had very little to do with solving the injustice of slavery, but everything to do with advancing the causes and interests of both parties. The initial attitude of blacks as niggers still existed, and the Black "cause" and struggle was eventually given support mostly because of the evolving white liberal movement's willingness to embrace causes that would further its agenda.

Once this happened, African Americans, as well as some of the other minority groups, started to come under the umbrella of the Democratic Party. But at the beginning, the racist influence of the old Democratic Party resisted this liberal change because of its racist unwillingness to abandon the political ideology of slavery, which produced much of this country's early wealth and power. Over time, they began fleeing to the Republican Party while bringing their Confederate and racist white supremacy ideology with them. Lincoln's assassination became the symbol of resentment against all anti-slavery support. Even as late as the sixties the Republican Party was more instrumental than some Democrats in pushing for civil rights legislation to be passed.

Eventually, it was the ability of the Democratic leadership within the Party to reinvent itself under liberal ideology, which helped social, economic, human rights, and civil rights progress even further. The Old Southern Guard of the pro-slavery, Democratic Party's political power began to wane after the Civil War. But, because they were still able to hold on to some of their political power and influence, they would not embrace any moderate ideas that were set forth by Lincoln. Once liberal ideology began to make a very powerful political push in transforming the Old Democratic Party, the politics of the Old Southern Guard began flipping to the Republican Party. Once their racist, white supremacy ideology and bigotry started to take hold within the Republican Party, it made conservatism and racism interchangeable.

As for the Lincoln-Republican Emancipation Proclamation, it proved that Lincoln's political ideology was closer to that of a liberal thinker and not a conservative one. But the Republican Party as it was recognized under Lincoln would end after his assassination. A little over a century later, during the beginning of the Nixon era, the Republican Party began falling even deeper under the influence of the Old Southern Guard's ideology of racism, which compounded the racist politics that already existed.

From that time forward, the Republican Party has been led by the Old Southern Guard's ideology of racism and slavery. Even the Democrat, Lyndon Johnson, racially politicized the black vote by saying that, "by giving niggers concessions, it would secure their democratic vote for the next two hundred years." Even though the objective was racist, the method worked in helping African Americans knock down and open key civil rights doors in this country. It is in the evolution, or lack of evolution of both the Democratic and Republican Party that has brought us to where we are today.

Chapter Four:

Slavery, Emancipation, and the "Nigger Identity"

I will shift the discussion back to the racist history of this country, and how the "nigger identity" evolved with our African ancestors.

By 1840, most slaves north of the Ohio River and Mason-Dixon Line had already been freed because of antislavery laws having been passed in 1804. To see blacks liberated from slavery by the Northern Union was not an open armed welcome because many of these ex-southern slaves would begin migrating and become exploited as cheap labor during the Industrial Revolution of the north. The deep resentment for freed slaves by most northern whites was no different than southern whites. The northern union had freed up cheap labor, but most of the country still held on to the racist attitudes of bitter hate and resentment towards these ex-black slaves. Exploiting Blacks to work for slave wages forced lower class whites to compete for factory jobs and all the other menial tasks. It only served to deepen the hate that racist whites already held towards blacks.

Even though these southern and northern ex-slaves were deeply despised as niggers by most of the entire country, the majority saw nothing about their "nigger identity" that would lessen their sense of freedom and liberation. Many of them only saw offense in the attitudes of racist whites who despised them for having been born black Africans. With the Civil War having come after the slave rebellions, it was these two pivotal events in American history that brought the open hatred of niggers by racist, whites to where it exists today.

The slave rebellions and the Civil War became the two catalysts that white racists have used as fuel to keep the flames of racism burning in this country. Once blacks started acting in organized and sometimes violent rebellions against slavery and the inferior class status that the racist ass, white, slave-master had branded them with, it caused Black slaves to become even more identified as violent, insubordinate, savage niggers who needed to suffer at the hands of even more brutal methods of control. And, once the South's secession forced the start of the Civil War, the position of the Confederacy was to crush the northern union along with its efforts to free insubordinate and rebellious nigger slaves.

According to Encyclopedia resources, "the Southern economy and military efforts depended on slave labor. As one congressman put it, "the slaves… cannot be neutral. As laborers, if not as soldiers, they will be allies of the rebels, or of the union." The same congressman and his fellow radical Republicans put pressure on Lincoln to rapidly emancipate the slaves, whereas moderate Republicans came to accept gradual compensated emancipation and colonization. Lincoln mentioned his Emancipation Proclamation to members of his cabinet on July 21, 1862. Secretary of State William H. Seward told Lincoln to wait for a victory before issuing the proclamation. Lincoln later said that slavery was somehow the cause of the war. Lincoln issued his preliminary Emancipation Proclamation on September 22, 1862, and said that a final proclamation would be issued if his gradual plan based on compensated emancipation and voluntary colonization was rejected. Lincoln issued his final Emancipation Proclamation on January 1, 1863. In his letter to Hodges, Lincoln explained his belief that, "if slavery is not wrong, then nothing is wrong ... I claim not to have controlled events, but confess plainly that events have controlled me."

Lincoln's Emancipation Proclamation, January 1, 1863, was a powerful move that promised freedom for slaves in the Confederacy as soon as the Union armies reached them, and authorized the enlistment of African Americans in the Union Army. Since the Emancipation Proclamation was based on the President's war power, it only included territory held by Confederates at the time. However, the Proclamation became the symbol of the Union's growing commitment to add emancipation to the Union's definition of liberty. Lincoln also played a leading role in getting Congress to vote for the 13th Amendment, which made emancipation universal and permanent. Enslaved African Americans did not wait for Lincoln's actions before escaping and seeking freedom behind Union lines.

From the early years of the war, hundreds of thousands of African Americans followed that path to freedom. African-American men served with distinction as soldiers and sailors with Union troops. Many of them joined the Union Army as workers and troops, forming entire regiments of the U.S. Colored troops -- most of whom were escaped slaves. The Confederacy was outraged by black soldiers and refused to treat them as prisoners of war. Many were shot, as was done at the Fort Pillow Massacre. Others were re-enslaved. It would be difficult for anyone to argue that these acts were not war crimes against Black soldiers. The evil intent was no less than those carried out by Adolph Hitler.

After the Confederacy was dealt a hard fought, but bitter defeat, and once freed blacks started their plight of trying to reach upward mobility, the racial hatred, and bitterness to brand blacks as niggers became even more intense. If it had not been for abolition and the

Civil War, slavery could easily have pushed its way into the twentieth century.

Before the constant threats of slave rebellions and nearly two and one half centuries before the Civil War era when slavery had first come to the shores of America, the "nigger" word was not being used in such a way that it easily marked a death sentence for black slaves. It didn't pack the kind of racial hatred and emotional explosion that it gained during the slave rebellions, the Civil War era, and onward.

Nothing could lessen the affront of the racist hate and lynching of black people as niggers. My attitude and emotional feelings toward a racist ass white man are atomic. From the time that the "nigger" word was derived, and has since evolved, all of its users have taken their emotional attitude and position of usage and aimed it at its black target. If we are ever to fully understand how we got the "nigger" word so deeply ingrained into our culture, we must start at the very beginning of slavery in America.

The start of slavery in America was a cruel act of human exploitation, racism, and class warfare by white oppressors to label poor whites alongside blacks because of the perceived notion of inferior class status. It made both of them a prime target of oppression. However, as I explained earlier, racist slave codes were put in place to deny black slaves indentured contracts of which they would be able to serve out and gain their freedom. The enslavement process against black people in America became a very brutal and cruel method of human exploitation by racist ass whites to gain prosperity and higher class status. This also included the fulfilling of racist white's, perverted gratifications gained by enslaving and dehumanizing African people.

It is vitally important for us to understand that our slave captivity by the racist ass, white slave-master was a very cruel and hateful violation of our human rights. It was initially based on their demand for human labor in the Americas as well as their racist perception of black inferiority. As for poor whites, their class status was no better than black slaves. The only real difference between these poor, downtrodden whites and black slaves was based solely on race. Therefore the attitude of racism began to take a more violent push to help keep the system of slavery intact. As the history of slavery continued in America, the attitude of racism became more brutal towards black slaves.

Before the slave rebellions and the Civil War, the "nigger" word was being used more like a systematic method for naming Black slaves.

For many whites, the "nigger" word was said to be of common usage when not using proper names to refer to black slaves. But as the slave rebellions began to pose a constant threat and the Civil War loomed, racial hate toward black slaves as "niggers" took center stage.

I have now reached a critical point in uncovering what I believe to be, the real truth about why we, as blacks here in America, have the "nigger" word so engrained in our psyche and so embedded in our culture. I have also reached a critical point to begin explaining why whites are utterly forbidden to use the "nigger" word.

The search begins at the shores of America where the first slave ships docked. It is very important to understand that many of our African ancestors came to America still clinging to their African, birthright names. But, with each generation of our African ancestors, children were birthed by their slave mothers with their "nigger" name already waiting for them. It is so vitally important to realize and understand the deep psychological impact that the slave culture had in shaping the identity of these newborn, slave babies. These precious, black, slave babies were born into a very abnormal and dysfunctional environment. And yet, they would grow up and not see anything wrong or offensive about their "nigger" name. In fact, under the cruel hands of slavery, their actual birthright names had become "nigger."

In retrospect, you must take a critical look at slavery and the "nigger" word's deep, psychological effect on these black, slave babies. The racist ass, white, slave-master forced their slave mothers to nurture them with the "nigger" name being burnt deeply into the psyche of their fragile, little, developing minds. These black, African, slave babies accepted their "nigger" name no differently than babies of today, learning to accept and answer to their names. As these slave babies continued to grow and develop mentally, the "nigger" name would take a deeper hold on their psyche. Once the first generation of African slaves died off, so did the names of their African ancestry and the second generation of African slaves' new names became "nigger."

The racist ass, white, slave-master made sure that these newborn, slave babies would not escape the "nigger" name. It is very important to understand that the power and authority of the racist ass, white, slave-master gave him the ability to strip away the parental rights of African slaves. He then slyly forged his way into the role of both surrogate and biological father. He made sure that the slave parents became no more than mere caregivers -- seen as no more than overgrown niggers who would never rise above the status of slave boys and slave girls. The racist ass, white, slave-master made it clear that little African slave babies were to be suckled and raised up under the "nigger" identity.

Once the racist ass, white, slave-master removed the parental rights of our African ancestors, it became more about how these African slave babies would take to their "nigger" name. The racist ass, white, slave-master made sure that the "nigger" name became well cultivated among his slaves so that it would become common place. These slave babies were taught their "nigger" name without any understanding about the growing hate and racism that whites would attach to it. But, for these slave children, the "nigger" word held no profane or derogatory meaning. As most of us know how the old saying goes when raising a child, if the child gets caught using profane language, and has to go before someone of authority other than the parent to answer for it, the authority figure firmly demands that the child tell where they learned such a profane word. The child then gradually lifts their head, looks up at the authority figure, and says, "I learned it from my parents." It's the same analogy as to how black, slave children learned how to use the "nigger" name given to them by their racist ass, white, slave-masters.

The racist ass, white, slave-master didn't separate any of his slaves from the "nigger" name, because in his system of slavery, all of his slaves were niggers. The only critical thing that he used to distinguish his slaves was good "nigger" slaves or bad "nigger" slaves. To this very day, within the vast population of the black masses here in America, we apply the very same attitude of the "good nigger" and the "bad nigger." But, during the long and painful history of our African ancestor's suffrage under slavery, what they were able to do with the help of the Union Army, was to overthrow the racist ass, white, slave-master in their rebellion. But, they held on to the "nigger" name given to them in America as their true African names had died off.

Our African ancestors took power and authority over their "nigger" name the same as their racist ass, white, slave-master/surrogate and biological father had once held. As ex-slaves, they'd taken control of their "nigger" name and would decide who was a good or bad nigger. And after becoming the master over their "nigger" name, our African ancestors handed this same liberated "nigger" attitude of rebellion to us as their descendants. If we use the "nigger" word to express ourselves towards one another without ill contempt, the usage of the "nigger" word is seen as an acknowledgement of acceptance. But, if the feeling towards another black person is filled with contempt, then that black person is seen as a "bad nigger," in the negative sense.

When the racist ass, white, slave-master was pleased with his slave children, they were good little nigger slaves. And when he was not pleased, they were judged as bad little nigger slaves. It was an attitude that the racist ass, white, slave-master ingrained into the minds of our African ancestors from the time they started to grow and develop. Out of this legacy of slavery, we carried on with the "nigger" identity from generation to generation. Our African ancestors had finally broken the physical chains of slavery held by their racist ass, white, slave-master father, but were still left to suffer its psychological effects. They had rebelled from the slave plantation and taken their "nigger" name with them. They had now become lord and master over their childhood slave "nigger" name.

You have to remember that within the long and painful history of the slave culture, our African ancestors lived, suffered, and died under their "nigger" identity. On one hand, the "nigger" word had become the symbol of rebellion and liberation. But on the other hand, it was still the symbol for all the vile and perverse things that the racist ass, white, slave-master forced upon and perpetrated against black slaves. It was this evil and perverse brutality that makes it utterly forbidden for whites to ever think again that they can openly use the "nigger" word against blacks under any circumstances.

We have to truly understand why our African ancestors held on to their "nigger" identity and why we, as their descendants, still cling to it. When our African ancestors rebelled, they didn't rebel under their original names, nor did they rebel under the name "black" or "negro" or "African American." Our African ancestors rebelled under their slave "nigger" name, and they became liberated under their slave "nigger" name. In essence, these ex-slaves had now elevated the "nigger" name into their badge of defiance and rebellion after having gained their triumphant victory over their racist ass, white, slave-master. From the very beginning of the slave rebellions and until the Civil War started and ended, it changed the perception of how freed slaves wanted to embrace their "nigger" identity. It was at this critical point in the history of slavery in America that the "nigger" word began to take on a historical and symbolic meaning of defiance, alongside its negative meaning for our African ancestors. This same transformation took a deep root at the very start of the post slave era and has survived in the culture of African Americans until this very day.

Our African ancestors had finally succeeded in their long and painful struggle against enslavement. They had rebelled against their racist ass, white, slave-master, and they had rebelled from the slave plantation and taken their slave "nigger" name with them. They were now masters over their childhood "nigger" name. They were now "physically free niggers" and they were now "liberated-minded niggers," and the only repulsive and unaccepted nigger was the "unliberated minded nigger." A great portion of the masses takes the very same attitude to this day. If a black person who thinks of themselves as a "liberated minded nigger" refers to another black person as an "unliberated minded nigger," it becomes one of the most heated conflicts among the black masses -- trying to distinguish themselves as "liberated niggers" vs. "unliberated niggers," as the latter means a "nigger" who has not liberated themselves from the sub-human and inferior mindset of a slave.

Out of the slave culture, I will refer to it as a "division," where blacks are at extreme odds about race behavior under the "nigger" identity. It's to say that this mentally "unliberated minded nigger" represents all the vile, lowlife, sub-human behavior that the racist ass, white, slave-master tried to brand the entire black race with. If not all blacks, then most blacks, inherently know and understand the subliminal message behind calling another black person a nigger, in this sense. Even the most uneducated and uncultured black person feels entitled to attack another black person with the "nigger" word. For those among the masses who use the "nigger" word, they feel entitled to use it regardless of the perception of being a "liberated-minded nigger," or not.

Regardless of who's making the attack, the attack is always charged with deep emotional feelings. Most blacks who use the "nigger" word within the subculture of black America inherently know that to be attacked as a low-life, subhuman, "unliberated minded nigger" is about the worse thing another Black person could ever be called in terms of existing below the threshold of being human. And, it becomes very unlikely that you will ever hear a politically correct Black person use the "nigger" word out in the open for white ears to hear.

Chapter Five

Racist Hypocrisy in Politics

It is as though these racist ass, white, hypocritical bastards in the news media will never get it. Look at the backlash their racist, white asses tried hitting President Obama with because he spoke the nigger word to make a point about racism. Not that it should matter, but he didn't even use the word in a social context. But these racist ass, White, news media bastards, along with their token ass, house niggers, who, themselves, have the word house niggers pinned on their backs tried to scold the President about the indignation attached to the word. But, all the indignation attached to it is about what their racist, white asses were allowed to inflict upon us during slavery. The nerve of these racist ass, white, hypocritical bastards, they call us niggers behind closed doors, yet they criticize blacks publicly when we use the "N" word in any context.

The real problem is that the racist ass, white, news media and the racist ass, white make-up within the Republican Party have been trying to give President Obama a political lynching from the moment that he was sworn into office as the first, African American president. Throughout his presidency, they have been willing to oppose him at every turn even if it meant destroying this country. For them to achieve their racist ass goal, they have tried to under mind, and destroy his Presidency and his legacy.

One of the sore spots for the racist, white element within this government and the news media, is that they will forever despise the fact that Osama Bin Laden was finally captured and brought to justice under the watch of President Obama. Because of their racist ass, political agenda, they could care less about having one ounce of sympathy in regards to the fact that Bin Laden's capture brought closure to many of the families of the victims of his heinous acts of terror. They could not care less that Bin Laden's capture also helped preserve the image of America as an effective world power in defense against any enemy that would dare carry out an attack against it.

If Osama Bin Laden had been captured and brought to justice under the watch of a white president, of all the ticker tape parades thrown for past presidents, his would have been greater than all other presidents combined. But, what did President Obama get? Instead of making racist ass, white America proud, it made them emotionally sick to see that what they deem as a nigger will go down in American history books for this accomplishment and not a white man. I guarantee you that if they could burn President Obama's memory out of their racist ass, white history books, they'd already be lighting up their racist ass, white KKK torches.

These racist ass, white, hypocritical bastards, have tried to block nearly every bill that President Obama has sought to pass. Then, their racist white asses, along with their so called intellectual, illegitimate ass, house niggers, they cried out to the American voters, falsely accusing the man of having made no accomplishments. In coded language, they cried, "What has this nigger accomplished as president for our precious, red, white, and blue, white United States of America?" And, to add even further insult, they have the racist ass nerve to say, what has he done for his race, struggling in poverty while being destroyed by Black-on-black crime?

From the very beginning, it has been a part of their racist ass scheme to convince white voters to never again in the history of this country take part in helping elect a Black president. They would have endorsed a white clown if it had worked in defeating President Obama, whom they call *The Nigger President* behind closed doors. Well, for the 2016 presidential elections, they have now elected their racist, white, Republican Party clown. In fact, we are finally able to re-gauge just how monstrous and deep bigotry and racism still exists in this country. For example, the white Republican nominee in the 2016 race to become the next president of this country has hit upon some of the most racist, political discord that goes back into the worse history of hate and racism in this country that has always been an unfortunate part of this white government's evil and racist legacy. And yet, this white Republican, presidential candidate became the nominee over the other Republican candidates in their party.

Here is why this has occurred. You see, for the last eight years, this country has been in an all-out race war and fight against President Obama of whom they see as a nigger. For the last eight years, the racist ass, white, Republican Party and the racist ass, white, news media has worked diligently to see this country destroyed rather than see it being led by someone whom they deem as a nigger. And now, racist ass, white America is not hesitating to finally vote out in the open, its true feelings of racist ass hatred that starts with black America while attacking other races in the middle, and then concluding again with their racist ass attacks on Black America.

For the last eight years, the racist ass, white, Republican Party and the racist ass, white, news media in their racist hate and resentment of President Obama, has been fueling and lighting the fire of racism and stoking the emotional flames of racist ass, white America. It now burns high and intense with the Republican nominee carrying their message of racist ass, white hate, and bigotry in this country. The Republican nominee, to his racist ass, white Republican supporters, has made some of the most disparaging remarks of mockery about people of color, the disabled, women, and people of different religious beliefs. He has spoken condescendingly about Hispanics, African Americans, women, and people seeking immigration. He has spoken as the bonafide, big bad, racist ass, white bully on the block. He has all but pulled his pants down and told this particular population to kiss his catering to racism, unapologetic, white ass.

These racist ass, white, news media, hypocritical bastards defend the Republican nominee by trying to explain away his repulsive and divisive language of bigotry and insults by trying to rationalize it as having anti-political establishment appeal. What shameless and pathetic, hypocritical bastards they are in their racist ass, white attitudes to openly embrace such ugly, brutal, and dehumanizing language of someone running for election to the highest office in the land. If this same Republican nominee had black skin and spewed the same, not so politically correct, language of bigotry and insults, they would, in their sudden, politically correct principles of hypocrisy, run him out of town like a hobo on a freight train, or round up a racist ass, white, Ku Klux Klan, lynch mob and have him hung from the highest tree as a filthy, hate mongering, repulsive mouth nigger.

At one of the Republican nominee rallies, one of his racist ass, white supporters shouted to a black protestor that we needed to go back to Africa as though Africa has no historical importance and value to human existence and civilization. Racist white, ignorant ass bastards like this are bent on the mindset of the racist ass, white colonizers who boastfully overlook the historical fact that they are not native to the Americas. Racist ass, white bastards like this, while they talk down on Africa, need to take their barbaric, raw meat eating, once cave dwelling asses back to the caves of Europe. And, to note historical facts, Africa was and is still being raped of its vast natural resources by racist ass, white Europeans while many of its people still live in poverty and out of the technological age. This goes on mainly because racist ass, white Europeans, since the time of their colonization of Africa, have desired to keep factions stirred up among impoverished African nations to continue their assault, exploiting the mother continent by tapping into her vast, natural resources.

The Republican nominee has struck a hateful chord of inciting violence among many of his racist ass, white supporters. An incident occurred at one of his rallies where an African American protestor was sucker punched in the face by one of his racist ass, redneck, cowboy hat, wearing supporters. The white cops handled the black protestor as though he was the villain and not the victim. But, the racist ass, white supporter was allowed to boast about having struck the black protestor in the mouth, and brag about how they might have to kill him the next time. He was later arrested, but only after social media publicized the incident. The entire event looked more like a Ku Klux Klan rally with the Republican nominee as the Grand Wizard, hosting the cross burning.

Shortly after this happened, a similar incident occurred. Only this time, it was a black supporter of the Republican nominee punching and violently kicking a white protestor at one of his rallies. This violent incident did more to help the Republican nominee because anytime a nigger attacks a white person, even when the incident is not as severe, the racist ass, white, news media will always exploit it by making it appear far worse than a white person attacking a black person. If this negro was not a hired supporter staged to carry out this violent act, then it has to be one of the most bizarre happenings to see a nigger at a political rally with a Ku Klux Klan type atmosphere, offering their support by striking a white protestor for opposing it. The entire incident looked more like an insane ass nigger trying to stop someone from preventing their lynching. This is exactly how I see house niggers when it comes to defending their racist ass, white slave-masters.

Let's look at the rude awakening -- the dose of reality -- the Republican nominee received in Chicago, IL, when his rally was shut down after violence erupted between protestors and the Republican nominee's supporters. He wanted to be the big bad bully on the block. Now he knows what it feels like to get punched back in the mouth. Despite this, his devoted, white, racist ass followers has assured him that they are willing to follow him into the pits of hell with their racist ass, white votes. They want no other Republican candidate to represent their racist ass, white voice. They have not had a candidate to speak their racist ass language since the days of George Wallace and the racist and brutal law enforcement of Bull Connor during the civil rights movement.

Herein lies the irony, the racist ass, white, Republican Party and the racist ass, white, news media, have for the last eight years used their racist ass hate for President Obama to galvanize and unite the votes of racist ass, white America. But, instead of producing the ideal, conservative candidate to lead their racist ass party, their efforts have produced what they deem as the mind of a Frankenstein monster that will destroy their party with the very racist ass, white voters that they have worked so hard to fire up during the Obama presidency.

After all is said and done by the Republican nominee, the racist ass, white, news media will still argue and defend him as not being racist. If their position holds true, then what do you call a white candidate who is adamant about giving an ear and their empathy to their racist ass, white supporters while acting extremely annoyed by the issues that concerns blacks and other minority groups? The racist ass, white, news media argued that what makes him so appealing to his supporters is that he is antiestablishment. But, if the racist ass, white, news media truly wants the American voters to get an insightful view of him as a businessman, all they need to do is take a critical look at some of the major collapses in his business deals, his casino investments and the demise of the university he founded. The first thing that should come to mind is corporate raider and Bernie Madoff's Ponzi scheme.

Adding even further to his bigotry, he denounced the judge presiding over the legal issues facing his failed university, saying he was unfit because of having been born of Mexican descent. His racist and biased argument is that the judge is incapable of showing judicial integrity because of his presidential campaign to build a border wall that Mexico would have to be financially responsible for.

I ask, what do you call whites in politics and in the news media who declare that they are not racist, but make it clear that they cater to racist views while slightly pulling against it? A two-faced racist? The real problem for those being racially discriminated against is which face will show up on a given race issue.

For example, when the Republican nominee was asked about the former white supremacist, Ku Klux Klan leader endorsing him for president, he equivocated on the question by giving the impression that he didn't want to lose any of his support from racist ass, white America by disavowing David Duke. But, the white, Republican Party nominee later tried to disavow Duke after pressure from the news media. He was not forced to do this because racist ass, white politicians, and the racist ass, white, news media is not in favor of the racist, white supremacy ideology of David Duke. Behind closed doors, David Duke embodies and symbolizes the core attitudes and feelings of racist ass, white America which includes some of the most powerful and wealthiest, whites in the world. They don't disagree with the racist, white support the Republican nominee is receiving; they disagree with the open mockery and disgrace that the Republican nominee is putting upon the face of their party. But, the racist ass, white Republican Party controlling the House and the Senate during the 2016, presidential election, shouldn't be allowed to run away from the monster that they helped to create by trying to destroy the Obama presidency.

In truth, the Republican nominee campaign and voter support actually represents the evil history of how American politics existed during the time of slavery and before the election of Abraham Lincoln, civil war, and emancipation. It's the very reason why the Republican nominee isn't fazed by all of his racist hate and bigotry. Racist ass, white America has owned it as being lawful and constitutional.

We finally get to see the ugliest and vulgar side of racist ass, white America through their support of their Republican nominee. It has unmasked their shameless and racist ass attitudes and feelings of wanting to run this country at all costs. It's utterly disgraceful, no matter how the racist ass, white, news media tries to spin it. The powerful vote of the American people to elect Obama as president of the United States has to go down as one of the most extraordinary votes on a single issue ever to be achieved in this country. But, it will also go down as one of the most extraordinary turn of events on uncovering just how deeply racist ass, white hate still exists in this country. It couldn't be more evident in the way the Republican nominee has been able to spew some of the vilest and divisive language of racism and bigotry and not be denounced for it. But, as long as it means erasing the memory of the nigger president, it has proven to gain even more support from racist ass, white America. Starting with the nominee, the Republican candidates, in their all-out effort to replace Obama at the end of his term, have used against each other some of the ugliest and vile language never seen before in American politics. In their efforts to destroy Obama, they have openly disgraced their party.

At the RNC, (Republican National Convention), the Republican nominee painted a gloomy picture of America having suffered a deep crack at its foundation in the areas of race relations, law enforcement, economics, and politics. But, what hypocrisy to argue that the problem itself is somehow the grand solution in resolving it? Much of why America is being cast in this place of gloom, is mainly because of how, since the election of President Obama, the racist ass led, Republican Party, has used every source of their power to exploit every violent act of terrorism to push their racist ass agenda. To destroy the leadership of a man that they deem to be a repulsive nigger, they have worked diligently to tear this country apart in the effort to regain full control of political power.

It could not be more evident that the Republican nominee in his efforts to be elected, will have rode the emotional tides of racial hatred that has been systematically manufactured in this country to stir up racial division between black America and white America. The racist ass, white, news media then sounds it out all across America. The death and destruction being exploited to push their racist ass, political agenda, truly demonstrates the degree of callousness and desensitization in this country. It did not start here, but began with the cruel history of slavery of racist ass, white America, who does not possess any genuine concern about the destruction and loss of human life.

The Republican nominee had the racist ass nerves to blame the Obama administration for causing the widening of our historical, racial divide. He went even further with his lying, racist insults by saying, "I am with you," as though he was including all of America. From the time of slavery, niggers have existed as no more than a political door mat to continue being exploited in unifying racist ass, white America while being thrown under the bus of this system of slavery over and over again. These racist ass, white bastards could not care less about how devastating it is for us to have our humanity crushed again and again.

Unless we unite to change this as a powerful, black nation, we will not be able to heal this deep, emotional wound inflicted upon us under this racist ass, white supremacist regime. The Republican nominee showed all of his racist ass, white hypocrisy nerves by saying that he will be the law and order president, while at the same time being investigated for his crooked dealings. He went on with his absurd lies about how his racist laden ass party will always tell the truth. But, when he uttered those fateful words to the effect of, no one knows this racist ass, crooked and rigged system better than him and how he alone could fix it. It was just another conniving way of saying that he alone knows how to put the *fix on* -- the same way he has done many times before in his crooked ass business dealings. It stood out as that one defining moment where he had a slip of the tongue. The expression on his face and his body language told the undeniable truth on himself in front of all of his racist ass, white supporters and house niggers.

This Republican Party nominee is no more than a modern-day, carpetbagger, moving from one political party to the next as an opportunist and exploiter. "I will be your voice," he vehemently shouted. The biggest question is, whose voice? Any nigger with the least bit of common sense knows full well that this racist ass, white bigot was talking only about racist ass, white America. Behind the smoke screen of all of his political rhetoric, it's no more than another racist ass, white supremacist speech crafted to appeal to racist ass, white America. True to form, lurking just below the surface in the minds of racist ass, white America is the thought that niggers are the targeted problem causing the social, economic, and political erosion in this country that all of white America must unite themselves against.

When he made his attack on crime and violence and restoring order and safety, he was talking exclusively about niggers while at the same time, praising this racist ass, white, police system of brutality and murder of niggers. I had mostly thought of the MSNBC talk show host of, "Morning Joe," whom I feel would like to be thought of as "*being for the cause of the common man.*" He gives the impression of being somewhat of a fair-minded critic on political issues. But, when he mocked President Obama with the Moses comparison and the parting of the Red Sea, and the lambasting of the Greek column prop used during his inauguration speech, it crossed the line of not showing the proper and politically correct acknowledgment for one of the greatest, historical achievements in American politics. His utterly disrespectful comments flowed into the hateful vein of racism.

In his effort to build up the image of the Republican nominee, it was easy for him to try and put down President Obama's inauguration promises, considering how his racist ass, Republican Party has worked the entire time of Obama's presidency to keep him from fulfilling those promises. He even went on boasting and praising how the Republican nominee was being well represented by his children. Well, barring racist ass, white attitudes, what does a thinly veiled, self-centered, wealthy, elitist ass, white family have to do with any real connection to middle and poor working class people in this country? A self-centered, wealthy, elitist ass, white family who had no problem plagiarizing the speech of the first African American, First Lady. Their racist ass actions were no more than the bold, symbolism of slavery where the wife of the racist ass, white slave-master is privileged and entitled to take credit for any redeeming qualities of her house servants. In other words, a black woman's virtue is better represented by a white woman. Blacks are not even qualified to represent the best of their own character.

Do you honestly believe that if a black candidate's wife had committed the same egregious, dishonest, shameful act, she would have gotten off the hook so easily? Now, whenever all of white

America shows sympathy for the wrongful act of any highly distinguished, white person against a nigger, niggers are fully expected to immediately withdraw their criticism, fall back into their submissive posture, and say nothing more about it. This exists as one of the core attitudes of racist ass, white supremacy and the determination to maintain its powerful influence of its slavery ass system over the minds of niggers.

But for the sake of their racist ass party trying to win back the White House, they are willing to turn their racist ass, hypercritical heads the other way, but not when it comes to attacking white liberals. Take for example the satirical skit that presidential candidate, Hilary Clinton, and New York's mayor, Bill de Blasio, put on about being on colored people's time (CPT). The hidden meaning behind this is the racial, stereotypical attitude about colored people always being late. How is it that the racist ass, white, news media, led by one of their most stanch, racist ass, news commentators, acted more upset about it than most blacks were about it themselves? This racist ass, white, news media commentator was quick to argue that blacks have a double standard when it involves racial issues with white liberals and white conservatives. But, at worse, all Hilary Clinton and Bill de Blasio did was make light of this racist white stereotype about blacks. The harsh truth is that racist ass whites actually say this behind closed doors and mean every racist ass word of it.

So, if Hilary Clinton and Bill de Blasio did receive a free pass and was not severely penalized for it, the reason is because they are not perceived to be a part of the same racist ass establishment entrenched deep into the white, Republican, conservative party. The Republican Party epitomizes racist ass, white America.

Obama broke the racist ass spirit within the conservative Republican Party twice by becoming a two term president. And, even after having done everything possible to destroy his presidency, they declared that it had only to do with his policies and nothing to do with race. The racist ass, white, news media even tried to make this boldfaced lie stand by alluding to the early 2015 Republican poll showing that the only Republican African American running for president in their party was polling well among white Republican voters. It was this ploy that they tried to use as an argument to dispel any notion that their attacks on Obama had anything to do with race. But, it would have to be an exception to the rule not to see a Republican, African American candidate not be used as a token, racist ass, political prop. Sadly, the majority of African Americans in the Republican Party are no more than token ass, house niggers, clamoring and pandering to racist ass, white politics to prove their worthiness for election and acceptance within the racist ass, white, slave-master's big plantation house.

By endorsing this racist ass, white bigot for president -- a racist ass, white bigot who referred to him as being mentally unstable and attacked him with other foul and demeaning accusations -- this Republican African American has finally proven himself to be no different than any of the token ass, house niggers that have gone before him. They even employed another house nigger on their racist ass, white, Republican Party team who once ran for president and got the same house nigger treatment. This racist ass, white, news media, house nigger has the same name of the brother of the biblical Abel and anyone who has ever read Genesis knows what that wicked ass nigger did to his brother. Even though the Bible warned against slaying this nigger, it certainly doesn't tell us to turn our backs on niggers of this sort.

I cannot believe that any of these racist ass, white, news media commentators who use token ass house niggers as props to try and dispel racism in the Republican Party, does not know how their own racist ass politics actually work. No personal disrespect intended. This is all about the fact that I have no political respect for these token ass, racist ass, piece of shit, white slave-master, house niggers. If the Democratic Party was to go back to its old, southern guard, ideology of Ku Klux Klan, racist hate towards niggers and the Republican Party went back to its history of the abolitionist movement against slavery, much of my attitude would be reversed about both of these white, majority, political parties.

How can any African American, within the racist ass, white led Republican Party who see themselves as not being a house nigger, actually believe that this is the same view that the racist ass, white Republican Party has of them? It's not out of character for the racist ass, white led, conservative, Republican Party to take the position that if white liberals could help elect a Black man into the oval office, they could also entertain the thought of electing one who'd be willing to be controlled as a house nigger in a last ditch effort to prevent a liberal candidate, white or black, man or woman, from ascending to the high seat of the oval office.

However, it is not uncommon for the racist ass led Republican Party to use blacks as house niggers in their party and then conveniently dispose of them. Just look at what took place with the Republican African American candidate during the 2016 Iowa caucus. False reports went out by one of his Republican opponent's staff members during the actual caucus, stating that he was suspending his campaign and returning home. His supporters were then asked to cast their votes for the other evangelical supported Republican candidate. Even though the opponent's staff tried to pin the false report on CNN, once the audio was reviewed, it became evident that categorically the language CNN used was not identical to the language being used by the staff of the Republican opponent.

This particular Republican candidate is Hispanic, but one of his racist ass, white staff members had no problem sending out the false report to gain votes during the voting process. Racist ass whites such as this epitomizes the racist led, Republican Party. They have no problem what so ever in scheming to undermine the voting process. Take a look at the voter ID laws. Take a look at their campaign to end early voting. Just take a look at how they gerrymander voting districts. Take a look at how they repealed the voting rights act. Just listen to the racist ass language, tone, and proposed politics they use to fire up their base. All of these dirty ass, unconstitutional schemes is how the racist ass, white led, Republican Party positions itself to cruise and trump their way to victory. The Republican nominee's presidential campaign should be a clear reminder to never forget what voting on the wrong side of history looks like in a racist ass, political party.

Even though President Obama was on point about having forced their racist, white asses to use the word nigger behind closed doors, it does not spell much progress for African Americans. Still, their racist, white, supremacist asses better not ever think that they can openly say the nigger word and not expect to be branded as the racist, white supremacist ass bastards that they are. Their racist, white supremacist asses in the news media, threw a racist ass shitfit over the issue of Obama saying the word nigger, though amongst one another within their culture, they can refer to themselves as good, old fashioned, redneck boys and it's no big deal. But let a black politician even slightly say the same thing about them and they're instantly seen as hateful and racist ass niggers no differently than white politicians if they say the word nigger in public.

You see blacks would have to deal with the same racist label. But again, it's their racist, white supremacist asses that are bitter because they still feel that as the racist ass, white descendants of the racist ass, white slave-master, they should have the same entitlement as blacks to use the word nigger even though using it convicts their racist white asses of all of their filthy, rotten, devilish, perverted history of slavery in this country. It's the defining difference between us and their racist, white supremacist asses when we use the word nigger.

It would be disingenuous to act as though the black race has shown no tolerance for the "nigger" word in our culture. But, we will never acknowledge it openly to whites and allow them to make it a point of argument to justify their racist ass position of calling Black people niggers. The mindset of whites is to call us niggers out of their racist ass feelings and attitudes derived from slavery and their false history of portraying blacks as being inferior and without any civilization. The racist ass, white man's hate is about the entire Black race existing as no more than subhuman, uncivilized, "nigger" animals. And, when we attack another black person with the "nigger" word, what we are saying to them is that they represent the sort of lowlife, ignorant behavior that the racist ass, white man uses to try and brand and destroy the entire black race. It would be impossible for us to use the "nigger" word in judging the Black race through the same eyes as the racist ass, white man. There is a very important distinction to be made here because we do not have the same wicked association and brutal history of slavery tied to the "nigger" word as does the racist ass, white, man.

It is virtually impossible to put our attitudes regarding our usage of the "nigger" word under the same perception of the racist ass, white man's, having judged all black people as lowlife, sub-human "nigger" animals. When we attack another black person with the "nigger" word, we are only able to use it as a simile or in a metaphorical sense. For example, we make reference to the "nigger" word by saying things like, "stop acting like a nigger," which in the racist white man's terms, it means animals, and every other racist and derogatory thing under the sun that the racist white man attaches to his attack on us. Even if we use metaphors like "that nigga is a beast," or "that nigga is an ox," it still cannot be put into the same context as the racist ass, white man's history of reducing our humanity to no more than chattel or livestock.

Chapter Six

The "Gatekeepers" and the Black Reformers

If any white person genuinely cares to understand the deep cruelty of our enslavement, they would also understand why it is utterly and forever forbidden for any white person to believe that it could somehow become acceptable for them to call us niggers. As for our African ancestors, when they came under the "nigger" identity within the slave culture, the "nigger" identity didn't evolve with us with the same identical meaning as it did with the racist ass, white, slave-master. We had to learn to see ourselves in a different way under the "nigger" identity other than how the racist ass, white, slave-master viewed us. Under the "nigger" identity, the racist ass, white, slave-master portrayed us as being dumb, ignorant, and submissive, subhuman animals. But even though we still had to bear the "nigger name," our African ancestors learned how to make it be something else other than what it meant to the racist ass, white, slave-master.

As I said earlier, it is impossible to have our usage of the "nigger" word tied to the same cruel and wicked slave history of the racist ass, white slave-master. Unlike using metaphors and similes when describing our association with the "nigger" word, the racist ass, white man is expressing absolute power over black people with no ownership of being human. Because of his power and authority over our African ancestors as slaves, he was able to reduce many of them into behaving like subhuman animals. One must understand that blacks within the subculture of the "nigger identity" do not frown so much on the usage of the "nigger" word by their definition, but more so against whites, and other races who eagerly join with them in their racist ass, white supremacy ideology of branding blacks as lowlife, subhuman, "nigger" animals. Again, it is crucial to understand how our African ancestors became connected to the "nigger" identity under slavery.

The racist ass, white, slave-master destroyed the original identity of our African ancestors, along with the institution of the black family. The racist ass, white, slave-master then forced slave mothers to birth, nurture, and suckle their little slave babies under the "nigger" identity.

In spite of this problem, we cannot get away from the fact that our African ancestors died and rebelled and became liberated under their "nigger" identity. And, what it has produced in our culture today are what I will call the "gatekeepers of the nigger word, niggers." Not all of these rebellious "niggers" are liberated minded, but they are the ones who express and sound out the "nigger" word openly within the black subculture. These "gatekeepers of the nigger word niggers" express what many of us think and feel about the usage of the "nigger" word, but will not reveal it publically. Hidden in secret, the "nigger" identity represents the symbol of our African ancestors' defiant rebellion and liberation against slavery.

Our African ancestors, while not being able to break the racist white man's grip on calling us "niggers" and degrading and dehumanizing the black race, were able to take the "nigger identity" and re-brand it with their defiant rebellion. The "nigger" name had now become the battle cry and symbolic representation of our African ancestors' pride of rebellion and black liberation. But for the racist ass, white, slave-master, the nigger name was no longer only a racist name for blacks, it had now become the official feared name of blacks. After having gained their liberation out of slavery, if their identity would still continue to be branded with racist hate, it would no longer be done as niggers under the power and authority of the racist ass, white, slave-master.

The racist ass, white man's hate would now have to be directed at niggers gaining freedom. And, a nigger also gaining power against the racist ass, white man is a feared, rebellious and liberated nigger. Now, with the "nigger identity" as the symbol of defiance, rebellion and liberation, and with the lost power and authority of the racist ass, white, slave-master, the masses of the Black race, still under the influence of the "nigger" word while not fully understanding how it was handed down to us generation after generation by our African ancestors, will secretly tolerate the "nigger" word within our subculture as a part of our black experience and expression. It even becomes foolish to think that a race-wide effort in America could ever be successfully mounted to prevent these "gatekeepers of the nigger word niggers" from keeping our ex-slave ancestor's "nigger" name alive within the sub-culture of Black America.

It would be dishonest for any black person of African American descent to act as though the "nigger identity" doesn't exist as a hidden norm within the sub-culture of the masses. It would be totally naïve to think that not even one black leader throughout the course of history has not used the "N" word the same as it's being used among the masses today. What if I were to say that someone of the likes of Frederick Douglas, Booker T. Washington, George Washington Carver, or Harriett Tubman could easily have allowed the "nigger" word to slip off their tongues? But, most black intellectuals and historical scholars, because of moral and political correctness, will never openly claim this position within the mainstream of black America because of the deep and bitter contempt we hold towards the racist ass white man for having branded us as despised niggers. Therefore, soon after the post slave era began, advocates of which I will refer to as Black reformers, quickly began putting together strong efforts of providing moral and intellectual leadership to the black masses. It was these black reformers such as Frederick Douglas who led the march towards moral and social stability. They also pushed towards educational, economic, and political growth. One of the deepest thorns in the side of their efforts was trying to get the black masses to shed all of the psychological and ill effects of the slave culture. The continued association with the "nigger" identity among the black masses would soon prove itself to be a problem which has carried on to this present day. The renowned writer, Langston Hughes once expressed his criticism of blacks because of their interest in wanting to read a book entitled, "Nigger Heaven," which was written by a white author.

Even though it was said that Hughes showed some interest in the book because of its depiction of the Harlem Renaissance, he still felt that many blacks paid far more attention to the title rather than its contents and that he felt that blacks showed more interest in it than any book written by a black author. But there were others such as W. E. B. Dubois who found the book to be very offensive. In my opinion, one cannot say that every Black person who read or chose to read a book of this sort is catering to racist, white stereotypes. As I wrote this essay, I had not read the book "Nigger Heaven," but I feel that any curiosity to read it should not convict me of catering to a particular racial stereotype. My first thought about the title of the book struck an interest to know if this white author was writing about some sort of segregated heaven for blacks. And, the only way to find out would be by reading the book or gathering information from another source.

Even though I have much respect for Brother Dubois' position, I feel that he lived in an era not far removed from the physical and emotional bondage of slavery. Brother Dubois was not born in a time that allowed him to see how certain aspects of the slave culture had evolved into the 21st century. Dr. Cornell West once wrote that the "N" word is of historical memory for black people. He goes on to explain that in his opinion, blacks in some instances use the "nigger" word as a form of rhythmic expression for connecting their thoughts to words. I believe that W. E. B. Dubois, like many early black reformers, were strongly set against promoting stereotypes that would suppress the progress of freedom. They had very little or no tolerance for any sort of attitudes among blacks that appeared to be the product of slavery. But, one of the difficult problems we are faced with is trying to fully understand how some of these same attitudes may not have hindered, but may have helped us by giving us some hidden advantage under our slave captivity.

Under their "nigger" identity, our African ancestors soon began to find ways of acting submissive to the racist ass, white, slave-master's perception of slaves, but in secret many of them would not allow themselves to be mentally broken into the behavior that the racist ass, white, slave-masters expected of their slaves. We know that the physical bondage of our slave captivity was a horrible and tragic suffrage of human life. But, the psychological bondage is far too complex to just concede here. We cannot take every circumstance of our submissive attitudes under slavery and conclude that all blacks were acting out racist stereotypes. If nearly every behavior we express is considered acting out racist, white stereotypes, it will only continue to hold us back as a race of people. It's all part of the racist ass white man's plot of keeping us behaving submissively. For example, if a Black person speaks with a firm tone towards a white person, they become stereotyped as a Black person acting too hostile or just simply acting like an angry "nigger animal." And, what this does is psychologically force us back into the submissive behavior of a "good nigger" of the racist ass, white, slave-master just as it was during slavery.

As the old saying goes, "You can't judge a book by its cover." Well, the same can be said for many of our African ancestors during slavery because not every black person under the "nigger" identity lived the racist white stereotype. While it remains true that some blacks do allow themselves to portray racist, white stereotypes, no black person should be afraid of dealing with stereotypes when the Black man becomes the target of the racist ass, white man in anything. The true "stereotypical niggers" are those who act like the low-life, subhuman, animals that the racist ass, white, slave-master tried to condition the entire Black race into becoming. Also included among them are those so-called, "intellectual ass house niggers," who thinks the racist ass white man has a monopoly on civilized behavior, and that the only way for us to obtain the quality of being human is by mimicking white people.

Let's get the facts straight. The art of civilization was founded by the black race on the continent of what is called Africa. But the racist ass, white man has so masterfully destroyed the black man's identity by cutting us off from the knowledge of our history. Now when we show our intelligence, he tries to conclude that blacks are trying to emulate the white man. And, when the Black man behaves ignorantly or with stupidity, he tries to conclude that he's acting like himself.

Because of the stigma of how slavery has portrayed us as wild, uncivilized, savage niggers, we are the only ethnic group in this country that has been psychologically forced into always feeling as though we have to hold our collective breath and hope that when the broad focus is on us that we not act and behave in such a way that will bring even more shame upon us as a race. Even though it becomes painfully embarrassing for us when niggers do behave ignorantly, we should never allow ourselves to be made to feel as though whites are our standard bearers and judges needed to validate whether or not we have passed the so-called, white, civilized, litmus test of having behaved intelligently. We should, first and foremost, be concerned about upholding our image of intelligence and achievements up to our own standards and not try to prove anything to racist ass, white supremacist elitist within the white race.

But, as for racist ass whites, they are not so willing to acknowledge historical facts that it was them who still existed as barbarians dwelling in the frozen caves of Europe, while blacks had already begun establishing human civilization. It should never be our goal to try and change the racist ass white man's perception of us. Instead, it should be our goal to succeed in spite of the racist ass white man's perception of us. It would be far worse to fail and be destroyed under the "nigger identity." There is no self-condemnation to be made by the black race as to why we still rebel and continue to fight back against this racist ass white system of government for liberation under the same bold and rebellious identity.

It is important to understand that in the minds of our once African slave ancestors, their emotional feeling of rebellion and liberation lived, breathed, and died under their "nigger identity." We know that the racist ass, white oppressor will always perceive us as a race full of worthless sub-human niggers to eventually be destroyed. But, like our rebellious African ancestors, many of us take the racist ass, white man to task under the same bold and rebellious "nigger identity."

Given the deep and painful truth about our enslavement by the racist ass, white, slave-master, and all the sick and brutal crimes attached to having branded us as niggers, the white race should also understand why blacks will never again in our history tolerate whites calling us niggers. The genocide of any race of people is the greatest crime against humanity. So when the world rightfully condemned the horror of nearly 6,000,000 European converts to Judaism being exterminated under Hitler's regime, how is it that the same European world is so willing to hide and turn blindly away from the fact that approximately forty or fifty million African slaves, of which many were Israelites and not Russian converts to Judaism, died all sorts of horrible deaths during the Transatlantic slave trade? It stands as one of the greatest, glossed over horrors and losses of human life in the history of mankind.

It is my effort that the racist ass, white man will finally get it, that the internal struggle and problems with the usage of the "nigger word" has nothing to do with validating and encouraging white racism to be cast upon the black race. Being the descendants of slaves in this country and not truly understanding the deep impact of our slave experience and how the "nigger identity" became a part of our African expression, have left us trapped in unwarranted guilt for not having broken our association with the "nigger identity." As the black race in America, we should not allow the racist ass, white man to justify his dirty ass by thinking he is somehow entitled to call us niggers because of our usage of the "nigger" word. We owe no explanation to this racist ass, white bastard about our internal struggle with the usage of the "nigger" word.

As descendants of our once African, slave ancestors, are we to be ashamed of the fact that they rebelled and liberated themselves under their slave "nigger identity?" Are we to shamefully disown them for handing this same rebellious attitude down from generation to generation? We have to understand historically that, despite the "nigger identity" being branded on our African ancestors by the racist ass, white slave-master. Yet, our African ancestors rebelled under it. They achieved liberation under it. And finally, it was they who understood that we as a race would always be perceived as a race full of lowlife, worthless sub-human niggers by the racist ass white man, no matter what we did. My point is this -- if the internal struggle with our usage of the "nigger" word causes some of our moral scholars, educators, and civic leaders to base their efforts to get rid of the usage of the "nigger" word because of white perception, then such efforts will never change anything externally. White racism has already indicted the entire Black race as inferior, worthless, lowlife, criminal, niggers who are doomed by our own racial make-up alone.

As we continue to grapple with the usage of the "nigger" word in our culture, let us move forward by letting go of this long-held, misconstrued notion that the usage of the "nigger" word in our culture is somehow actually hurting our external image to the rest of the world. Being perceived as niggers by racist ass white people doesn't make or break us, but our attitude, behavior, and course of action does. And so having been forced under the bondage of slavery in America, the attitude, behavior, and course of action by our African ancestors was rebellion under their "nigger identity." It's not the "nigger identity" itself that's actually hurting and hindering us. It's the attitude and behavior of these racist ass, white, slave-master, conditioned minded ass niggers. You see, we have to act more like the rebellious and liberated minded slaves who would no longer answer to the racist ass, white slave-master under their "nigger identity."

It didn't matter if he tried saying "good niggers" to these rebellious and now liberated minded slaves, because everything he tried to say to them, going forward, was seen as bad. They didn't reject their "nigger identity," but they now despised what their racist ass, white, slave-master surrogate father did to them under their "nigger identity." They had not forgotten all the perverted and sick things that were done to them. They had not forgotten all the times they were whipped, beaten, and lynched even when they had behaved as so called "good little niggers." In this day and age, if a racist ass, white person dared to call a black person a nigger, it sets off a very confrontational attitude in many black people. Even amongst ourselves, some Black people will become very angry if another Black person calls them a nigger with the same negative intent as a racist ass, white person.

The "nigger identity" was handed down to us by our ex-slave African ancestors, and now many of us among the black masses have taken the same ownership of the "nigger" word with a free pass to use it however we see fit. Even though our African ancestors had rebelled and finally gained liberation from slavery, the deep historical truth still remains that the "nigger" identity was branded into our psyche by the racist ass, white slave-master, while acting as the surrogate and biological father of our African ancestors. He was able to do this after our African ancestors were brought to America under the cruel bondage of slavery. And now tragically for many of us, the deep psychological problem of rejection still exists among blacks because of the unwillingness of the racist ass, white man to accept them. It is this sort of twisted and dysfunctional slave-master father and nigger slave child relationship forced under slavery that keeps many of us still pandering up to the racist ass, white man for acceptance.

Just as Brother Malcolm spoke, even to this very day, we have blacks among us who continually act like the "house niggers," who were dead set against the "field nigger's" rebellious attitude; the same "house niggers" who scratched, clawed, and screamed because of not wanting their racist ass, white slave-master to lose control over them and their "nigger name." But, now racist ass, white people have been forced into using the "nigger" word in private to degrade and mock black people. So now if the racist ass, white man wants to continue with his racist ass coalition of branding blacks as niggers, they would have to keep carrying it out in the dark. The racist ass, white, man has been very successful in making the "nigger" word a plague and a symbol of universal hate and racism towards black people.

There are probably only small pockets of the entire world where the "nigger" word has not been used or heard in making racist attacks upon black people. In the past, no matter how determined our moral scholars, educators and civic leaders have been in their efforts to discourage the use of the "nigger" word in our culture, their reasoning has fallen on deaf ears and now comes across as them being no more than apologists for the black race. It would be delusional for us to actually believe that one would be able to reach out into all of urban Black America and erase the "nigger" word from our culture. If digging deeper into the history of the racist ass, white man doesn't bear further charges as to why white people are forbidden to call black people niggers, it is certainly my effort not to fall short of a revealing argument about the evil atrocities that the racist ass, white slave-master was allowed to force upon black people during slavery.

Regardless of what the racist ass, white man will not stop at to further his racist ass causes, our moral leaders should not have to go on acting as apologists for the sub-culture within the black race where the "nigger" word still exists. We must come to grips with the stark reality that the racist external perception of black people as niggers has already been set within racist, white supremacy ideology that exists within the white race. Because of the ills of slavery against the black race, our usage of the "nigger" word will never allow the racist ass, white man, or any race for that matter, to judge us from the outside when they have not suffered what we have from the inside. One of the most important and critical things that we are left to deal with out of the slave culture, are the attitudes that developed under the "nigger identity."

It is very crucial to realize that one of the things that the racist ass, white, slave-master did to justify slavery was to portray our African ancestors as being no more than subhuman, nigger animals. After having done this the next goal was to condition our African ancestors into behaving like sub-human animals. Even to this very day the racist ass, white man uses the same blueprint to demonize, de-humanize, and systematically destroy the Black race as a form of genocide.

The racist ass, white, slave-master, along with his own sick and perverted behavior promoted all sorts of savagery within the slave quarters. There were those among our African ancestors who caved in to this sub-human animal like conditioning, while others resisted, even to the point of death. But those who became broken under their "nigger identity," began acting as willful savages among their own people. They quickly learned that their acts of savagery served a useful purpose for the racist ass, white, slave-master. Under their "nigger identity" these sub-human acting slaves knew that murdering another slave would only become severe to their racist ass, white, slave-master if they were not able to make up the workload for the slave who had been slain. But on the other hand, those slaves who resisted and did not allow themselves to cave in to this sub-human conditioning, became the real threat to the racist ass, white slave-master. It was these slaves who became the black revolutionary leaders of the slave revolts.

As a race of people, we cannot allow the racist ass, white man's history of slavery to quietly and tactfully be dismissed as being one of the single most evil and wicked horrors against humanity. No perversion imaginable would be farfetched as to what the racist ass, White, slave-master was able to force upon our African ancestors. Many of them were no more than vile and perverted beasts who raped black mothers. And they were pedophiles along with other racist whites who forced their perverted lifestyles upon black slaves.

Even racist ass, white women had a part in the exploitation of black slaves. It was decided among some of them that if not under the laws of the racist ass, white man, then by way of his own pervert deeds, they held half ownership of the property owned by the racist ass, white slave-master. But even just the thought of a white woman having a sexual interest in a black male slave the same as the racist ass, white, slave-master had for black female slaves posed a serious threat. It was this sort of sick and perverted sexual exploitation of our African ancestors that remains at the very root of why the black man is still so deeply despised by the racist ass, white man in regard to any association with a white woman. Black men were already being murdered by lynch mobs and it was out of this sort of racist hate that led to even further hate and the castration of black men. The racist ass, white man now suffers from some sort of twisted, white male, emasculated complex when comparing his manhood to that of a black man. But he has no one to blame but himself because he was the one who marched black men and women in chains naked, and half-naked, exposing their body parts as they were being led off to be sold on the auction block.

Chapter Seven

Racism in Sports

Let's put aside the sexual myths about black men and remember Jesse Owens in the 1936 Berlin Olympics, and the so-called Aryan, white supremacy in the world of sports. You have to remember that the racist ass, white man started this racist, white supremacy ideology shit in sports. And, what did black men and women do to dispel it once the racist ass, white man could no longer keep us from competing in the world of organized sports? We obliterated this racist ass idea of Aryan white supremacy. And what honors did we receive for it! We became even more despised as "niggers." Oh, and I might add "beautiful, shiny, black, gold medal, winning niggers," at that. Against racist oppression in this country, we have raised the American flag in some of the most prominent and prestigious events in Olympic sports history. Yet, racist ass, whites in America have stood up in patriotic hypocrisy with their hands across their chest, pretending to support us while still despising us in their racist ass hearts. They never stop scheming and hoping for our demise no matter what area of achievement we strive for.

In this age of the steroid culture in sports, do not allow yourself to believe the racist ass hypocrisy about only wanting to clean up the use of performance-enhancing drugs to protect the integrity of sports. The very reason they had their racist ass, white, scientists experimenting with performance-enhancing drugs was to find a way to catch up as well as gain an edge on the superior athletic skills of black athletes. Imagine if the steroid culture had existed during the time of Hitler's reign. Look at it from this perspective - average white athletes were taking performance-enhancing drugs to try and bridge the gap between themselves and the extraordinary natural talent of black athletes. But, once black athletes started getting hold of performance-enhancing drugs, white athletes when using them, were only going from average to good. But, black athletes, went from great to even greater. In the end, it negated white athlete's hopes of getting ahead of the same curve.

In this respect, the use of performance-enhancing drugs became counter-productive for whites in their efforts to overtake Black athletes. You see, the problem within the white race involving the world of organized sports is that we, as blacks, display far more genuine fairness and integrity when it comes to putting our Black athletes on the face of sports. Unlike most white athletes and white coaches, black athletes and black coaches care very little for race favoritism over talent. It is very important for us to know that we are at the top because of our ability and not because of our racial makeup. But, racist ass, whites are very satisfied with doing the exact opposite.

For example, white racism still plays a major role in scouting baseball talent. There are three essential skillsets that go a long way in helping baseball players achieve success: speed, hitting, and fielding. Hands down, niggers have proven themselves to be very gifted with speed. Imagine having all of that speed gap-to-gap at all three outfield positions. Imagine all the hits and runs that can be taken away from the opposing teams. Imagine all of that blazing speed along the base path and the stolen bases and runs that could be scored. And, last but not least, check the record book and see where niggers stand in hitting and home runs. I think they have held their own on defense in the gold glove category.

It's by far one of the greatest sport's tragedies to realize just how long white racism in both amateur and professional baseball has robbed African Americans from displaying their baseball talent. But, in all of their racist ass hypocrisy, racist ass whites still have the damned nerve to pay tribute to the old Negro League while all of this racist ass shit continues to plague America's favorite pastime. Whenever the racial make-up is black vs. white in sports competition, racist ass whites have no problem cheating blacks or employing token ass house niggers along with them to assist in carrying it out. Tragically, because of the history of slavery and the ongoing racism in this country, blacks and whites will never be able to fully escape the attitude of being driven by race pride when pitted against each other.

Even in our most sincere efforts to keep up good and impartial race relationships between ourselves, it still becomes difficult for us to keep our feelings of race pride suppressed. Racist ass whites have always held the upper-hand and have a well-known history of not playing fair against niggers in sport's competition. And now, look what is happening to us today in the world of sports. Blacks are allowed to play sports, but rarely are they able to manage or coach amateur and professional sports programs proportionally to whites. For blacks to hold a majority ownership of a professional sports team such as basketball, football, and baseball is a feat that, unfortunately, has to go down as the rarest of accomplishments in the history of professional sports in this country.

When not exploiting us for their own financial gains, they discriminate against our race and our athletic talent. And because whites dominate ownership and control over sports organizations, they hold the power of hiring racist ass, white coaches, and managers. And whenever possible, they then discriminate against black athletes by putting less talented white athletes ahead of them in all facets of amateur and professional sports. Sadly, amateur and professional baseball from the bottom to the top is a prime example of the most fierce, racist ass efforts still in existence to keep African Americans discriminated against when it comes to their baseball talent. It's also the same in management. They care very little about supporting youth baseball programs for inner-city youth. But, they have no racist damn problem whatsoever in financing and supporting youth leagues for suburban white kids.

Their racist ass goal is to get African Americans out of competing in both amateur and professional baseball as well as suppressing them from holding managerial positions. Baseball is one of the last frontiers in sports in which racist ass whites see themselves having their faces plastered at the top. And yet, African American athletes still hold some of the most prestigious records in professional baseball history. Blacks have been dominating in basketball, football, and specific areas of track and field. And, even though we are not dominating in heavy weight boxing as we once did, we still hold the title of having been its greatest champions until another great, black champion ascends to the throne to carry on the tradition. Rest in peace, brother, Muhammad Ali.

Racism and segregation in sports were two of the essential reasons in making black, college, athletic programs so vital in helping blacks develop in sports. The black hall of fame coach that had much to do with Black achievement in sports was the legendary Grambling football coach Eddie Robinson.

The historical importance of Black colleges is steeped in the history of racism in this country, and we should always give honor to those African Americans who founded, as well as supported them. Not long before I was born, Jackie Robinson was breaking down the color barrier in baseball. And, not too long after I was born, two African American students were breaking down the walls of segregation at the University of Alabama. The racist ass, white power structure in this country has kept the doors of opportunity locked for African Americans, even after slavery had been abolished. Therefore, establishing black colleges was vital in helping blacks make progress in both academics and sports. It was one of the very reasons that inspired me to enroll at Jackson State University as a freshman student athlete. And, to show a small example of racist ass politics in sports, at Jackson State, a small black college was a sophomore football player by the name of Walter Payton, who was competing for the Heisman Trophy. Walter Payton became one of the NFL's greatest running backs of all time. Anyone who ever saw him in football practice, or saw him play in college football games and have any knowledge about sports greatness, knew that the NFL Hall of Fame in Canton, Ohio, had a place already waiting for his statue. May he rest in peace.

Unfortunately, racist ass politics in sports is still alive and well. Archie Griffin, another African American athlete was competing for the Heisman Trophy during the time of Walter Payton's college career. But it was Archie Griffin who succeeded in winning the Heisman Trophy, twice, and no one can argue the fact that it still stands as one of college football's greatest achievements. In my opinion, either one of those Heisman Trophies could easily have been sitting on Walter Payton's mantle. To witness Archie Griffin win two Heisman Trophies was a proud moment for African Americans. But, to have seen Walter win one would have been even sweeter. Unfortunately it was not to be, due to the influence of legendary, football coach Woody Hayes, and the biased ass, white, selection committee. They couldn't fathom the thought of a black athlete from a small, black college winning the Heisman Trophy. It would have been bad business for a powerful, white, athletic, collegiate program like Ohio State that uses achievements like the Heisman Trophy as a selling pitch to recruit, as well as achieve great financial gains.

I refused to buy their racist ass garbage about the level of competition in black colleges during the time Walter Payton competed. Because during Walter's era in the S.W.A.C., (Southwestern Athletic Conference), the black athletes on the defensive line, linebacker position, and cornerback position, were just as good or better than the talent at any of the major Division I schools. Much of the same could be said for the offensive side of the ball and especially at the skill positions that produced the likes of the great legendary and hall of fame, wide receiver, Jerry Rice and history making, Superbowl winning quarterback, Doug Williams. On the offensive line, there were elite linemen such as the all pro, hall of famer, Jackie Slater. The rich and talented history of Black college football could go on and on.

Shifting from collegiate football to professional basketball, let's examine the front office management that involved the Michael Jordan and Scottie Pippen led Chicago Bulls. Unless their remarkable feat becomes surpassed, they will most likely go down as the greatest championship team assembled in NBA history. They went on a remarkable run, winning three consecutive NBA championships, and then took a loss trying to make it four straight. But during that year, Jordan went on a short hiatus from the sport in pursuit of a professional baseball career. Jordan returned near the end of the season, but it was not enough to keep the Bulls reigning on their throne. But, with Jordan back at full force the following season, the Bulls went on another remarkable run for three more consecutive NBA championships.

Barring the year that Jordan left the sport, the Bulls could possibly have won eight NBA championships in a row. But the racist ass, white management, and ownership broke the team up after winning their sixth NBA title. Aside from the conflict between Coach Phil Jackson and the Bull's front office, Michael Jordan and Scottie Pippen held zero leverage to retain Jackson as coach. To that white management and ownership, Jordan and Pippen were seen as no more than two great, prized niggers on the racist ass, White, slave-master's plantation. It didn't matter one bit that the Bull's fans were robbed of at least two more championships with the tandem of Jordan and Pippen. Instead of keeping the team together with Jackson as coach, management and ownership wanted it to be known beyond a shadow of doubt that the racist ass, white plantation's owner signed the paychecks and not the niggers working under his racist ass, white supremacist authority. This is just one case in many of which racist ass, white ownership in sports has been able to continue keeping the upper hand over niggers.

As a blueprint example of sports solidarity working in our favor occurred at the University of Missouri. The African American football players launched a protest against racism on their campus. We have to show that we have no tolerance for complacency towards racist ass behavior, and one of the places it should not be tolerated is on the campuses of learning institutions where diversity should be allowed to exist and flourish. Racist expressions shouldn't be allowed to hide behind the First Amendment Right of free speech.

Bringing down the white establishment at the University of Missouri for showing complacency and tolerance for the status quo of resurging institutionalized racism, was by all measures the right protest. Youth movement protests against the political establishment have a historical past of having been launched from university campuses, and the University of Missouri is no different in this respect. But, what will become uniquely different about the University of Missouri's protest is how it was carried out and the swift effect it had in bringing down the once thought to be untouchable white administration.

The African American football player's threat to boycott their games and the potential financial and political fallout was too great a risk for the governing body of the University of Missouri to take. The act of solidarity taken by the African American football players and the student body that supported them should be used as a blueprint for demonstrating how to force change within white institutions unwilling to act swiftly against racism. We cannot afford to allow racism to revive an atmosphere of racist hate on college campuses as it once existed during the time of segregation of the 50's and 60's. And yet the racist ass, white, news media is all for supporting this kind of blatant interpretation of the First Amendment right in order to continue reviving and promoting an open atmosphere to freely express hate and racism against African Americans throughout this country.

One racist ass, white, news media commentator even tried to discredit the University of Missouri protest by criticizing the team for not having a winning record. What does a losing damn football record have to do with allowing racism to be victorious? It's a clear example of how the racist ass, white, slave-master views niggers on a slave plantation. In other words, this racist ass, white, news media commentator is saying that these are lazy niggers producing no value and should not be allowed to question the white administration's tolerance of allowing a racist ass atmosphere to be created on their campus.

What we are seeing is simply more racist ass, white supremacy, hypocrisy shit by the racist ass, white, news media. If the *Black Lives Matter* movement can be condemned for exercising their First Amendment right of free speech, then how is it that the racist ass, White, news media could so quickly use the First Amendment right of free speech to come to the defense of racist ass, white, hate speech on the University of Missouri campus? You see, nothing has changed about the history of slavery with these racist ass, white bastards, because they still have the same racist ass double standards regarding the constitution when it comes to them and niggers.

And then there was Donald Sterling's racist ass remarks about blacks. Just think about it for a moment. If NBA ownership like Mark Cuban would dare cross the line by appearing as though he was willing to defend the racist ass behavior of Donald Sterling, how do you think the more conservative white owners felt in defense of Sterling? But, with black players and the player's union stirring up support against Sterling, he was eventually forced into selling his NBA franchise. It is this sort of racist ass behavior of management and ownership that stands as a clear example of how many of these powerful white owners of professional sports organizations think when it comes to having Black athletes competing for them.

I was a student athlete in grade school, high school, and college, and I am well aware of the kind of sheltered world that is built around amateur and professional athletes. Living mostly in a pacified and pampered world might be ideal for some black athletes, but the problem is that it is nowhere near the real world of how niggers are viewed by the culture of racist ass, white sports institutions. There are some unique and exceptional sports related relationships being created among whites and blacks that, because of the human enrichment it brings to race relations, should not be undermined. But, these kinds of relationships sadly exist as a small bubble and will never be allowed to have great influence over the racist ass culture of white ownership in both professional and amateur sports when it comes to accepting niggers on an equal playing field and not based solely on exploiting their athletic talent.

The bubble exists mainly because of sport's politics and is, in most cases, easily ruptured. This is why so many of these racist ass, white, sports organizations are now finally acting chummy with niggers. Remember, the seed of racist white sports politics was planted when Jack Johnson stepped into the boxing ring, when Jesse Owens exploded out of the starting blocks during the 1936 Berlin Olympics, and when Jackie Robinson was allowed to put on a major league, baseball uniform. But, none of these extraordinary athletes were accepted on an equal playing field involving their human rights. As much as the sports world involving racist ass whites still despise niggers, they began suppressing their racist ass attitudes in favor of diplomacy in order to exploit both the political and financial value that niggers bring to the world of sports.

From the very time that the racist ass, white man began exploiting the black man and woman during slavery, he became well aware of our extraordinary ability to persevere even under the worst conditions. But, before the racist ass, white man began understanding the financial and political value of exploiting our talents, it was their racist ass goal to keep us out of every prosperous industry in this country. Professional sports is just one prime example. But, just look at the sport's world alone, blacks have shown the extraordinary ability to excel at the top of nearly every sport that they take a profound interest. Take a close look at women's gymnastics and the dominance by Simone Biles and the Olympic gold medal winner, Gabriel Douglas.

As for Biles, she's already being considered the greatest women's gymnast of all times. And yet the sports body and media of women's gymnastics have kept her sports dominance as quiet as possible. Biles is the three time, all-around champion from 2013 to 2015. She is the first woman to win three consecutive titles at the World Artistic Gymnastics Championships. She has amassed fourteen world medals, ten of them gold, two silver, and two bronze. She owns the most world gold medals in women's gymnastics history. Biles and Douglas took gold and silver, respectively, at the 2015 women's all-around finals competition at the World Artistic Gymnastics Championships. They even followed it up by striking gold at the 2016 Olympics and, just maybe, Biles will receive the recognition in the world of women's gymnastics that she so well deserves.

Another example is Simone Manuel who made sport's history by becoming the first African American woman to win a gold medal in an individual, swimming event which she followed up with a silver. She also added another gold, and a silver medal in team events.

It was another great moment for African Americans when Debbie Thomas ascended to the top of women's figure skating as a 1986 world champion and two time national champion. But during her climb, she was often met with discrimination by figure skating judges not wanting to accept an African American woman at the top of their sport.

Racist whites who control the sports world are well aware of the fact that when Black youth take a keen interest in a particular sport and is given the chance to develop, they show an uncanny ability to excel. In this respect, they resent and envy and fear niggers more than niggers realize, no differently than it was during the time of slavery.

The racist ass, white man still makes billions upon billions of dollars off exploiting the extraordinary gifts of blacks as niggers. Therefore, the racist ass, white man's main goal is to keep us laboring under his authority while receiving the least amount of gain on the backend. Racist white sports powers have learned how to craft and suppress their racist ass attitudes towards niggers for profit as well as other political exploits. When it comes to the racist ass, white man in power, niggers have to be very careful on how we claim and defend progress with whites, or we will be left continually having to defend regrets. Otherwise, in the words of Brother Malcolm, we are getting hood-winked.

I only say this about rebellious, field niggers because house niggers would never allow themselves to feel hood-winked by their racist ass, white slave-masters. They will quickly and repeatedly argue, "Why what's wrong with you, you crazy, ungrateful ass nigger? Can't you see how good boss done been to us niggers by allowing us to work and live on his big plantation?" You know how impossible it is for hell to freeze over? It is just as impossible to get a racist ass, white, slave-master ass, house nigger to separate, or go against his racist ass, white, slave-master.

Let's take another look at racist ass politics in sports. Serena Williams is arguably the greatest female athlete in sport's history. We know that in the world of women's tennis, she already owns this mantle. These racist ass, powerful corporations who pay millions of dollars for professional athletes to promote their products, put Maria Sharapova financially ahead of Serena Williams in endorsement deals. Somehow her brand is supposedly more marketable than Serena Williams. You're damn right it is, seeing how these racist ass, white, powerful corporations have based it on her lily white skin and not on her sports greatness when compared to that of Serena Williams.

The racist element within the sports body of women's professional tennis tried to dismantle the William's sisters by plastering Sharapova as the face of the sport. And, just as I said, during this same time, racist ass, white corporations quickly jumped on Sharapova's band wagon and began offering her major endorsement deals. And look how they were rewarded, she ended up testing positive for a banned substance. Still, not one of them is willing to laud the fact that it was the William sisters who transcended women's professional tennis from being primarily seen as a teeny bopper, professional sport. The William sisters changed it into a highly glamourous and fashionable, women's professional sports. As sisters, they have practically dominated women's professional tennis well into their mid-thirties. Their extraordinary athletic ability of still being crowned as champions has set a new standard for sport's dominance.

They have also brought fashion, style, and glamour to the sport in such a way that had never been done before. Maybe someday the world of women's professional tennis will honor them for their extraordinary and remarkable feat. It's a very legitimate argument that the William sisters have achieved something that will never be duplicated or surpassed. For anyone who is unwilling to acknowledge, or cannot comprehend, the William sister's greatness, forever is a long time for someone to try and equal or overtake them in their sports achievements.

Chapter Eight

Racism in Sports, Up Close & Personal

As I stated earlier, I attended Jackson State University as a freshman student athlete. I had received offers to attend several local small colleges in the Midwestern state where my family had moved as well as a couple of letters of interest from Division One schools. But, instead of responding to their interest, I wanted to return to my southern roots and play football at an all-black college. Looking back, if I had made the football team as a walk on, I would not have transferred to some small, racist ass, white college in another part of Mississippi. At Jackson State, I had to wait until spring practice to try out, and one of my closest friends tried out with me, but the coaches had already had an interest in him coming out of high school as a six foot two, wide receiver from Natchez, Mississippi. Ray did make the team as a walk on, but later quit because of siding with the fact that I did not. At only five feet eight and a half, I played running back in high school but converted to wide receiver once I attended college. Fortunately, for me, I did because Walter Payton, a sophomore at the time, owned the running back position.

The Jackson State football team had talent stacked at just about every position. They had a wide receiver named Isaac Bridges. In my eyes, he was one of the greatest college talents that never became known. For those us who believe jet black skin is beautiful, Ike was it. But, unlike that old racist cartoon character that racist ass whites used to poke fun at dark complexions, none of that could be branded on Ike. You know the old cartoon character of the black fellow with smut black skin, big lips, and big, white eyes? No nigger who has not been brainwashed would accept such a racist ass stereotype in regards to African people with beautiful, jet black skin.

Ike must have been about six foot three, and when he put on his helmet, all you could see was that jet black, silhouette image from inside. I had never seen a wide receiver with so much explosive quickness and raw speed. Ike had footwork like a ballerina when he pivoted or cut in and out of routs. It was a thing of sheer beauty to watch -- poetry in motion. But, the big brute of a head coach would not let him compete except in certain games because the rap on Ike was he did not like to practice. The big, towering, head coach only allowed him to play in big games such as Grambling and Alcorn. I think it might have been a home game against Grambling when the head coach decided to allow him to start.

Jimmy Lewis, the quarterback, threw a rainbow bomb straight down the middle of the field. All you could see was Ike with that blazing speed, separating from the defense as though the sea had parted. He made an electrifying, over the shoulder catch for a touchdown. The NFL should've come calling and rescued Ike after that very game. Instead, oddly, I remembered him getting kicked out of practice the same night I got cut from trying to make the football team. I only lasted for two sprint drills. I was so nervous that I nearly jumped off sides on the first one, but when I jumped off sides on the second one, the big head coach who struck sheer terror in me called me over and said, "Son, you're too small to be in here," and sent me packing. Other than not being able to be a part of that Black, elite, football team, the thing that bothered me even worse was getting humiliated in front of Walter Payton, one of the greatest football players to ever play the game.

I remember Ike catching up with me and trying to console me. I don't know if Ike felt sorry for me or what. But what I did know was I was dealing with the worst hurt and dejection I had ever felt in my life at that time. Still, for that brief moment, it made me feel better to have what I felt to be one of the greatest, college, wide receivers ever to play the game walking next to a nobody. But once I made it back to my dorm, the only thing that I felt like doing afterwards was packing my bags and leaving with my shattered dreams. The best way that I can describe the situation was that it felt as though the Gladys Knight song, "Midnight Train to Georgia," had been written especially for a sport's tragedy like the one I'd just experienced. And, as fate would have it, shortly afterward, I remember Walter showing up one night in the same little, off-campus, food restaurant that I frequented. He walked in wearing shorts, flip flop sandals, and a sleeveless, cut-off sweatshirt, looking chiseled like a Greek God with an air of confidence surrounding him as though he was already standing on top of the sport's world. But, here I stood with my crumbled little dream of having to choose between feeling great admiration or envy towards him.

After I got cut, I would sit in the stands and watch practice. I watched everything Walter and Ike did in practice down to the smallest details; their moves, the route running, their footwork, even the flashy way they dressed out in their uniforms during games. So, after my freshman year when I transferred to that little racist ass, white college, I took all the things I learned from watching the greats. I only decided to attend this little, racist ass, white college because Ray explained to me that a couple of his high school friends would be enrolling there the following year and that it would be a good idea for us to play football there as well.

We finished out our freshman year at Jackson State and then our sophomore year we transferred to this small, predominately white college in another part of Mississippi. We were not far into summer camp before Ray's two hometown friends quit the team because of the racist ass attitudes of the white coaching staff and some of the white players. They had a white defensive back on that team who was not shy about his racist ass feelings about black athletes. Other than hitting and tackling, he did not want to be anywhere near a nigger. One day, during practice, he and Ray got into a scuffle, and Ray busted his racist, white ass up pretty good, nosebleed and all. Seeing how Ray and I were close friends and roommates, the old, racist ass, White, head coach hated both of us even worse afterwards. Ray didn't want any part of that racist ass football program, so he left.

My family had already moved from Mississippi to Milwaukee during my freshman year of high school so I didn't want to leave the little racist ass college and return to Milwaukee without having found another university to enroll in. Besides, if I had not stayed there, I never would have met my new roommate, Jesse, another African American, and one of the most talented art students on that campus.

I remember, at that same, little, racist ass, white college, the Commodores were booked to do a gig at a time when they were still virtually unknown and trying to find their way onto the map of fame. It was Jesse who insisted that we go to the small assembly hall where they would be performing. Once we arrived, it was evident to us that this black band was being greeted by a small, white, redneck crowd. Along with Jesse and I, there was a small group of African American students in attendance. Despite how sparse the white crowd was, they kept themselves separated from the black students during the entire performance.

The little, white, redneck crowd was so sparse that you could walk right through them and up to the performance. There was no stage, so the band was at floor level. Their performance was both mellow and high energy from start to finish, but the crowd was lukewarm at best. Allow me to explain it this way. Do you know that feeling of embarrassment you get for musicians who're struggling to become successful, but no one is showing any real enthusiasm or support? This describes the atmosphere the Commodores were experiencing. Now, for anyone who does not believe the Commodores didn't pay their dues to become successful musicians, here's one small testimonial.

I remember Jesse saying something to the effect, "bro, these country rednecks don't know the making of a famous band when they hear one." He said, "bro, once the performance is over, let's go up and shake their hands and show our support, because when they become famous, we will have been the only ones to have ceased the moment of recognizing it." So, no sooner than the concert ended and they started taking down their band equipment, that little white, redneck ass crowd, along with the small number of black students, began to vanish. But, Jesse and I immediately approached the group and went on a handshaking and fan admiration mission as though we were the two hippest, young niggers on that small, racist ass, white campus. And, just as Jesse discerned it, the rest is history.

Jesse only participated in track, but I owe it to him for inspiring me to take art seriously. One odd thing about that little, white, racist college is that you didn't feel the racism in the art department the same way that it was felt in some of the other departments. It certainly wasn't felt the way it was inside the athletic department. Right after Ray had that fight, I don't know if that old, racist ass, white coach was trying to take it out on me, but at our next practice, he called for the nutcracker drill. The quarterback, the center, and ball carrier on offense and on defense, two line backers split out on both sides of the center and between the guard and tackle gap. That old, racist ass, white, head coach then called me out first as the ball carrier. They had one linebacker in the drill that was African American and was being touted as NFL caliber. The other linebacker was white. But, I had been at Jackson State the year before and knew close up what real NFL caliber linebackers looked like. With no disrespect, neither one of those linebackers in my eyes fit that description.

At Jackson State they had Robert Brazil, and, if I am not mistaken, he became a seven time Pro Bowler. At about 6'5 and over two hundred and fifty pounds, Brazil was so menacing, vicious, and violent on contact, that I once thought to myself that if I were to make that team I might have to pack a small pistol somewhere in my uniform just in case I survived the hit and the big fella didn't want to acknowledge that the whistle had blown. The real frightening part about it was that there was at least three or four other linebackers built in a similar mode. So, when the center snapped the ball, I was able to go untouched on the first run. But, instead of allowing the next ball carrier to run the drill, that old, racist, white coach screamed out to me, "come back here and run that damn play again." It was one of the most gratifying feelings that I could've felt at that moment.

Shortly after that practice, I suffered a severe hamstring pull during sprint drills, but there was no way that I would not have practiced if I could've gotten back on the football field. But that old racist ass white coach would not allow me enough time to heal and forced me back on the field a few days after the injury. I could barely run and limped through practice and contact drills. And much as I hated it, but after several more practices of this kind of treatment, I decided it was best for me not to stay in that racist ass, football program.

After leaving Jackson State University, it was as though I could not escape from enrolling in predominately white universities that didn't have a racist ass, football program. When I finally transferred to a northern school in the Midwest, I ended up experiencing some of the same racist ass problems. Not that it signifies a racist ass sports program, but the entire football coaching staff at that university was white. There were only five black athletes on the entire team, but I didn't learn how much racism was on that staff until just before the season started.

We were about three weeks away from breaking summer camp to begin the season. We had just finished our afternoon practice and was starting for the locker room when the head coach yelled and told me to stay on the field. I jogged to where he was standing, which was somewhere near the middle of the practice field. The head coach took a knee then told me to take a knee next to him. He then looked me straight in the eyes and the first thing he said was, "you know the last wide receiver at this position from a year ago is now in the NFL." The brother he was talking about was another African American who was drafted in the third round by the Buffalo Bills. He then said to me, "I am going to give you the same chance to go to the NFL at the same position." After all the hard work and sweat from Pop Warner Football League to high school and college, the only thing that would've been more gratifying was reaching the ultimate goal.

Once we broke that little meeting, I thanked the coach then got up off my knee then jogged back to the locker room feeling as though my feet were floating on clouds. But no more than a week later all of it came crashing down. This was a division two university in the Midwest and with barely a handful of niggers on campus when compared to the white population on campus. The problem started when I was approached by this white female student. I first thought of her as a groupie when she told me that she knew I was a football player. But eventually, her persistence led to casual involvement. Soon afterward, I learned that her boyfriend was one of the white grad assistant coaches. My instant fear was that my entire football future would be destroyed. I knew that if this got back to her boyfriend my chances to continue playing football at that school would be over. So, the next time this white female and I met, I explained to her that I didn't know she was the girlfriend of one of the grad assistant coaches. I then explained to her that the relationship had to end. But, what that white girl said next, I could not believe my ears were hearing. She said that before she would allow this to happen, she would tell her boyfriend. Still, regardless of what she threatened to do, I knew I was not going to be involved with her again.

A few days after being back at football practice, I got my answer as to how this would play out. Out of nowhere, I went from being the number one receiver on the depth chart to the third string receiver on the scout team. The racist ass, white coach that I felt was responsible for it was another grad assistant coach who had just been cut from an NFL team as a free agent wide receiver. I was later told that he was friends with the grad assistant whose girlfriend that I had encountered. To make things even worse, this racist ass, white, grad assistant coach was also my position coach.

As if things was not already bad enough, shortly afterwards it got even worse when three of my white, female friends showed up at my dorm window after curfew. My white roommate and I were both awakened by all the loud knocking on the window. I immediately got up from my bunk and opened it, then tried to get them to leave before their presence got me into even more trouble with those racist ass, white coaches. But, it was too late. When I peered down the side of the building, I spotted two of those white coaches at the far end corner of the dorm. And, as the three females broke and ran away, I saw one of the coaches step out from alongside the building and begin counting window slots that led right up to where the girl's had been standing. With my roommate already having been awakened by the noise, I was now busted.

I felt my dream of getting the opportunity of becoming a professional football player was being shattered. Even though I was now dying inside, I had so much passion for the game that I didn't want to give up and quit playing. But the tension between me and this racist ass, White, assistant coach was so thick that you could cut it with a knife. Still, that only motivated me to work even harder in practice. It didn't matter if it was on the scout team, the doghouse team, whatever, as long as I was able to put on a uniform and touch a football.

I remember one practice I was on the scout team going against one of the schemes of the starting defense. One of the old, racist ass, white defensive coaches called up what he felt was one of their best linebackers and placed him on me in bump and run coverage. He said, "Now if this was the wide receiver who just went to the NFL, we would not be in this coverage." He made the entire play call feel like a subpar, nigger boy athlete against and All American white boy athlete.

When the quarterback started calling the signal, the linebacker broke down in attack mode. With his arms and the palms of his hands facing me, he was positioned for immediate contact to jam me. But, when the snap signal was called, that linebacker was still at the line of scrimmage, feet frozen, hands still tucked. I was already slanting down field with one hand raised, asking for the football to be delivered. But, those old racist ass white coaches were so pissed they refused to allow the quarterback to throw me the football.

Once the season started, not having any quickness or speed at the wide out position, only made things worse for their team's struggling offense. They already had a losing record of around zero and four, and the racist, white, head coach was fed up with his all white starting receiving corp not making plays during games. We were just getting ready for the next game and balls were being dropped, and routes were being run poorly without getting any separation from the defense. But there I was on the sideline as a third or fourth string scout team player eager to play, but still having to stand there agonizing and watching. Even though the racist ass, white coach was unwilling to put me back as a starter on the depth chart, he had seen enough of this ineptitude in practice by his white receivers ahead of me. So, out of nowhere, the head coach angrily screamed at me and said, "Dammit, Mitch, get up here and show these receivers how I want this damn play ran!"

Again, they put this white kid on me who they felt was their best corner. The play was meant to be a fifteen yard out route for the first down. But, the cornerback, already knowing the down and distance, played off of me for about ten yards. I quickly drove him down to about twenty yards and then dug in on an inside pivot. He bit on the fake and was frozen near the spot I had just vacated. I then took the route to the sideline. The ball was already in the air, traveling as though it was on a rope, but angling too far out of bounds for me to make the play with both hands. So, as the ball arrived, I dove for it while reaching out and extending my right arm and hand to their full limit and caught the ball and tucked it as I slid, dragging both feet inbounds. As I looked up with my head turned back towards the coaching staff all I saw was a bunch of white coaches and players jumping up and down like cheerleaders. I then jumped up with the ball, jogged back, and took my rank with the scout team. After practice, the big defensive coordinator walked up to me and said, "Boy, you know you are a pro, don't you?" I replied, "Are you talking to me, coach?" He then said, "You're the only one standing here besides me, aren't you?" I then said, "Yes sir, coach."

I remember that things were going so bad for the team that a player's only team meeting was called by the team captains. But, only the seniors were allowed to address the team. Once it was my turn, it was as though all of those white players couldn't wait to hear what I had to say after seeing how I had been demoted to the scout team and a bench warmer. But, dead serious as I was, when I finally spoke, it startled me that I drew a big round of laughs after having shouted at the top of my voice, "What is wrong with you guys? I got girls in the stands!" It didn't dawn on me at the time, but they were probably thinking, "Nigger, fooling around with our white women is what got your black ass in this predicament in the first place." It certainly would have been a position from which I would not have had any defensive argument against.

But, even while all of this was happening, I knew that tempers between me and that racist ass, white receiving coach was on the edge of exploding and, shortly afterwards, it finally happened. The racist ass, white, assistant, receiving coach had the wide outs running crossing routes, and he was throwing the ball probably no more than ten to twelve yards away from us. I was the only receiver that had not dropped any balls and the more balls I caught, the harder he tried to throw them. Finally, he threw me a ball that was traveling with so much velocity that I had to jump near the height of my waistline to have any chance of catching it. But, during the catch, the force of the ball caused my body to lean into an arched shape. Even though I was able to make a clean catch, I was pulled too far to the side, and my lead foot didn't give me enough balance to keep my body from making contact with the ground. Once I returned to the receiver's line, some of my teammates were giving me hand slaps. While watching, this racist ass, white, receiving coach hastily said, "Yeah, but next time stay on your feet."

It was those words that finally became the straw that broke the camel's back. The anger wasn't about what he said because, as a player, your entire goal is to get better. So, it was not hard for me to except the criticism from that perspective. But, I was already at a boiling point because of what I had been going through with these racist ass, white coaches. So, the problem was not what was said, but who said it. Before I could think the words "fuck you" was already out of my mouth. The next thing I heard from that racist ass, white coach was, "go turn your equipment in. You are off this team."

Boy, I knew he had to have been waiting a long time to finally utter those words to me. Part of me wanted to say, "Coach, I didn't mean it." But I knew if he didn't accept my apology, I probably would've tried to kill his racist, white ass right there on that football field. My only other option was to respect his racist ass, white, authority and leave the field. I was so devastated that I couldn't sleep that entire night. The next morning, my only chance to try and get back on the football team was to talk to the head coach. As I walked into the athletic department that morning I felt as though I was going before a racist ass, white coach with the power of giving me a lifetime ban from ever playing football again. I nervously walked to his office. There he was, the door already open, and sitting at his desk as though he was expecting me. The first thing I said when I walked through that door is, "Coach, why are you'all doing this to me? I believe in God too." He looked up at me from his desk, making eye contact. He then said to me, "Mitch, you are the best wide receiver on this team. But who am I going to keep, you, or my receiving coach?

I knew it had to be a rhetorical question, so I stood there utterly defenseless and dejected. But I either had to be desperate, naïve, or both when he said, "I tell you what, Mitch, if you go back and apologize to your position coach and he accepts you back on the team, I will go along with it." I left that office so fast to go back and try to apologize that I couldn't think straight. And not that it would have mattered, but instead of going to this racist ass, white coach in street clothes to apologize, I was so desperate to get back onto that team, I decided to put my practice gear on and then head to the practice field. But, now that I've looked back on it, that racist ass, white coach must have thought to himself that I had to be one cocky ass, over confident, ass nigger. But, that walk to the field was filled with deep anxiety. Once I was able to sort this racist ass, white coach out from the hoard of players, it was as if they all rescinded and left all of this open space for us to talk. I then walked gradually up to him, practice uniform on, helmet in hand.

He was about six foot two in height, and the first thing I did when I looked up at him was say, "Coach, I was really out of line about what I said the other day at practice, and I apologize for it, and I promise it will never happen again. Coach said that if you accepted my apology and allowed me back on the team, he would support it." But, this racist ass, white bastard looked me right in the eyes with this racist ass, sour look on his face and said, "No." He stood there with his head tilted as he said it. My first thought was to take my helmet and try and crack his racist ass, white skull wide open. That racist ass, white bastard didn't know just how close he came to being killed or knocked unconscious. I don't think his racist, white ass would've even seen it coming, seeing as he was too preoccupied with the gratifying thought of having just officially kicked this nigger off his lily white football squad. At that point, I did everything in my power to try and hold my peace as this sudden rage of blind anger took hold of me. So, instead of exploding, my parting words for his racist white ass were, "pro athletes recognize each other and that's why you were cut from the NFL team that you tried out for."

I then turned and took the long walk back to that locker room for the last time with the painful feeling that my football future was now essentially over. Afterwards, I submitted at least four or five letter to NFL teams in hopes of landing a free agent tryout, but all I received back was some very polite rejection slips. It's strange sometimes how fate would have it. I remember growing up in Mississippi in the sixties, and the Green Bay Packers was the only team that I knew by name. The first time I witnessed them lose a game, I couldn't stop the tears from pouring from my eyes. And to think that destiny guided my family to relocate to Wisconsin, the home of the same professional football team that I idolized as a little boy. I even kept their rejection slip as a memento.

I knew this void could never be filled. Playing professional football was my greatest passion and lifelong dream and the deep pain of it ending so abruptly that too much thought of it still brings agony. Many tears were shed over it. But, before I ended up leaving that little, white, Midwestern town, I applied for a job as a freshman, assistant, football coach. After interviewing, I was hired. The head coach was white, and the freshman team was also made up of white kids. I remember the first day that I was introduced to the team and took charge of my group. But two of the white players in my group said that they didn't want a *nigger* coaching them. At first, I was not sure what to say, so I hesitated and tried to ignore the comment. But some of the other white kids reported it to the head coach.

Immediately, he stopped everything and called the entire team back together and began addressing the issue of race. First, he apologized to me and for the team, stating no such attitudes would be tolerated. Then, he said those two players were off the team. But, I immediately stepped in and asked the coach to allow them to stay. I felt that if I allowed those two players to be kicked off the team, we would all be losers. I won those two white kids over that very moment, and the entire team got behind me for the way I'd handled the matter. Those two white kids apologized to me and from that day forward I could not have asked for a better work ethic from both of them.

Before I arrived at that school, I was not sure if the head coach was new at his position, but from the information I was getting the freshman, program had not had a winning season for years. In fact, they were said to have been at the bottom of the conference year after year and had not won a single football game the year before. For some reason or another, the head coach designated me as the team's motivational speaker.

Once the season started, coach and I took that freshman team on a winning roll that had not been seen at that school. We were the talk of the town and was only one game away from an undefeated season. We had started the week out having good practices, but all of a sudden the bottom fell out at the last practice. We were unable to get through the entire practice with the head coach because he had to leave because of an emergency. And since practice had not finished, he instructed me to carry out the final practice details. But, I didn't realize just how big headed these kids had gotten until I was left to complete the final practice without the head coach. When I tried going through the final drills, it was as if the majority of that team had decided to take the remainder of the practice off. After trying several times to get a full team effort, I decided to end the practice. I told those kids that if they were not going to give me a hundred percent team effort, then it was a waste of time for me to be there.

As I walked off, I saw a bunch of heads hanging as they walked back to the school locker room. Here we were with the last and biggest game left on our schedule, and these kids felt as if they were just going to show up, walk on the football field and the game was going to be handed to them. When I got home, I called coach and first asked if things were okay with him and then told him what had happened at practice. The last thing we both wanted was to hammer these kids seeing how important this game was for an undefeated season. So, during the day of the game, I asked coach if he would not bring any of it up. He stuck to his routine, but the only thing that was left out of the equation was me giving them a pep talk before the game. I think coach understood how I felt about what had happened the day before. No sooner than the game started, it didn't matter what plays coach called, our kids couldn't execute any of them.

At halftime, we had not scored a single point and was down by two touchdowns. All the team could do was sit quietly with their heads hanging. I stood with my arms folded, not saying one single word. All of a sudden, Coach yelled out to me and said, "Coach, talk to these kids!" I said something to the effect of, "do you see what happens when you get too big headed and take your opponent lightly?" I then ended the speech by saying, "you are better than that team. Now go back out there on the field and prove it."

We didn't allow that team to score another touchdown. We came back to win that championship game. With barely over a couple minutes left, the other team had to punt the ball. So, I pulled our punt returner over and told him that we had to have a good return in order to have good field positioning on the final drive. And, if we had not scored, there would have been no undefeated season. Our punt returner received the ball deep within our territory and brought the ball across midfield to about the forty yard line. When the offense went onto the field, I told our other running back that it was his job to finish. That kid must have broken at least three or four tackles before he finally broke loose for the game winning touchdown. It was not only a great sports achievement for that school and community, but it was also an enriching experience in race relations.

I only coached there that one season before I returned to Milwaukee, WI. It didn't take long for me to find another coaching job. This one was in Brookfield, WI. Again, it was in a predominantly white community and the job was for the same position that I'd just left in Minnesota. But, as an assistant freshman coach, we were also assigned to help out at times with the varsity football team. The racist encounter I had there did not involve a racial slur. Again, it was more about racist politics in sports. We had this white kid at running back who I felt had legitimate, big time, college ability. I became very supportive of his desire to play football at a major university, but he didn't feel the white head coach felt the same way. I told him not to worry about it, just continue playing football at a high level and I would take care of the rest. I later asked him what he thought about playing football at BYU. Quickly, he said that it sounded like a great opportunity. So, I kept compiling his stats and then called up Brigham Young University and spoke to the legendary Lavelle Edwards.

It was the year shortly after he had won the national championship. It was simply amazing to have actually been speaking to him on the other end of the phone. The man was so down to earth and accessible that it would have most likely been too hard for someone to believe if they had no knowledge of the kind of public relations coach this man was. It certainly was the case for me. The conversation was very cordial as he listened to me tell him about this young man's character and football skills. Coach Edwards actually called the young man's home and spoke to his parents about their son's interest in attending Brigham Young University. But, to his own disappointment, the young man told me that his father spoke to the head coach and with his advice they decided that I was out of line for overstepping the head football coach.

All of the discussions were then quickly called off. I honestly felt that young man had the ability to fit into a D-1 program academically and athletically. I found it odd that the white, head coach never mentioned one word to me about the fact that I had contacted Coach Edwards at BYU. After that season, I decided not to return to that football program, and the next and last football coaching job that I would ever take was in Milwaukee, WI, during the next football season. This job was as an assistant, head football coach at a high school in the Milwaukee public school system.

When I attended high school in the early seventies, this particular high school was predominantly white. But for the two seasons that I coached there in the late eighties the face of the program was trending towards predominantly black athletes, though the face of the administration and varsity level coaching staff remained white. Once again, it was racist ass, white politics in sports. I didn't know it at the time, but the racist, white, head coach was under pressure to hire an African American, head assistant, coach because the majority of the players on the team were black. There were already two freshman black coaches in the program whom I felt were far more qualified in X's and O's than I was. But, seeing how they knew this racist ass, white coach's M.O., he wanted nothing to do with hiring either of them. Instead, he felt that it was safer for him to hire me from the outside to serve as a *token nigger* to satisfy the race quota. Even though it worked in causing some dissention between myself and the two other African American coaches, I would not allow it to destroy our sense of unity altogether.

I stayed in that racist ass program for two years out of obligation to protect those Black players by trying to stem off some of the unfair treatment by this racist ass, white coach, and it was astounding to learn just how sick and deeply rooted his racist ass attitude was towards black people. No matter how backwards this racist ass occurrence sounds, it is true. The movie Top Gun had just been released into the theaters, though I had not seen the actual movie until sometime later. That racist ass, white coach had already introduced the music sound track into the locker room as his motivational theme song before games. I could not help but notice that, almost around the same time, he suddenly stopped calling me by my last name as a coach. Instead, he started calling me by my first name. For the world of me, I could not figure out why this racist ass, white coach would do something like this and it bothered me.

Still, I never confronted him as to why he started addressing me as coach by my first name and not my last name. But, when I finally saw the movie, "Top Gun," I got my answer. The lead character, played by Tom Cruise, had the same last name of Mitchell that was given to my family's ancestors by their racist ass, white slave-master. Can you believe it? This racist ass, white bastard couldn't bring himself to continue calling me by my last name because his white hero in the movie had my real-life slave name. Attitudes like this demonstrates just how warped some whites are in their racist ass attitudes.

Chapter Nine

African Americans, Gains or Losses?

I know there are some critics set to argue that since slavery ended, African Americans have made substantial, measurable progress. But, in order to say that blacks have made significant progress, you first have to understand how far slavery set us back and the size and magnitude of the racist ass mountain in front of us. The progress becomes small when your eyes become open, and you finally see how much further up that racist ass mountain we still have to climb versus how much further the black race would have been up if not for the devastation and stagnation of white racism and its exploits during the time of slavery. It depends on how you choose to look at progress. For example, why has there been only one Black president in the entire history of this country? It's obvious that the basic principles of institutionalized racism have been alive and well throughout the history of this country. It was first built into the racist, white controlled, constitutional laws of this country during the time of slavery. It was then built into other white institutions of America and has been kept intact under various underhanded methods that could no longer exist after the abolishment of slavery.

Blacks are denied opportunities and have been discriminated against in every facet of American society. So if this system of institutionalized racism is still ruling at the top of this racist ass mountain, then blacks will only get so far before the vices of racism force us to slide back down to the bottom and further into the pitfalls of poverty. With our health, educational, economic and political progress continually declining, how will we be able to gain enough power to keep pushing our way back up that racist ass mountain again?

Just look at the ill conditions of health and nutrition in this country for African Americans. Look at the ill and failing conditions of education. Look at the ills of social, economic conditions. Look at the ills of injustice within the judicial system. Look at the ills of racist politics. Do we realize the gravity of how this racist ass mountain exists against African Americans? Do we realize how far slavery set us back in denying us the same opportunities as white people in this country?

How can we begin to tackle such a disadvantage, when at the same time our mental and physical health is continually being destroyed? It's by design that the racist elements within this government are working to accelerate the decline of both our mental and physical well-being. The most effective method of destroying anything with life is by destroying the root that keeps it alive and growing. Those of us who do not see it, nor understand what this racist ass, white man's system is doing to us as a race of people, are walking to our fate like blind sheep to the slaughter.

The ills of poverty along with the illegal drugs being dumped into our communities are causing many of our children to be brought into this world sick and unhealthy. With such devastating deficiencies, black children don't get mentally smarter. Instead, they fall further behind in mental and nutritional development. With the opposition of this racist ass system already in place and against us as a race, how can we continue producing elite scholars in the field of academics? How then can we continue producing elite athletes in the world of sports? In truth, we are producing them at a consistently declining rate. Now, by conspiring to destroy the black man's health, the racist ass, white man sees it as his one great equalizer in his white male, inferior, emasculated complex and hidden fear of the Black man. The racist ass, white man, knows that by diminishing and destroying our mental and physical health, it will eventually eliminate our ability to reach goals of higher achievement. It will hinder and destroy our ability to achieve great progress in the field of academics and the field of sports as well as all other areas of career opportunities in this country. It exists as the racist, white man's greatest divisive scheme in his vicious and hateful attempt to take away from us our extraordinary, natural, God given gifts. It's the only way that the racist ass, white man feels that he will be able to cure his racist ass, white male, inferior, emasculated complex.

Their envy and hate for us run so deep within their racist ass, white hearts and minds that they want to exploit and destroy us simultaneously. Niggers brought to this land under slavery are the true Israelite nation and covenant people of Yahweh (God), that the racist ass, white man fears and wants to see destroyed.

Again, our inability to achieve is due in great part to the impoverished conditions that we are continually being forced into. Out of all of this, the racist ass, white man has tried to label us as the inferior race. But, why has he been so hell-bent on destroying us? As I said before, on the continent of the blacks, now known as Africa, the Black man had already begun building civilizations when the racist ass, white man was still living and laboring within the primitive conditions of Europe. We were the world's first nation builders and it is our blueprint that the racist ass, white man uses to this day.

Along with this fact, and the racist history of slavery, it has much to do with why the black man is so despised in this country.

Chapter Ten

Black Lives Matter

Because of all of the injustice that the racist ass, white man brought upon the black man, he has created this racist ass, white, police militia, out of his deepest fears, as part of his racist ass, "white male emasculated complex" against niggers. I seriously doubt today that you have black men walking around, caught up and obsessed with some sort of sick and perverted emasculated male complex of feeling inadequate to white men in regards to their manhood.

As black men, we have to be made fully aware of where much of the racist ass, white man's desire to violently attack us is coming from. One of the most gratifying things these racist ass, white devils have at their disposal to help them deal with their white male emasculated complex, is the ability to wear a police badge and carry a gun with niggers as their primary target. A racist ass, white man with a police badge and a deadly firearm coupled with this white male, emasculated complex, equals a very volatile and dangerous situation for black men when facing him. Because of their sick, emasculate, white male complex, it takes nothing to provoke them into violently beating and murdering niggers.

To these racist ass, white, police bastards, there is no such thing as the First Amendment right of free speech -- to question their racist ass, white, police authority and tactics when they are not acting within the framework of the law. If we question them, we are subject to be brutally beaten, murdered, or both. These racist ass, white bastards actually believe and demonstrate by their actions, that having been given a police badge and a gun by this racist ass, white, police system gives them the authority to take away a nigger's First Amendment rights of lawful, free speech.

Black people as a race do not want "gang-banging," gun-carrying, criminal, thug ass niggers lurking among them. But, we do not want them removed at the expense of targeting the entire Black race as a race of criminals. When we as black people depend on law enforcement to protect us from criminals, we do not expect that in the same instance we become judged as criminals instead of victims, due to our racial makeup. But, because of their bitter and racist hate, instead of equally enforcing the law against all criminals, these racist ass, white devils, are hell-bent on using excessive and deadly brutal force, targeted mainly towards niggers.

They feel that the only way of gaining confidence within their racist ass, white male emasculated complex is by enforcing their racist ass authority of treating black men as "nigger boys" with no rights of being a man, and waste no time beating and murdering us when we question their racist and blatant abuse of police authority. Let us as black men not be blind as to why the racist ass, white man so despises us as niggers.

He hates the fact that mankind and civilization began with the black race and not their racist white asses. They hate and fear the thought of the black race becoming a threat to their own racist ass, white power. They hate admitting to Biblical evidence that points towards the black race possessing the mantle of being the true, chosen, covenant people of the Bible and not their racist, white, European asses. They hate having to live in the shadow of the black man possessing the mantle of having been the first world rulers. They hate our extraordinary physical prowess in the world of sports, and, lastly, they hate the very thought of black men having any involvement with white women. And now, with these racist ass, white devils controlling the political system, the criminal justice system, and law enforcement, we have to learn how to be very meticulous in how we go about dealing with them.

The racist ass, white man of today, has the same white, male, emasculated complex as did his racist ass, white, slave-master forefather. Many of these racist ass, white, wicked, and devilish, illegitimate bastards of law enforcement commit their racist and brutal acts of cold blooded murder behind police badges, and then run back and hide out within the white race. It's almost impossible to weed them out of the police force as it should be done, because they do not consider our civil rights when going after criminals. Instead of using lawful procedures in apprehending criminals, these racist ass, white cops are more intent on judging all black people as no more than unlawful, criminal niggers whose lives literally mean nothing.

To compound matters even more, the racist ass, white, news media quickly defends the brutal acts of these racist ass, white cops by citing black-on-black crime. The norm is that human beings are against becoming victims of crime by any person or persons, regardless of race. So, what is the point of argument for these racist ass, white bastards, when involving black people as victims of crime?

Let us not be fooled by this errant defense of white cops. The good are the minority. The bad are the majority. If we were to line up a thousand, white cops out of the view of the public and police body cams and dash cam recorders and let one nigger slightly rub them the wrong way, ninety percent of those white cops are going to take a hostile positon against that nigger. They are going to be itching to beat or murder his ass. This is the stark reality of the culture and racist atmosphere that exists in this racist, white supremacy, police system of America. It's both sad and tragic for niggers that the white, police system, empowered to enforce the laws of protecting American society, exists, in part, as a smoke screen that allows it to continue brutalizing and violating the civil rights of blacks.

The very defense of using black-on-black crime to take racist ass, white cops off the hook for brutally violating the civil rights of black people, carries deep, racist implications. Does black-on-black crime somehow excuse the argument against racist ass, white police brutality against Black people? The horror and violence of black-on-black crime and racist ass, white, police brutality, causing the wrongful loss of the lives of black people, are terrifying to the black community. What the racist ass, white, news media is actually arguing, along with racist ass, white politicians is that we value the safety of our lives far less when it has to do with black-on-black crime and that we only protest about the value of our lives when the complaint is against racist ass, white, police brutality. But regardless of the amount of traction that this sick and twisted racist ass point of view might gain, we cannot allow it to be used to make racist ass, white, police brutality any less of a crime against black people. Even when we suffer from a profound lack of black leadership within our communities, it should not be misconstrued and used by the racist ass, white, news media and racist ass, white politicians to suggest blacks are not outraged by all of the violence, including that of black-on-black crime.

When we have blacks violently beating, robbing, and murdering other black people, we shouldn't have to debate over which cops will show up under the law - the non-racist white cops, or the racist ass, white cops. Just like any other victims of crime, we are seeking immediate protection under the law. Why should our next fear have to be that we may be mistaken for being the actual criminal? If the racist ass, white man is so hell-bent on brutally beating and murdering innocent black people, shouldn't this be a powerful message to those niggers who choose to commit violent crimes against other citizens? It's not that racist ass, white cops care about protecting innocent black people. We serve as no more than pawns through which they impose their will to brutally beat and murder us without discretion.

Racist ass, white, law enforcement only perceive us as being criminal niggers under siege by other criminal niggers, and the racist ass, white, news media will quickly jump to the defense and support racist ass, white, law enforcement on the same position. Sadly and tragically for niggers, to these racist ass, white, murderous, police bastards, we are no more than a race of criminal niggers pleading for help from other criminal niggers within our race. The police system in American is tainted with racist, white supremacy ideology, and has no will to see black people as being innocent victims of crime. Again, no matter how clear and compelling the evidence, the racist ass, white, news media never concedes in their efforts to support, defend, and protect racist ass, white law enforcement.

It then should be obvious to any unprejudiced and commonsense mind what these racist ass, white bastards in the news media and politics are trying to do in their efforts to protect, support, and defend racist ass, white, police brutality. The racist ass, white, news media is quick to argue that because of the disproportionate crime rate in the black community, compared to the white community it should somehow add credibility to criminalizing the entire black race. We as black people must deal with the fact that the racist ass, white man will never stop exploiting the ills of crime in our communities as a tool to indict us as a race of criminal niggers. The racist ass, white, news media and racist ass, white politicians will always stand together and argue that in order to effectively police our neighborhoods and communities, this sort of racist ass, white supremacy ideology way of thinking should be acceptable by us as a race. We would like nothing less than to have murdering, criminal, thug ass niggers removed from among us, but we want it done by effectively profiling criminal activity and not the black race itself.

Considering the history of mass shootings and murders of whites by other whites in this country, why isn't it the case that these same, racist ass, white hypocrites in the news media and politics support the same criminalization of white communities? They do not want to see themselves cast in the same light as blacks when it comes to violent crimes being perpetrated by whites. And, if this is not the case, is it that violent, white crimes get a free pass from the racist ass, white news media and racist ass, white politicians when compared to violent, black crimes? And if so, again, why?

It's very clear that the predominately white police forces of America, police black communities with a different mindset than that of white communities. And, if this is the case and there's nothing wrong with it, why not create a predominately black, police force and allow them to patrol white communities with the same mindset of white police patrolling black communities? Now, we know that such a thing will never be permitted because of laws being governed by racist ass, whites. However, my point certainly stands that, if this sort of policing is wrong in protecting the civil rights of whites, then it should be wrong when it comes to protecting the civil rights of blacks.

No civilized society would ever allow itself to be without a system set against lawless and violent behavior. The real problem for niggers is having these racist ass, white devil descendants of the racist ass, white slave-master ruling over the police and criminal justice system. In this regard, for niggers, the criminal justice system has become the modern day slave market. I know that the racist ass, white man and his token ass, house niggers will quickly and biasedly argue that I have nothing on which to base my position. But, though they willfully overlook the facts, the obvious truth is, under the authority of the racist ass, white man, prisons have become the extension of a huge business corporation tied to the criminal justice system with niggers being targeted as its most valuable commodity that keeps bread on the table of the racist ass descendants of the racist ass, white slave-master.

Shamefully, this is where the criminal justice system now has its primary interest involving niggers. Their motto is to let the crimes of the ghetto keep pouring in. Even in prison, rehabilitating niggers back into society is counterproductive for these racist ass, white bastards because they believe that after slavery ended, the best place for all niggers is in the graveyard or the penal system. But, regardless of race, no one in their right mind would want to see violent ass criminals on the street or have them released back into society without an effective form of rehabilitation. The racist ass, white man, as the overseer of the criminal justice system, has the biased agenda of keeping the status quo intact involving the incarceration of niggers. They are well content that the poverty of ghettos is continuously producing a steady flow of niggers back into the slave market and into the penal system. By keeping niggers personified as the most dangerous and violent threat existing in American society, it helps to market how important the criminal justice systems and prison systems are as a tool to keep the racist ass, white man safe and fed.

These racist ass, white bastards, ruling over the criminal justice system, keep the prison system overflowing with niggers while they easily sit back, financially stuffing their pockets, eating expensive steak and caviar and sipping on vintage wine. This is what I mean when I say that the criminal justice system and prison system has become the new, modern day, slave market for niggers. These racist ass, white devils love coming to work while feeding their racist ass appetites and getting paid by prosecuting and controlling niggers, as well as giving niggers a good and long send off into the prison system or a short one to the electric chair as often as possible.

As for the flawed crime bill that was crafted and passed under the Clinton administration, the Republican Party had no problem casting their racist ass, bipartisan, white vote like fleas and ticks jumping on a defenseless dog. But, how can any nigger with a conscience, argue shamelessly against the crafting of a just crime bill which targets *all* criminals, considering how the black community is under siege by violent and murderous ass criminals? The problem is that the crime bill under the Clinton administration needs to be repealed on how it was crafted within a racist ass, white system of government that targets the entire black race as criminals. However, in no way can this long standing, racist, white system of government with the bipartisanship of both the Democratic and Republican Party, place the crafting of this failed, crime bill solely on the shoulders of the Clinton administration. There is enough blame to go around in both parties.

When the time fits the crime, I am all for it - prosecute the culprits accordingly. I have no problem seeing ruthless and violent ass criminals of any race given life prison sentences, or the death penalty, by a fair criminal justice system. The violent and treacherous, murdering ass niggers who, along with the racist ass, murderous, white, police system that's creating all the upheaval in black communities and spreading violence to the masses, must not be allowed to continue overpowering us. Any reasonable minded person of any race would clearly want to see criminals punished and removed from the communities of law-abiding citizens. But, it must be done fairly -- a lawful right that does not exist for niggers today.

In the racist ass, white criminal justice system in this country, even before the actual crime becomes attached to the sentence, we are already facing three to five additional years just for being a nigger. So, when it comes to the racist ass, white, criminal justice system judging niggers, the death penalty becomes a very disturbing and questionable method of punishment, especially considering that they do not miss a night's sleep when they wrongfully sentence niggers to death. The mere thought of having to go before a racist ass, white judge handing down nigger time and not white time, and nigger penalties and not white penalties, frightens the shit out of niggers.

For those who refuse to accept the fact that there is such a thing as black time and white time when it comes to this country's racist ass, criminal justice system, let me make quite plain the disparity of justice between blacks and whites. At the time of writing this essay, there was an estimated population of forty-three million African Americans living in the U.S., and just over two hundred and forty-eight million whites. Considering that there are about six times more whites than blacks, and, throughout history, the same criminal and civil crimes have been committed by both races, it becomes quite obvious that the higher ratio of incarcerated blacks, as opposed to whites in this country, is astoundingly unjust.

As I said before, the racist ass, white man will never allow his criminal acts to be seen in the same light as blacks, especially seeing how he has already judged us as being no more than an inferior race of lowlife, subhuman, and violent, savage, criminal niggers. But what if the table of history had been turned and it was his racist, white ass that had been enslaved by us, and stripped bare of all social, economic and political freedoms and growth? Then, what if we kept these unjust, inhumane restrictions intact by employing institutionalized racism? Would they not be faced with many, if not all, of the same plagues and internal strife facing the black race here in America? So, why do these racist ass, white, hypocritical, bastards continue to dare paint themselves as being more inherently forthright and honest than we are as a race? As black people, we have to stop allowing their racist, white asses to continue hammering and de-humanizing us with such racist ass hypocrisy.

The racist ass, white man within this government is very content with not owning up to the fact that from the time of physical slavery in America and until the time it ended, racism and discrimination helped manufacture a poor system of education for niggers. A poor system of education continues in the manufacturing of poverty for niggers, and poverty continues in the manufacturing of crime, and crime helps to manufacture the prison systems for niggers, of which, in this country, niggers are being placed in disproportionate numbers.

Now, because of all of our economic strife, the racist ass element within this system of government tries to paint African Americans as being the face of welfare and entitlement in this country. But, in truth, the racist ass, white man in nearly all of his wealth and prosperity is the biggest recipient of welfare entitlement that was afforded to him through slavery, through discrimination, and through racism against niggers in this country. The racist ass, white man refuses to admit that his race's stability of economic and political growth is deeply tied to the history of slavery, and that he "slave-mastered" his racist, white ass into economic and governmental powers that have afforded him great advantages that have never been afforded to niggers. The history behind him having gained this power, is the cruel, brutal, and inhumane acts of slavery that the racist ass, white man is still unwilling to come face-to-face with. Even though other people of color suffered racial injustices by the racist elements within this government, none have been so readily used as a target of racist ass hate, and despised as have blacks in this country.

As I explained earlier, no matter how clear and compelling the evidence might be, the racist ass, white, news media never concedes in their efforts to defend and protect the racist ass laws within this government. For example, in some critical instances, our eyes act as the perfect camera, capturing what we see, and processing it down to the smallest detail. But, when such critical moments occur with niggers when confronted by racist ass, white, law enforcement, our credibility means literally nothing to the racist ass, white, news media in their efforts to support the cover up and brutality of racist ass, white cops. Instead of supporting the evidence when niggers have been openly brutalized and murdered, they quickly shift the focus away from the criminal behavior of racist ass, white, law enforcement by referencing to black-on-black crime. They quickly revert to this racist ass method as a way of cutting off the attacks against racist ass, white cops.

Racist ass, white, police brutality against niggers throughout the history of this country has led to riots and rebellion. But yet, the racist ass, white, news media quickly tries to use looting and destruction of property as the main basis for Black protests, not for seeking justice itself. Instead the racist ass, white news media puts the focus on looting and the destruction of property, to satisfy their racist ass desire of portraying the black race as a race of criminal, thug niggers. In their racist ass eyes, there exists no such thing as "niggers" marching for justice, or rioting because of racist ass, white oppression and police brutality in this country.

The nerve of these racist ass, white, hypocritical bastards. They never condemn any of their own people throughout their history of uprisings against oppressive governments. When they loot, pillage, and destroy everything in their path, they call it a just revolution for freedom. And, these racist ass, white bastards want to call us a bunch of law-less, law-breaking, criminal thug niggers? They know what the real face of revolution looks like when an oppressed people come to a boiling point, and revolt against oppression and brutality. All of their pinned up anger is like an active volcano, about to erupt. It then becomes a revolution, destroying any and everything in its path. In fact, looting, pillaging, and destroying all semblances of that government is the actual eye of the storm in a revolution.

Revolution is like a blind tornado that destroys virtually everything in its path, and once the storm settles, miraculously, there might be a few, scattered structures left standing. One of the first things these racist ass, white bastards try to argue is that we destroy the establishments within our own community. The very notion of such a racist ass white position is pathetic. First of all, most of these establishments are not even owned by niggers. The majority of them are owned by racist ass whites. In fact, of the small percentage of these establishments that we do occupy here in America, the majority have a racist ass, "white man's mortgage" attached to it. Personally, if it were somehow at all possible, I would say to niggers who turn to looting in a massive protest against this racist ass, white establishment - not to destroy any property where the deed is owned by any non-racist or blacks who are not token ass house niggers. Otherwise, my position is just as Brother Malcolm -- by any means necessary.

Oppressed people under an oppressive government see no empowerment or ownership of any sort. The unfortunate truth about this racist ass, white system of government, is that their racist ass, white, news media will always defend the brutality of racist ass, white cops as being more important than the civil rights of the entire black race. In other words, the career of one racist, white, devilish ass cop is far more valuable than all of the black lives in this country.

This is the attitude and feelings of racist ass, white, supremacy ideology in America. These racist ass attitudes exist as the true indicator of the depth of the racist ass fire that burns and brings niggers in this county to a boiling point. Now that these racist ass, white bastards cannot openly call us unruly and rebellious ass niggers anymore, they have slyly hand-picked their word that acts as the equivalent -- "thug." In other words, it has an ambiguous meaning when they use the word "thug" against us. For them, it means nigger. But, you know the old saying, "if you can't beat them, join them." So let's start calling their racist, white asses thugs, and make it the equivalent of calling them racist, white, asshole, redneck, peckerwood bastards. Let's make it the equivalent of calling them the racist white asshole descendants of perverted ass, white slave-masters who raped black women while committing all sorts of pedophilia upon little black slave children. Let's make it the equivalent of calling them racist, white, asshole, psychologically emasculated, white, slave-masters who castrated and lynched black men.

If these racist ass, white bastards want to turn the word "thug" into a race war of words, this is how it's going to be for us when we call their racist, white, asses a race of thugs.

I know by definition what the word "thug" actually means in its proper context. Anyone who profanely breaks civil laws can, by criminal definition, be labeled a "thug." And while I do see these "slavery-time" ass, subhuman minded, murderous ass niggers as thugs, I also see these racist ass, white bastards on the police force as the kingpins of murderous ass thugs. Along with them, the racist ass, white news media is the kingpin, thug ass bastards that support them. In no way am I saying that whites are not entitled to use the word thug. But racist ass, whites better be damned sure that the label is about criminals and not about race whenever the perpetrator is black.

If these racist ass, white bastards are intent upon continuing to take the word "thug" out of context of its definition, and use it to label the black race as thug criminal niggers, then we are going to take the word "thug" out of context the same damn way for the racist ass, white man and hope that our equivalent definition is translated universally into every language on this earth.

Again, if these racist ass, white bastards truly want to know what the face of rebellion and revolution looks like once niggers reach a boiling point, all they have to do is remember the revolutionary abolitionist, Nat Turner, whose memory is still bitterly profaned and despised as one of the most notorious "niggers" in the history of Black revolt in this county.

Another thing about this racist ass, white, news media is that it will go to any length to try and dispel the notion of racist ass, white, police brutality. In the tragic death of Freddie Gray in Baltimore, MD, three of the six cops charged in his death were Black, and the other three, white. So, as soon as the racist ass, white, news media bloodhounds got hold of this information, they quickly jumped on it as an opportunity to try and rule out racist ass, white, police brutality as part of this criminal act. But, we know that throughout this country, black police officers patrol regularly in police vehicles with white cops, as well as serving in some other capacity of law enforcement with them. Even though none of these cops were convicted, the Department of Justice later reported, after their investigation, that they found a history of racist patterns within the Baltimore police department.

It's not impossible for black cops to be involved in an excessive force case with white cops who have a racist ass motive for their actions, while the black cop's brutal actions are motivated by something entirely different. For example, in South Carolina, a black cop arrived on the scene in the shooting of Walter Scott by a racist ass, white cop. Under such conditions, if a black cop upheld the code of silence among police officers, and did not give an accurate report of the incident, thereby, deciding to become a part of the cover-up, it still cannot be used to deny the fact that this white cop was racist. Tragically, in this country, we do have situations where bad black cops become involved with racist ass white cops in the brutal beatings and murder of black citizens.

These racist ass, white, news media, bastards need to own up to the fact that slavery created a cultural, slave mentality that has many blacks hating themselves, and if these sort of "niggers" find their way onto the police force, it would not be surprising to see them act out brutality upon other blacks, especially seeing how they crave acceptance from their racist ass, white slave-masters. It's just like arguing that if a slave was the whip holder in the brutal beating of another slave, it somehow is supposed to nullify the racist ass, white, slave-master from being a brutal racist ass bastard. But, this is exactly how far these racist ass, white, news media bastards are willing to go in their efforts to try and deny, as well as hide racist ass, white, police brutality. After the death of Freddie Gray, the racist ass, white, news media was still at it, defending the slowdown of these racist ass, white cops along with any "house nigger ass cops," siding with them and not wanting to uphold their sworn duty.

In Baltimore, these racist ass, white, cops decided they would not respond expediently in protecting black citizens from crime in their neighborhoods and community. These racist, white, asshole bastards took the stance of solidarity that if they were not allowed to police our community as a brutal, racist ass, police force, they would refuse to do their job. For them, to negatively and unprofessionally behave this way is not being un-American when done so against black citizens in this country. In fact, it's the all-American, white, racist ass way of life - a textbook display -- on how to deal with niggers.

You can believe, these racist ass, white, news media bastards had themselves a "racist ass, fucking orgasm" reporting it. They want us to plead for racist ass, white, police brutality in order to get the least bit of protection from becoming victims of violent crime in our community. Just as I said before, these racist ass, white police are the "kingpin, thug ass bastards" who place themselves above the law, and the racist ass, white news media are the "kingpin, thug ass bastards" who support it.

We are the only race in which this racist ass, white tactic is so readily taken when our civil rights become violated. The loud and clear message they are sending by exploiting the unlawful behavior of violent ass, murderous niggers, is that it justifies their own violent and vicious ass, unlawful acts of murdering black people as niggers. How can they be trusted when they commit these same kinds of brutal and murderous crimes against African Americans, as do these murderous and treacherous ass niggers, and the racist ass, white, news media supports it? When the racist ass, white, news media becomes so fixated on pointing out black-on-black crime, they deliberately sidestep the critical difference and overlook the fact that cops are hired with a sworn duty to uphold the law and not behave like the piece of shit ass criminals hell-bent on breaking the law. Yet, this is exactly what they do, and the racist ass, white, news media takes a very callous and inhumane position in continually supporting it. We were the ones who suffered the sick and perverted indignation of slavery, yet we are the ones so hated and despised. In their racist ass eyes, by exploiting the behavior of violent, criminal ass, niggers, this is all they need or care about when it comes to justifying their involvement of brutalizing and murdering black people as niggers.

Whenever there is racist ass, white, police brutality against blacks, these racist ass white bastards in the news media, along with the racist ass elements within the political and judicial system, continually defend their racist, white supremacy ideology of murdering and destroying niggers without feeling even one thread of guilt. They continually fend off our charges by using black-on-black crime as a defense against their own wrongful violation of our civil rights. The real truth about these racist ass, white bastards is that no matter what side of the law black people find themselves, we are already judged as an "inferior race of lowlife, subhuman, welfare-dependent, criminal niggers." But, when these same racist ass, white bastards had us in the brutal chains of physical slavery, we were considered valuable and productive property.

It was these racist ass, white, slave-masters who were the big welfare recipients, gaining vast wealth by exploiting black people as slaves. Because of this unjust and inhumane imbalance of power, which is still being protected by racist, white laws, it will continue supporting white people as the biggest welfare recipients in this country. And yet, to this very day, the racist ass descendants of these racist ass, white, slave-masters are still able to control these ideological brainwashed and so-called intellectual ass "house niggers" into supporting racist ass politics in this country that continually targets the black race as the face of welfare. Instead of unmasking the racist ass, white man within this white system of government, these so-called, intellectual, brainwashed ass, "house niggers" do everything in their power to help fortify the racist white man's political position.

The racist ass, white, news media even went and brought this supposedly High Sheriff, ten-gallon, cowboy hat wearing, red neck bar going ass house nigger, from Milwaukee, WI, to their news network to score himself some political points at the expense of our human and civil rights. He kept kissing his racist ass, white slave-master's ass until he landed himself a speaking slot at the Republican National Convention. It just goes to show you that you can't vote for someone just because of them being of the same race that you are. If blacks have been paying attention, and if this piece of shit ass, house nigger who needs a spur kicked against his token ass would have been making these same statements prior to his last election, there's a damned good chance that his pathetic, traitor ass would have gotten very little support from black voters.

This ear-to-ear, grinning ass, house nigger completely discredited the *Black Lives Matter* movement as being no more than the mixture of misguided, rogue, activists, and criminal thugs with no legitimate grounds to base their protest. This piece of shit ass, house nigger had the audacity to accuse former Secretary of State, Hillary Clinton, of politically prostituting herself for black votes. But, if this whore ass, piece of shit, house nigger wants to stoop to this sort of political mudslinging, then he has had his token ass bent over, touching his toes, and personifying the real definition of a political prostitute for his racist ass, white slave-master.

House niggers like this commit the greatest blasphemy to our black, revolutionary struggle to overcome this racist ass, oppressive system of government in this country. What these white, slave-master ass, house niggers fail to accept is, tragically, sometimes it takes just violence to fight unjust violence and hate in order to gain liberation out of the grip of tyranny. But, these piece of shit ass, house niggers want to keep the black race bound and gagged under all of this racist ass, slavery-time shit. Black lives have not mattered and have been devalued and destroyed from the time of slavery. And, for a racist ass, white, slave-master, piece of shit, house nigger to denounce a movement for saying "*Black Lives Matter*," is an affront to the entire black race in this country. This pathetic ass, house nigger even went on to state that he could not find one ounce of evidence that supports the position that black males are seen through different lens than white males involving racist ass, white, law enforcement. What is the fucking problem with this token, badge wearing ass, piece of shit ass house nigger? If white law enforcement justifiably kills a thousand white ass criminals, then unjustifiably kills one black man or woman out of their racist ass policing, it becomes a problem in *Black Lives Matter*.

As for these racist ass, white politicians and news media commentators and their flunky ass, house niggers who have denounced the narrative, *Black Lives Matter*, do these morons need to be retaught elementary education on pointing out a specific issue occurring within a general subject on which the narrative being used is not meant to undermine, nor take away from the basic subject itself? In this case, the argument by the racist ass, White, news media is "all lives matter." But, just look at how these racist ass, white devils and their piece of shit ass, house niggers tried to refute and distort the message of *Black Lives Matter* by quickly using the phrase, "All Lives Matter." If all lives actually mattered like these racist ass, white, hypocritical, asshole bastards have tried to argue, then why did Black lives not matter during slavery, and why do they not still matter?

Don't these racist ass, white bastards get it? It's extremely insulting for these racist ass, white, hypocritical bastards to look us in the face and say, "All lives matter." Don't these racist ass, piece of shit, white idiots, and their dumbing down ass, house niggers realize how contradictory that statement is when the behavior of these racist ass, white bastards clearly demonstrates that black lives matter least among all human lives?

Some white police officers threw a little national, racist ass, white, news media shit fit over being protested against by having the slogan "*Black Lives Matter*" written on their coffee cups at several Dunkin Donut shops. Now if these acts really angered and offended them regarding their civil rights to be served in a public restaurant, how do they think niggers felt about nearly four hundred years of slavery and open Jim Crow laws? These racist ass, white bastards need to own up to it. Niggers are neither welcomed, nor accepted, in the majority of suburban neighborhoods and public places in white America.

Again, the *Black Lives Matter* movement is not saying that the "only" lives that matter are black lives. But, I cannot bring myself to actually believe that these intellectual, racist ass, whites and their so-called intellectual ass, house niggers could be so damned ignorant about the real message of *Black Lives Matter*. So, in this respect, I have labeled them racist ass, white morons because they would go so far as to insult their own intellect in order to try and make their racist ass point of view stand up. And I would also call their so-called, intellectual ass, house niggers the ass kissers of racist ass, white morons. As I said earlier, I cannot believe that these racist ass, white intellectuals are not aware that what really insults the *Black Lives Matter* protest movement is hearing racist ass, whites and their piece of shit ass, house niggers use the term, "All Lives Matter," only to refute their message when in fact, all lives do not matter in this country.

The lives of blacks matters least among all human lives, because of all of the external negative forces of racism by whites which cause much of the internal negative forces among blacks. No matter how unsettling it is, we have to be prepared to deal with the treason of these house niggers against the black race in favor of their racist ass, White, slave-masters.

Under their "nigger identity," these slavery time-minded ass, conditioned, "house niggers" will always hinder our progress. We should not be surprised by their continual longing for acceptance from the racist ass descendants of their former, racist ass, white slave-masters. It doesn't matter to these "house niggers" that the racist ass, white man has us all judged as a race full of born criminals. These "slavery time-minded, conditioned ass, house niggers" do not possess the willingness to understand, nor accept the fact that regardless if we justifiably or unjustifiably criticize our own race, these racist ass, white bastards will still judge it as an admission of race guilt. Even when they invite liberal, black, news media spokespersons onto their racist ass, white news media networks to offer a counterpoint argument, they still try to treat them as though they are no more than little nigger boys and girls getting out of line with the racist ass, white slave-master.

You see, they do not invite them onto their networks for the integrity of journalism. Instead, they do it only to try and dispel any notion that they are a racist ass, biased, news media with the goal of only wanting to report their own racist ass interests in the world of journalism in this country. These racist ass, white, hypocritical bastards have no problem defining the entire black race as criminals based on the criminal act of one nigger. But, they have a serious problem with it when we make the same sweeping charges against their racist ass, white, police system.

The point that I make here is that, when we criticize the criminal behavior of black individuals, the racist ass, white, news media sees it as a validation that supports their racist ass position, that acknowledging the wrongdoing of one nigger criminalizes the entire black race. In the eyes of the racist ass, white man, the criminal behavior of one nigger condemns the entire Black race. And, when we are in error, or appear to be in error, of defending the criminal behavior of niggers, the racist ass, white, news media also sees it as a validation that supports its racist ass position of us all being a race of criminal niggers, not wanting to defend the law but more set on defending the unlawful and violent acts of niggers. In other words, within the racist ass, white man's eyes, we are damned niggers if we do, and damned niggers if we don't. You see, the racist ass, white man has us already judged as a race full of guilty, "false-charging, criminal ass niggers," set against the good, upstanding, and lawful governing power of white America. By them having perceived the entire black race as criminals, no matter what position we take, be it right or wrong, the outcome of how we become judged will always be the same. And, nothing is more gratifying to the racist ass, white, news media than getting these so-called "intellectual, self-glorified ass, house niggers" in politics to support their racist ass position on the Black race.

Chapter Eleven

Technology the 'New Savior,' Terrorism, & the 2nd Amendment

Under their "nigger identity," racist ass, white, slave-master ass, house niggers only work to hinder progress and stir up division within the black race.

While this goes on, the position of racist ass, white, law enforcement is that we have to be continually racially profiled because of having no existence other than breaking laws created solely for the purpose of protecting the well-being of its white citizens. The racist ass, white, slave-master receives immense gratification from hearing his "house niggers" defend and support his racist ass, white supremacy ideology of blacks being inferior to the white race, as well as the human race, itself. But, we should not be surprised by these "house niggers' good nigger" relationship of wanting to be accepted by their racist ass, white, slave-master. It doesn't matter to these piece of shit ass, "house niggers" that the racist ass, white man has judged us all of not having a rightful place within the human family.

In the eyes of the racist ass, white man, we have already been judged and found guilty of being a race of criminal niggers, always pursuing vainly after race credibility that could never be supported nor accepted by him. And, because racist ass, whites have incorporated institutionalized racism within practically every aspect of what they deem a just government of judicial laws, there is no tolerance or acceptance of a black counter-attack when they unjustly carry out brutal assaults on niggers. They have us judged as a race being born below the threshold of humanity. And, therefore, it becomes impossible for them to acknowledge or see us as having any form of civil rights. No matter how clear and blatant their racist ass acts become, for them to denounce it would be seen as self-incrimination within their racist white supremacy ideology. It is precisely why the grand jury system in America has become no more than a predominately racist ass and corrupt, white jury system that sanctions murder and brutality of niggers by racist ass, white cops.

Take again the tragedy of April 4, 2015, when a racist ass, white cop in South Carolina, fatally shot a 50 year old, unarmed, African American male in the back four times. If it had not been by fate that the shooting was caught on a civilian cell phone camera, it could have easily been a racist ass, white grand jury case in which this racist ass, white cop would have most likely been exonerated. But thanks to divine intervention, the incident was caught on camera. The evidence was so compelling that the racist ass, white news media could do nothing more but try and treat this horrific event as not being newsworthy. But once the cell phone video that captured the murder became public, the initial police report was refuted. The racist ass, white news media, seeing how they could not defend this racist ass, white cop, quickly called on their "house niggers" to do it for them. One of these piece of shit ass, "house niggers" tried to defend this racist ass, white, murderous cop by trying to bring Mr. Scott's character into question. Another piece of shit ass "house nigger" on the same racist ass, white, news media network tried thanking and praising Mr. Scott's family for not playing the race card. Still, it baffles me to see how this so called, intellectual ass, "house nigger" didn't realize that Mr. Scott's family didn't have to play the race card because the evidence on the cell phone camera did it for them.

As you can see, in such a horrific and racist ass crime like this, the racist ass, white, news media had to employ one of its "house niggers" in defense of this racist ass, white, murderous cop. But, when you have a racist ass, white commentator on the national news pretending to refute one of their "house niggers" for defending this racist ass, white cop, it's both hypocritical and utterly disgraceful.

Just a little over three months after Mr. Scott was murdered, another racist ass, white cop in a somewhat similar, eerie situation on July 19, in Cincinnati, OH, murdered another African American during a minor traffic stop. Mr. Dubose was shot in the head at point blank range for trying to close his car door and drive off. And, just like the racist ass white cop in Mr. Scott's murder, he tried to distort the facts. But, in his erratic efforts to do so, he forgot about the police, dash cam recorder. Once it was reviewed, it clearly contradicted his police transmission of the incident as it was occurring. Clearly, these racist ass white police are using deceptive tactics that exist as the unwritten rules throughout the entire white police community in this country.

Then there was the October 14th, brutal murder of a seventeen year old African American by the name of Laquon McDonald, by a racist ass, white, Chicago, police officer named Jason Van Dyke. The entire incident was captured on police dash cam, but was suppressed for thirteen months until a court order forced the release of the graphic video depicting the murder. And, once again, the racist ass, white news media exploited black-on-black crime to try and deflect the vicious murder of African Americans by racist ass, white police. Again, it is clear that these racist ass, white, hypocritical bastards in the racist ass, white, news media don't give a damn about black-on-black crime. They exploit it with their sick minded asses, only to push their own racist ass, political agenda. These racist ass, white, news media bastards have no problem using black-on-black crime to marginalize the murder of African Americans by racist ass, white cops.

Then there was the violence that erupted in Dallas, TX, on July the 7th, where five police officers were murdered. Just days before, two African American males were shot dead in Baton Rouge, LA, and St. Paul, MN. And, not even two weeks after, in the early morning hours of July 17th, violence returned to Baton Rouge, LA, and another retaliatory attack against police took place. I will expand on those tragedies in a later chapter.

Before the advent of body cams and police dash cams, we will never know the truth about how many African Americans were brutally beaten and murdered by these same racist ass tactics. Racist ass, white cops know that a dead nigger can't talk and a nigger who lives to talk behind a brutal, police beating, their word will not stand up in a racist ass, white criminal justice system that has sworn to defend and protect the actions of racist ass, white cops. The last thing this racist ass, white, system of law enforcement wanted was to find itself being policed by the technology of body cams and police dash cams. But, if given enough time, the next tactic that these racist ass, white cops would try will be to fix it so that their body cams and dash cam equipment will either be off, or conveniently malfunctioning during their brutal attacks of beating and murdering niggers. The truth of the matter is, non-racist, white cops have the difficult task of trying to uphold their lawful duties while trying to manage and police these racist ass, white cops. It becomes a golden situation for niggers when white cops patrol our neighborhoods and do their jobs effectively by fighting crime without harboring a racist impulse towards us.

But, as for racist ass, white cops, they still operate under the same racist ass, white supremacy of the slave-master's authority over niggers. If a nigger questions their racist ass, white authority, no matter how minor the infraction, it's still seen as the ultimate insult and can easily cost a nigger his or her life. The white police system in this country that polices niggers within the inner-cities of urban America, is mainly made up of racist ass, white, death squads. The KKK merely traded in their white sheets and hooded masks for police uniforms with badges and guns and the legal authority to brutally beat and murder niggers. Let us not be deceived because non-racist, white cops are the exception and not the rule. Yet these racist ass, white politicians and the racist ass, white news media have the damn nerve to continually argue against this fact.

Racist ass whites within the political and criminal justice system have positioned themselves in such a way that they control the policing system of this country. Upholding the sworn duty of the law by treating all citizens fairly regardless of race is the exception because the racist atmosphere and culture of bad and unlawful policing is the rule in this country. But, the racist ass, white, news media is quick to give credibility to these racist ass, white cops of being America's finest, first responders. The problem with this backwards ass defense is that niggers are not arguing against them as white, patriotic, racists in their defense of white America because they have lived up to this racist ass, white supremacy image throughout the brutal and racist history of this country. In fact, to try and condemn African Americans for protesting this kind of white patriotism is racist itself.

I seriously doubt that racist ass, white cops would be at the center of nigger's complaints if they would stop brutalizing and murdering niggers, keep their personal beliefs to themselves, and not act upon them as they have taken a sworn oath to uphold the law by protecting all citizens regardless of race. Yet, these racist ass, white bastards are continually hired and allowed to remain in law enforcement. To our detriment, these racist ass, white cops pride themselves on being nigger harassers and murders.

Regardless of race, no citizen who is in need of immediate protection from criminals, is going to question the personal belief of a cop when the only thing that matters is them upholding the law without bias. But, as for these racist ass, white cops who willfully beat and murder blacks, our protest against them should forever stand as a lightning rod that strikes at the nerve of all racial injustice that we have suffered in this country. It should also reveal that the murderous acts of racist ass, white, law enforcement reflects the rules and not the exception of how racist ass, white cops abuse their authority by using criminal methods to cover up evidence and distort facts when they brutalize and murder black people as niggers.

Less than three months after Mr. Scott's brutal murder, the state of Carolina suffered another heinous act of racist hate and violence against African Americans. On June 17, 2015, Dylann Roof traveled from Lexington, SC, to Charleston, SC, and entered Emanuel AME Church during a night of bible study. He sat among the congregation for nearly an hour pretending to fellowship with them before he cold heartedly began massacring them. Nine African Americans died from the barrage of gunfire. One of the things he was stated as saying during the time he was committing this heinous, terrorist, hate crime was that all black men are the rapists of white women. His racist ass statement somehow suggests that black men are the historic rapists of white women. But, the facts show that it was the racist ass, white slave-master who was the historical rapists of black women along with all the other perverse violations against black people in this country during slavery.

In the case of these white, mass murderers, white psychologists and psychiatrists shouldn't be so quick to rush in and use mental illness as the lone reason for their psychopathic behavior and the convenient go to explanation for committing these heinous acts. Even when it can be proven that such demonic individuals suffer from a form of clinical mental illness, it is my position that more should be done in analyzing how this warped and deranged behavior becomes embedded in their minds. I believe that in the case of these hate crimes racist white supremacy ideology only helps to nurture and influence their psychopathic behavior in society. I take this position based mainly on how in some ways the male dominant, ego becomes gratified. You see, regardless of how abnormal and dysfunctional this psychological complex might be, I am of the position that much of the alpha male, egotistical persona is based on the portrayal of the dominant, tough guy image. Or, to be even more precise, the glorified *bad guy* image.

And, because racist, white supremacy ideology, by itself alone, has targeted black men as the ultimate villains who owns the mantle of male violence in this country, and because of the deep desire of some males to connect to this dominant tough guy, bad guy image, it could well be one of the psychological problems driving some white males to feel emasculated. With this being connected to their already racist and hateful views, it becomes even more of a threat for blacks already having to deal with a race war lead by racist ass, white cops with the support of the racist ass, white, news media and the racist ass, white system of injustice. I believe that many of these psychopathic, white males have a longing, desire, and obsession to prove to society that they possess the same kind of male violent behavior that makes them just as capable of carrying out the same kinds of violent, criminal acts that the racist ass, White, news media only want to depict and attribute to niggers.

And, when these psychopathic, dysfunctional, white males begin to feel that they are not able to receive the same kind of violent stature and attention that the racist ass, white, news media eagerly associates with niggers, psychologically many of these white males could easily feel that, in order to overcome their deep psychological sense of male weakness, they have to prove themselves by gaining power and control over others through violent acts of their own instead of continually feeling like the weak and pathetic sociopaths that they have become.

Regardless if these psychopathic, white males commit heinous hate crimes against people of color, or society itself, it is my belief that racist, white supremacy ideology being bent on making black men out to be the perennial, bad guy villain, has much to do with producing these white, psychopathic mass murderers. And, once this racist, white supremacy ideology of portraying niggers as the ultimate, criminal villains becomes injected into the racist ass, white, news media, into law enforcement, in politics as well as society itself, it is my position that it contributes to helping produce, nurture and influence some white males into becoming psychopathic, mass murderers. And, when it comes to committing the kind of racist ass, hate crime like that of Dylann Roof, I believe it's not just by some strange coincidence that it occurred at a time of violent white, racist, police brutality against Africa Americans.

And, to make the problem even worse for niggers, this racist ass, white system of law enforcement has also become the model for breeding and influencing white racist, vigilante groups throughout this country. Under such racist ass influence, racist ass, white psychopaths like Dylann Roof could've easily began feeling that it was part of his racist ass, white supremacist duty to join in the racist ass fight of murdering African Americans.

I believe that how niggers are portrayed in the racist ass, white, news media involving violent crimes has much to do with shaping and influencing the minds of these deranged, white, psychopathic, mass murderers regardless of who becomes their victims, be it out of racist ass hate against blacks or against society itself.

Just over two months after Dylann Roof's heinous crime of racist ass terror, a Black assailant in the township of Roanoke, VA, brutally murdered a young, white, female reporter and her white cameraman on live TV. The assailant was an ex-news reporter who was fired from the same news station where the victims were employed. The shooting occurred just a little over two years after his firing. The murderer stated in his suicide note that the Dylann Roof massacre and racist discrimination, harassment, and homophobic attitudes by those at the news station pushed him to this senseless and evil act of cold blooded murder.

Months earlier, Roof stated that he committed his acts of terror out of his racist ass beliefs of white supremacy and hate for the Black race. Again, it's obvious that Roof is under the powerful influence of racist ass, white supremacy ideology that's being injected into nearly all facets of white America. Both of these deranged murderers gave a chilling look inside their mental state of mind. And, regardless of how we, in our anguish, manage our emotions on judging and dealing with both of these horrible tragedies, we cannot escape the fact that both murderers saw their heinous acts stemming from a race war occurring in this country between blacks and whites. As I alluded to earlier, the racist ass, white, police system in this country exists as the motivational tool in creating racist ass, white, vigilante, militia groups targeting niggers.

Regardless of race, in self-defense to protect oneself from vicious criminals, I too believe strongly in the Second Amendment right to bear arms, even though it was created for whites and not niggers. Under slavery, niggers were not allowed to bear arms. And, even though the abolishment of slavery eventually gave niggers the same rights to legally bear arms as whites, racist white's attitudes of not wanting niggers to bear arms under the Second Amendment rights, still exists. Now, the racist ass, white political and criminal justice system has enacted an elaborate scheme of trying to make all niggers into felons so that we are not able to legally purchase firearms under the Second Amendment right. Restoring the Second Amendment right to felons after they've paid their debt to society should be a very stringent process. The problem is, the racist ass, white scheme within the criminal justice system is designed to turn niggers into felons, despite the degree of the offense. Another driving racist force behind this scheme, along with the racist ass, white, news media, political, and criminal justice system, is the NRA (National Rifle Association).

It shouldn't come as a surprise that the NRA gave its racist ass endorsement to the Republican nominee in the 2016 presidential race, seeing how both hold the same ideology of bigotry. It was an open-arm embrace by both parties. Not even the worst mass murder shooting and terrorist act on U.S. soil that took place in the early morning hours of June 12, 2016 will force the racist ass, white, KKK, NRA to change its tightly held position against supporting stricter gun control laws. Instead, along with the racist ass, white, news media, they would quickly accuse the Obama administration and gun control supporters of politicizing this horrific terrorist act in order to threaten their Second Amendment rights to bear arms. But both the hypocritical racist ass, white, news media and the racist based white governing body of the NRA wasted no time exploiting and politicizing this horrific act of terror by attacking the Obama administration and the left for not using the term "radical Islamic terrorist," to describe ISIS and other jihadist extremist terrorist groups.

The NRA has become the most politically powerful, racist, white, KKK militia organization in this country. The NRA has now become the modern-day, vigilante, KKK watchdogs of racist ass, white America with its target placed squarely on the backs of niggers. Niggers would have to be a race full of blind ass fools not to believe that these racist ass, Second Amendment right supporting, white people have niggers as their primary target and reason for stock piling guns no differently than they did during slavery and our slave rebellions. It's their core tactic and racist belief that niggers are public enemy number one within racist ass, white America. And, it's the very fuel that drives the NRA into wanting to recruit and arm the entire white race, thereby creating its racist ass, white, KKK militia. At the same time, they want all niggers to become felons.

I don't give a damn what these racist ass, sons-of-bitches try to argue about crime, because the residuals of slavery along with continual racism, discrimination and oppression, broken families, no education, poor education, and joblessness is at the very root of why so many niggers are becoming felons. It's all part of the racist ass ploy that turns niggers into felons and prevents them from exercising their Second Amendment rights. These racist ass, white bastards within the criminal justice system has devised it so that even the most minor offense can be used to put a felony rap on a nigger; they're going to employ it without hesitation. The NRA has this racist ass, white, news media, political and judicial system firmly in its hip pocket to do its racist ass bidding against niggers.

Every nigger in their right, God given, common sense mind should support the Second Amendment right to bear arms, seeing how we are the ones being targeted for destruction as a race by these racist ass, white bastards. But on the other hand, no nigger in their right, God given, common sense mind should support the NRA knowing that it has recruited and built the most powerful, racist ass, white, KKK militia organization in this country armed against niggers. I cannot emphasize it enough. Racist ass whites don't argue the Second Amendment right to include niggers even when they scheme and tokenize niggers into supporting the NRA. If the racist ass, white, KKK NRA could stop every nigger from owning a firearm in this country, it would conveniently do so without the least bit of hesitation, because it's a lot easier for a racist ass, white bastard to murder an unarmed nigger than an armed one. You got racist ass, white, NRA, vigilante, KKK sons-of-bitches patrolling throughout America with legal firearms just looking for situations to start up some racist ass shit with niggers in order to blow our brains out. But, as for us niggers, what do we have? A bunch of treacherous, thug ass, gang-banging, mentally deficient minded ass, murderous, felony, criminal ass niggers ravaging our communities with illegal firearms. As for the rest of us niggers who are not these treacherous and vicious criminal ass niggers, the majority of us are economically poor ass niggers left to live in fear while trying to protect ourselves mostly with unregistered firearms purchased from the illegal gun markets of inner-city ghettos. To add to this problem, this racist ass, white system has judged all niggers as criminals.

Now, psychologically, for many of us niggers, we have no incentive of going through a background check to legally purchase and own firearms. The background check, under the Second Amendment rights, is far more difficult for niggers than it is for whites who have both the financial resources and approved skin color. The vastly, powerful, financial lobbyist of the racist ass, white, KKK NRA is determined to keep this requirement firmly intact so that it can keep a racist ass, white, militia ready and armed against niggers without being threatened nor rivaled. So, it would be wise for niggers to know that when the racist ass, white, KKK, NRA says that its racist ass, white freedom's safest place, its actually talking about the safest ass place armed against an entire race labeled as criminal ass niggers.

Let's have another honest conversation about race because racial conflicts between blacks and whites in this country has found its way back into an extreme holding pattern. And, now it appears as though both sides are anticipating the next violent act against the other as a way of pointing out just how evil and wicked the other side is. This is not the mindset that any civilized society should be hinging itself upon. And now, with this having been said, one should be able to see through the disguise of how the racist ass, white news media wanted to use Vester Flannigan's horrible and senseless act of murder as a direct portrayal of a wicked race of violent criminal niggers set against the puritan image of white America.

But, in light of the Dylann Roof massacre and slaughter of nine African Americans, they could not fully exploit this horrible tragedy. They had to be very careful not to let their racist ass attitude show by attempting to portray the loss of innocent white lives as appearing more meaningful and valuable than the loss of innocent Black lives. With Flannigan having brought up the Dylann Roof massacre, what the racist ass, white, news media hated about it was the fact that it got right in the way of their racist ass attempt of wanting to portray the black race as the evil and envious villains set against the good, honest, hard earned, success and prominence of the white race.

Morbid and macabre as it might sound for some whites to actually believe and especially for those families of the victims, the racist ass, white, news media was sorely disappointed that the white casualty rate wasn't even higher so that the deaths could be classified as a mass murder by a psychopathic, violent, criminal ass nigger. But, in light of all of the mass murders that have sprung up from the white race, these racist ass, white, news media bastards still want to brand the mark of mass murderers solely upon the black race.

In any of these horrific cases where one of these deranged, mass murderers are found in the black race, and white law enforcement ends up killing them during their attack, the racist ass, white, news media wastes no time treating it as though it's a message being sent to an entire race of criminal ass niggers having one of their own killed by their white, All American, hero cops who gallantly and courageously defend them from a psychopathic race of criminal ass, mass murdering niggers. But, the real truth of the matter is that, regardless of race, any police force who prevents society from mass murder attacks are heroes.

But, let's keep it real, these racist ass, white bastards are well aware of the fact that mass murder in this country shows a pattern of being more prevalent within the white race than any other race. And, what makes it even more appalling is the fact that at one point in their racist ass history, it was legal for them to commit the mass murder and lynching of black people. In the horrible mass murder that took place in Roseburg, OR, on October 1, 2015, twenty-six year old Chris Harper-Mercer described himself as being of mixed race. He may or may not have been mixed with black, but if a terrorist, mass murderer is mixed with nigger, you can be assured that it's going to be the nigger half that will get the full blame for the act and not the other half, especially, if the other half is white.

In the aftermath of this horrific, terrorist act, the Republican, African American candidate for president at the time, came under fire for the position he took on how he would've handled himself if he had been one of the Roseburg victims. To show the hypocrisy by the racist ass, white, Republican supported, news media regarding this heinous act of mass murder, they quickly screamed that racism was coming out of the white, liberal, news media for suggesting that the candidate was victim blaming. It is not my position to defend racist ass, white bias by any political party. And, while I despise any black person who would allow themselves to become a house nigger, the real irony, hypocrisy, and burning question in this matter is, "how can racists condemn racism?" If the African American candidate had been a Democrat, the racist ass, white, conservative, news media would have attacked him the same way they accused the liberal, white, news media of being racist. One would have to be a blind fool not to believe that the reason the African American candidate received a free pass on not being attacked by the racist ass, white, Republican supported, news media had everything to do with him being perceived as one of the conservative, right-wing, house niggers within the Republican Party.

Now, these same racist ass, white bastards are waiting to exploit the casualties of white lives being caused by niggers in order to keep justifying all the unjustifiable evil and cruelty they inflicted upon niggers from the very first time we were brought to this country in the iron shackles of slavery.

As I see it, exploiting this tragic occurrence in Roseburg, OR, reveals just one of the ways in which racist, white supremacy ideology helps cause further infection within this society. Shortly after the Dylann Roof massacre, I listened to racist ass, white, news commentators ask African American news contributors and political leaders did they agree that progress was being made because of how swiftly the white police community worked with the African American community in apprehending Roof. As far as I am concerned, why should it take these sort of horrific acts of racist hate and terror against African Americans before the predominantly white police community demonstrate their ability to effectively uphold their sworn duty to act in a consistent and professional manner when it comes to protecting the civil rights of its citizens regardless of race? The racist ass, white, news media expressed their view that African Americans, owe the white, police community special recommendations of valor when they protect us from criminals. But why? The white police community serves white citizens with the attitude that it is their inalienable rights to be protected under the same laws that black citizens are denied.

White citizens expect this without feeling as though they have to reward white police with the kind of apologetic, ass kissing attitude that racist white cops expect from black citizens when they respond to our call for help. We are treated this way because it is all part of their racist and biased history of slavery. We are still seen as not being worthy of the same protection and human rights as white people. So, when they help us they feel as though they are actually going far above and beyond their own racist ass, white supremacy ideology duties. Whenever the racist ass, white, slave-master decides to show any mercy on us as niggers, they demand that we be far more grateful to them than white citizens. Racist, white supremacy ideology teaching has done a masterful job in shaping the minds of whites that even in their intellectual expressions of trying to be politically correct in their racist ass hypocrisy, they are still unable to avoid making racist ass gaffes or statements that reflect racist thinking.

White intellectual racists are not racist because they are ignorant of the fact that all human beings are individuals. But for those of us to which this matters, it does make a difference in how we relate to one another as human beings. It's somewhat foolish to try and school intellectual, racist ass whites on such a notion regarding race. Again, they are not ignorant in this regard if you can understand my point of view because they are clearly aware of why they are racist. Take a good look at the racist ass, white, power structure ruling this country and you will quickly abandon any notion that they are somehow misguided individuals just waiting for the grand revelation to reveal the light to them that they are racist, be it by other human beings or Almighty God Himself.

Scripturally, these people are racist ass, white devils. So, if these racist ass, white devils do not hesitate in rejecting the word of God in doing their racist ass evil, one must understand that they have been given up to reprobation and are on their way to becoming hell bound. The only way to fight them is by gaining power within this white political system of government, because they will never accept us in this country of having the same human rights as they do and will only tolerate us whenever they are able to exploit us.

Tragically, Dylann Roof's racist ass attitude typifies the racist white supremacy ideology teaching in this country. The racist ass, white element in this government supports it. The racist ass, white element in the judicial system supports it. The racist ass, white element in law enforcement supports it. The racist ass, white element in the news media supports it. And finally, the racist ass attitudes within white America supports it. When it comes to race hatred, all this racist white supremacy ideology does is help nurture and influence the attitudes of the Dylann Roofs within the white race. What racist ass, white supremacy ideology does is teach deranged ass whites like Dylann Roof to distort racial history between whites and blacks.

To add even further to the lack of news integrity, at the same time that Dylann Roof massacred nine African Americans in a terrorist, racist, hate crime, the racist ass, white news media quickly ran an entire segment about a violent incident that occurred at a food distribution center in Moore Oklahoma.

A deranged, black individual who had just been fired, returned days later and carries out a brutal assault upon several employees. He used a knife to brutally sever the head of a white female employee before he was eventually shot by a chief, administrative officer inside the building. It was no doubt a heinous act of terror by a warped individual who was later found to be under the influence and teaching of the terrorist group, ISIS. But the entire tragedy will never take away the fact that the racist ass, white, news media used the timing of it for political exploitation and not so much for reporting it for the sheer horror of what happened to those who were victims of it. It was totally shameless and disgraceful to the integrity of journalism.

This racist ass, White, news media commentator actually tried to make the crime of Dylann Roof appear less horrific than the horrific crime committed by this deranged, black individual. Because in the case involving the black attacker all of the victims were white. And in the Dylann Roof case all the victims were African American. This racist ass, white news media commentator desecrated the memory of those nine slain African Americans even before they had been laid to rest. Though these two heinous acts happened nearly a year apart, this racist ass, White, news media commentator slyly used the timing of this situation for political exploitation.

She wanted to plant into the minds of the country that Dylann Roof, the white, boyish looking psychopath committed a crime that was not as horrific as the one committed by the menacing, nigger psychopath by emphasizing to the viewers the graphic details of his heinous crime. Yet for both cases, her racist ass, political exploitation only caused further emotional harm to all the families of the victims who tragically lost their lives in both senseless and evil acts of terror. This racist ass, white, news commentator only wanted to exploit this tragedy in order to say, "Look white America at one of their vicious, animal, nigger psychopaths and how he savagely brutalized someone in our precious, white race."

The obvious point that she was trying to remind the country, as well as drive home to racist ass, white America is that a violent, vicious, criminal nigger thug is far worse than a supposedly, mentally ill, psychopathic, white, racist terrorist like Dylann Roof who committed a somewhat harmless crime because the people that Roof brutally massacred were all African Americans. It's a clear example of how the racist ass, white news media uses its power in promoting racism in this country no matter who gets hurt.

One of the victims of the Dylann Roof massacre said Roof also stated black people were trying to take over *their* country. Again, his racist ass attitude is a part of the teaching of racist, white supremacy ideology.

Chapter Twelve

Free Stuff Entitlements - Whites vs. Blacks

"They all want free stuff."

When racist whites make statements like this, all they are saying is that we are the welfare government dependent, entitlement race only wanting to take from white America. Unlike unsophisticated, racist bigots, racist ass, white politicians and the racist ass, white, news media say the same things about blacks, but in coded language.

They use statements like, "As Americans we pay our fair share of taxes," but what they are saying is that niggers are not respected as tax payers, but whites are. They will quickly make reference to entitlement programs while knowing they are specifically targeting African Americans. They will say things like they all want free stuff which is just another way of saying that niggers want free stuff. When they say this, they are not referring so much to other under-privilege minorities and poor whites, but more specifically to African Americans. They will go on and on with this sort of racist coded language while knowing all along that they are targeting black people in this country. But, when it comes to being charitable in this country in common everyday life, blacks are far more generous than we are given credit for.

Racist ass, white politicians, and the racist ass, white, news media, have labeled us as the "poor people" race filled with vagabonds, homeless beggars, and criminal bums. And even though there are poor, down trodden whites who are in just as bad, if not worse, conditions, racist, white, supremacy ideology have many of them brainwashed into believing that being white still somehow places them above niggers. But, racist ass, whites who are above poverty look down on these same down trodden, white trash, racists for having fallen into the shameful conditions that slavery and racism reserved solely for niggers. Racist whites who are above the economic fray of poverty will pass these homeless, white beggars by with tightened purse strings no differently than they do towards homeless, begging niggers -- they frown upon them as being just as repulsive.

Here, let us remember Mark 12:44: "for they all put in out of their surplus, but she, out of her poverty, put in all she owned, all she had to live on." But, you see, with niggers having been labeled as the poor people race, all the pennies, nickels, dimes, quarters, and dollars we help give to homeless and destitute people, beggars in our community, and to those standing alongside roadways day after day, month after month, and year after year do add up. It doesn't end there. We have blacks who have gone on to become very wealthy philanthropists in American society, and they do just as much, if not more, charitable work in this country as whites. But, when the majority of charity organizations owned by whites receive donations, regardless if they are wealthy recipients or not, how often are those donations redistributed to causes not connected to white communities? These racist ass, white bastards have slave-mastered their racist, white asses into becoming the "free stuff" entitlement race for centuries. They have the damn audacity to try and place this label solely on niggers.

They are also saying that we are a race full of lazy, criminal niggers with no other purpose in life but to try and rob, murder, and take what they feel they rightfully own in this country, though whites are the biggest 'free stuff,' welfare recipients in this country.

In light of this, we still have, under the "nigger identity," these so-called, intellectual ass, ideologically, brainwashed ass "house niggers," who're still under the tutelage of their racist ass, white, slave-master who willfully feeds the racist ass appetite of the racist ass, white, news media and the racist ass element within this government.

The racist ass, white man, will never stop his argument in slandering the black race, and then branding us as a welfare entitlement race of criminal niggers. But the true history of how this country was built points towards the racist ass, white man as being the head and face of criminality and welfare entitlement in this country. The exploitation of black people as slaves gave the racist ass, white man unequaled wealth and governmental power in this country, of which he has not relinquished and is also unwilling to allow us the opportunity of becoming equal participants. At its very best, this is how the real corporate welfare system of the racist ass, white man was built.

We as niggers have been mainly forced into living at the very impoverished end of how real welfare and entitlement exists in this country. And through slavery, the racist ass, white man has afforded himself to live at the very wealthy end of welfare in this country. So how can these racist ass, white, hypocritical bastards attack the black race as being the face of criminality and welfare entitlement? How is it *not gaining* 'free stuff' when an entire country of white's wealth increased exponentially, generation after generation, after having forced niggers to work nearly a combined four hundred years with no wages, and later, slave wages? The brutal enslavement of our African ancestors was at the core of helping build the 'free stuff,' corporate, welfare system of the rich, and the unjust laws still enacted here in America against our race, in many ways, is no more than using a different method -- a do-over -- of all the evil and unlawful criminal acts of slavery.

The racist ass, white man, has built much of the great financial wealth of this country off the backs of slaves and the Transatlantic Slave Trade. Generation after generation, these racist ass, white bastards have fed their families with a 'free stuff,' welfare entitlement, silver spoon. But, they have the audacity to look niggers in the eyes with a straight face and label us as the biggest welfare recipients in this country.

Unless this government makes up for niggers under slavery, generation after generation of not having wages, a vote, or a voice in politics, and unless all of the wealth and land ownership in this country is redistributed in a progressive way, niggers will never be satisfied under this racist ass system of government. But, it is not my position that this can be achieved under a socialist government which already exists in many ways with racist ass, white America at the top. Until this economic imbalance becomes bridged, whites will always remain the undeniable face of welfare entitlement for the rich.

For this racist ass, white system of government to continuously falsely labeling the black race as the face of welfare in this country is an affront to all of the cruel and inhumane suffering inflicted upon us during slavery. Slavery put these racist ass, white, piece of shit bastards at the head of the table of entitlement and welfare, and they now have the damn audacity to keep pointing their racist ass finger at niggers.

The racist ass, white man within this government, has sworn to live and die by his oath that there is never to be any real form of restitution for having enslaved black people as niggers. Even though welfare of the poor helps the needs of underprivileged people, the racist ass, white man in government sees it as the only form of restitution that niggers will ever be able to force his hand. And now, he has finally decided that he will not allow his hand to be forced any further. The racist ass, white man now tells us that after not being paid a day's wages for slave work for nearly three centuries while boldly enacting slave wages and ongoing discrimination against niggers, it's time to pull the plug on welfare for poor niggers. He has decided that we have finally used up our big, 'free stuff,' welfare entitlement payday of restitution for slavery. But, as for their own great welfare state of wealth, it should be allowed to continue without even the slightest question or protest from niggers. They have decided that niggers will no longer be spoon fed the crumbs off the vast wealth gained from slavery. These racist ass, white, piece of shit bastards actually believe that they have more than made up for slavery.

But, as I look out across America and see how niggers still suffer from the aftermath, all I have in my heart towards this racist ass, white system of government is scorn and contempt. On behalf of our African ancestors who were enslaved in this country, we should not abandon a demand for restitution. Neither should we allow the racist ass, white man to wash his filthy, piece of shit ass hands of all of the evil and wicked deeds committed against our humanity because of slavery.

To show just how far some of these racist ass, elected, white politicians are willing to go when it comes to demeaning and labeling niggers as a bunch of freeloading criminals, the white, racist ass, piece of shit, one-time, college dropout governor of Wisconsin has fixed it so that niggers are no longer allowed to buy certain types of food as food stamp recipients. Even though the law affects all poor people in the state of Wisconsin, the bill, beyond a shadow of doubt, was crafted and aimed specifically at niggers. Racist ass ploys of this sort are not new to the racist ass games of politics targeting niggers. It's the long held, racist ass, white, political blueprint of how to galvanize and rally up the support of racist ass, white voters. But, as for this racist ass, white, union busting governor against the working class, he feels privileged and entitled to continue living high on the lifestyle of the 'free stuff,' welfare of the wealthy while using his magic wand to exact more racist ass laws that will further impoverish niggers and help accelerate their rapid flow into the prison systems of this country. It goes right back to what I explained earlier about how the criminal justice system is being used as a modern day slave market primarily targeting niggers.

Welfare of the poor doesn't even begin to pay us the interest on the financial losses and damages of slavery. The horrors of slavery more than justifies such demands of having the great wealth of this country redistributed to us because we have more than earned it. Until we receive the wealth that measures the depth of our suffering and our anger, niggers will never be satisfied under this racist ass, white system of government. We are not asking for something free because it is owed to us. It is their racist, white asses, through having enslaved niggers, who are the real "free stuff" race in America. The cruel act of slavery was a socialist ass program for racist ass, white America.

Regardless of their political affiliations, racist or not, the masses of the white race in this country have been raised and influenced by the idea of the inherited, silver spoon of wealth and prosperity of corporate, white America. Much of it was obtained from having enslaved niggers. Regardless, of whether they embrace racist attitudes and practices, or not, racist, white supremacy ideology is the culprit and caretaker that has played a major role in shaping corporate white America. Because of this, a vast portion of white America is spoiled on the notion of the inherited, silver spoon of white privilege. As were their parents before them, generation after generation is becoming influenced by the same idea under the capitalist system of private enterprise. But, when it comes to socialism, in spite of how well it's being masked, whites have no problem gaining wealth and prosperity by utilizing socialist methods. To add even further to this point of argument, when the Democratic candidate, running for president in the 2016 election, launched his campaign on the promise of creating a socialist government, just look at the overwhelming support from the masses of millennial, white kids on college campuses. He has gained their support all across America wherever he has taken his campaign and idea of a socialist revolution and government.

Even conservative whites within the racist ass, white led, Republican Party couldn't force these spoiled, millennial, white kids not to take the white race socialist, "free stuff," wealth and prosperity mask off. Be it in a capitalist or socialist system, whites will always be firmly positioned at the front of the line. You see, the goal of racist ass, white America is to keep niggers pushed further and further at the back of the line of economic and political growth. Racist ass whites are already ruling a dual system of both capitalism and socialism in this country. And now, all of these spoiled, millennial, white, college kids who are already benefitting from the vast financial wealth amassed within the private enterprise of this capitalist system are just itching to find out if the grass can become even greener for them on the other side of a full-fledged, socialist government. And, because of how racist ass whites have so skillfully set up this system of government to always work in their favor, niggers shouldn't want to see themselves pushed even farther behind at the back of the line in a socialist government while whites remain firmly positioned at the front.

Niggers should not want to merely exist in a full-fledged, socialist government, receiving even smaller portions of "free stuff," trickle down, economic crumbs. For niggers, a socialist government would exist as no more than a step-child to a communist government. So why should niggers, after all, that we have suffered and died for under slavery, have to settle for supposedly poor, equal down, economics that would still be unequal while pushing niggers even further to the bottom instead of upward toward economic and political stability? I believe that niggers would have a better chance if we were only to push for more effective legislation based on socialist reforms that will help overhaul this grossly, one-sided, racist ass, white, capitalist system of Wall Street.

To touch a bit further on the socialist candidate's stance on a "free stuff," socialist government, I would be the first to support the idea of black youth receiving a free, college education alongside white youth. But, even if a free, college education was somehow made possible for all students, how would the majority of our black youth obtain the level of education to attend college free when racism and poverty have Black families trapped in some of the worse social and economic conditions in this country? How will they be able to arrive at the level of a free college education when failing schools expose an alarming percentage of them on the path of becoming dropouts even before they reach high school?

And, while I believe that the socialist candidate campaign to break up corporate, Wall Street's monopoly of welfare is vital to the economic stability of middle and lower class wage earners, I am firmly against advocating a socialist government becoming the charted course in our efforts to achieve economic growth and stability for African Americans. Why should niggers have to settle for more, poor, trickle-down, welfare entitlement programs after having been forced throughout slavery to help build a great capitalist system of vast wealth of private enterprise for racist ass, white America only to end up being rewarded with the bottom end of more socialist program's crumbs falling off of the rich, "free stuff," table of the racist ass, white man?

I believe wholeheartedly in niggers unifying and becoming a powerful, independent black nation within this country by establishing vast, private enterprises and gaining the great capitalist wealth that these racist ass, white bastards built off of the backs of our African ancestors, but have done everything within their racist ass, white power to prevent us from obtaining. Whites have been governing a white, nationalist system of power from the very time they arrived here and began their colonization of the Americas. For niggers to not expediently begin building a black nationalist system of power in this country, would push us even closer to the borderline of social, economic, and political extinction.

We have been forced to live at the poor end of the welfare system, while powerful, white, financial institutions that were initially tied to the slave trade continue to allow whites to live at the wealthy end. In fact, the poor end of the welfare system was implemented to help poor whites survive and not niggers. One of the core principles of racist, white supremacy, ideology, is that, under no circumstances, can racist ass, whites ever be made to believe that their indictment of niggers as a lazy, dishonest, inferior, welfare-dependent race of criminals is wrong.

Even the great financial mecca of the Western world has ties to slavery and the slave trade. A wall that was built with the help of slaves became known as Wall Street -- the first slave market established in New York by its city council. Behind this wall, our African ancestors were placed on auction blocks, naked and half-naked, to be sold to the highest bidder. The New York Stock Exchange was founded not far from it, with one of the prime commodities on the exchange being niggers. And, it doesn't stop there. When the abolishment of slavery began to force the end of the Transatlantic Slave Trade, the same racist ass, white European powers quickly began the colonization of nearly all of the continent of Africa for its vast riches and natural resources. Many of their powerful, White, financial banking systems and business corporations are all a part of corporate welfare.

Chapter Thirteen

More on Slavery

When the racist ass, white, slave-master was not forcing his own sick and perverted behavior upon our African ancestors, he was forcing them to breed like livestock. They were being bred under their "nigger identity" to do all of the brutal, back-breaking, slave labor while allowing the racist ass, white slave-master to gain great political and financial power in this country.

For 246 years, 1619 until 1865, (the year of the Emancipation Proclamation), our African ancestors held virtually no rights to social, economic, and political power.

Generation after generation, they were forced to work before sun up and long after the sun had set, while receiving not one cent of a day's wages. They were denied an education. They were beaten, violated, and psychologically traumatized. They had the institution of family destroyed. And, after the Emancipation Proclamation to end slavery, for nearly the first 100 years leading up to the civil rights movement, those years, in many ways, were no different than the first 246 years of slavery when our ancestors arrived in Jamestown, VA. It adds up to nearly 400 years of unbroken, racist oppression against niggers.

Many of the problems we suffer today have much to do with the evil and wicked horrors of slavery. And while it remains true that some African kingdoms had their own Judas and traitor ass hand in helping European slave traders with the enslavement of the Black Israelite nation, it should never be allowed to be used as some sort of crutch to lessen racist ass, white European's wicked and horrible deeds of having masterminded the transatlantic slave trade.

The racist ass, white man, cannot move the minds of the black masses off the ills of slavery fast enough. He now prefers for his evil and wicked deeds of slavery to finally be forever forgotten. However, with each passing generation of black youth, we should not allow them to forget the kind of sick and filthy, immoral history that the racist ass, white man has involving us as a people. Because the same racist ass, white supremacy ideology that he had during slavery, he still has now, but has become more sophisticated in carrying it out. And the worst thing that we could ever do as a race is to become lured asleep by it. The racist ass, white man, tries to brush slavery off as being no more than a trivial act against a bunch of low-life, subhuman, savage niggers. He has succeeded in his efforts by gaining the support of other nations in despising the black race above all other nations. By having promoted worldwide hate of the black race, the racist ass, white man, by some statistical accounts, has successfully been able to turn the deaths and murders of nearly fifty million Africans, (while being transported to the Americas), as slaves into nothing more than an exaggeration. He has the gall to give the impression that slavery wasn't all that bad in this country by trying to portray us as having been no more than a bunch of low-life, savage niggers of whom he should be given credit for civilizing. And, sadly but true, under slavery, niggers were conditioned into believing this heinous lie after being cut off from the origin of our civilization. In truth, it was the racist ass, white slave-master who forced many of our African ancestors into behaving like uncivilized, savage, sub-human nigger animals under slavery.

Would slavery not have been all that bad if whites were the slaves with black slave-masters who were responsible for the deaths and murders of nearly fifty million white slaves, many of them being women and children? Would whites say that slavery wasn't all that bad if their black slave-masters shackled and marched them naked and half-naked onto slave ships? Would they say slavery wasn't all that bad if their racist, black slave-masters packed white slaves in the dungeon of slave ships to defecate on themselves and sleep and die in their feces? Would they say that slavery wasn't all that bad if white slaves had died of diseases from filth and starvation? Would they say that slavery wasn't all that bad if countless white slaves had their live and dead bodies dumped into the ocean as a burial place and a source of food for sharks? Would they say that slavery wasn't all that bad once they arrived on the shores of America and their racist, black slave-masters led them off in chains to be sold naked and half-naked as chattel on slave auction blocks? Would they say that slavery wasn't all that bad if they had their identity destroyed by their racist black slave-masters? Would they say that slavery wasn't all that bad if white slave mothers were forced to raise their little white, slave babies without their own ancestral identity, but instead with one given to them by their black slave-masters?

Would they say that slavery wasn't all that bad if racist, black slave-masters destroyed the institution of their families and sold them off to slave plantations in all directions? Would they say that slavery wasn't all that bad if racist black slave-masters forced white slaves to breed like animal livestock with no regard to what their family relationship was? Would they say that slavery wasn't all that bad if racist, black slave-masters forced and forged their way into becoming the surrogate and biological father to their children? Would they say that slavery wasn't all that bad if their racist, black slave-masters raped white slave women, white slave mothers, and were pedophiles and enforcers of all sorts of sick and perverted lifestyles upon white slaves? Would they say that slavery wasn't all that bad if the racist, black slave-masters beat, burned, lynched, and castrated white, male slaves? Would they say that slavery wasn't all that bad if their racist, black slave-masters forced them into doing all sorts of back-breaking and brutal slave labor before sunrise and long after the day's end? Would they say that slavery wasn't all that bad if their racist, black, slave-masters made them work without receiving one cent of a day's wages for economic survival?

Would they say that slavery wasn't all that bad if the racist black slave-masters denied white slaves the right to learn how to read, write, and receive an education? Would they say that slavery wasn't all that bad if it had been blacks as slave-masters ruling this country over the course of history while gaining great financial wealth directly and indirectly from the transatlantic slave trade? Would they say that slavery wasn't all that bad if it would have been blacks as slave-masters denying whites of any rights of participation in the political process? Would they say that slavery wasn't all that bad if it were blacks as slave-masters who ended up possessing all the land while white slaves were barely afforded a small burial plot?

These are just some of the countless reasons that the racist ass descendants of the racist ass, white slave-master are forbidden to think they could ever again be allowed to call us niggers. For the white race, these were all just "what ifs." But for the black race, all of these horrors exist as the deep, unhealed wounds of our suffrage at the hands of the racist ass, white slave-master. The tides of the racist ass, white man's hate still continue to beat un-relentlessly against our humanity.

I honestly believe that blacks don't possess the same kind of racist ideology on the order of race the way it exists in the white race. I believe that, even though still being far from perfect, if we had been the dominate power and majority population in America with whites as the minority, having been oppressed under biased laws that blacks created and that needed to be met with forced change, they would be much further along than we are as the minority in having attained their human rights. The one critical factor I base this on is they would not have been forced into being pushed so far down below the threshold of humanity because of their racial make-up the same way they have done in penalizing us with hate and racism because of the color of our skin. Their social, economic, and political fight with us would have been more about the true fight between the haves and the have nots and not the frivolous one that racist ass whites have made up and so cleverly and connivingly argued and would have us believe.

The historical saga of Alex Haley's family, "Roots," and the movie, "Amistad," and "12 Years a Slave," all give what I believe to be a very credible depiction of our African ancestor's brutal and inhumane slave experience. But, despite how painful and emotional, we are only seeing a small glimpse into the cruelty of how evil and beastly these racist ass, white, slave-masters were in the inhumane treatment of our African ancestors.

Because of the evil of the racist ass, white man's desire to destroy us by preventing us from having any sense of acceptance, blacks have been almost psychologically forced out of feeling a sense of normalcy within the human race. We are the only race of people on earth with a racist ass target squarely on our backs that has us feeling uneasy about how all the other races perceive us. When we go out among the rest of humanity, we are continually concerned about confronting racism. Our physical appearance and behavior is under the microscope more than any other race. Our social, economic, and political existence is under the microscope more than any other race, regardless if we are at the bottom, or have achieved success at the top. We always have to deal with the constant thought of other races hating us, mainly because of the racist ass, white man leading the charge and promoting it. When we walk the streets where public establishments exist, it is difficult for us to avoid wondering if we are walking past racist ass whites. When we become employed among whites, or by some exceptional circumstance, become their employer, we are still left wondering if there are racists among them, mocking us and calling us niggers behind our backs. Do they greet us with a smile, yet despise us as niggers in their thoughts? Do they greet us with a handshake while harboring racist hate in their hearts for us as niggers?

Out of fear of retaliation, from the time of slavery, niggers have spoken ill of their racist ass, white slave-masters in secret. But, back during the time of physical slavery and even more so in this day and age, niggers have no problem what so ever in their rebellion to express out in the open their deep feelings of resentment towards the racist ass descendants of the racist ass, white slave-master. While whites today, do it behind our backs to hide their racist ass, white feelings towards niggers because of not being able to do it out in the open as they once did during slavery.

Chapter Fourteen:

Racism, Up Close and Personal

As I was writing this essay, I had gone on one of my routine, early morning jogs. As I ventured eastward where the great white flight still borders near black neighborhoods, I came across a middle-aged white couple walking a large dog on a leash. I was jogging just off of the sidewalk, and as I approached to pass them, the dog became a little riled up on its leash. As I began to jog by them at a gradual pace, I spoke kindly, and they spoke back, and the woman pulled the dog back as it raised up on its hind legs. Before I'd gotten passed them, the man said suddenly and in a subtle tone, "the dog acted this way because he was a black guy," meaning, "nigger." The woman quickly refuted him saying, "It didn't matter." I guess he was implying that both he and the dog was racist. A few days later, I jogged past the same middle-aged, white woman and the dog, without the middle-aged, white man. But this time, when the dog riled up, she quickly said, "No, no, no! He's a good man." I don't know why she said this. Maybe she felt bad about what the man had said only days earlier.

This kind of encounter was just one more example of the typical, racist ass, attitude some whites hold towards blacks. All it took to spark racism in this white man was me jogging past him, as a black man. It's this sort of racist ass behavior that explains why racist whites should stop trying to find ways to justify their racist ass attitudes towards black people when it takes nothing but our racial makeup for them to judge us.

This immediately brings to mind another situation I encountered when I was still attending this predominantly white university in central Minnesota. I met this young, white lady and would later learn that her parents had adopted children of color as she was growing up. She made me aware that one of these children was an African American, and I think the other child was of Asian descent. After our first encounter, I did not speak to her until several days later. Even though she was a student at the same university, she lived in an off-campus apartment. The worst thing I could have done that night was show up unannounced, but that's exactly what I did. When I knocked at the door and announced who I was, she graciously opened the door. What happened next, threw me for a loop. I see this white guy, who appeared a bit older than both of us, sitting on her living room couch, in front of her coffee table.

The strange part was her inviting me in, then her sitting on the couch between a black guy and a white guy. What was even stranger, was the white guy talking and drinking, whatever he was drinking at the coffee table, and acting as though all was normal. The situation became more awkward and uncomfortable by the moment, so I abruptly asked her if I could speak with her alone. We walked into the inner hallway of her apartment, where I asked her about our earlier encounter and the one that was now taking place in her living room. She said that our first encounter stood, meaning she had more interest in me than the other guy. She was quite nervous and said that I would have to explain it to him. We then returned to the living room and took the same seating arrangement as before. I could not help but notice how nervous and completely uncomfortable she was being caught up in the middle of such a male egotistical thing like this.

When I began trying to break the situation down to the white guy, that he was making the situation crowded, all hell broke loose. It became a war of words about who would stay and who would have to go. Finally, she'd had enough of the back and forth words of war. What came next was a shock to me, the white guy, and her for that matter. She screamed at the top of her lungs, "both of you niggers get out of here!" Total silence fell over the room. Then, the white guy suddenly uttered in deep, emotional anguish and dejection, "he's the nigger, not me!"

She was already in a state of hysteria, so I kept my mouth shut. But, after hearing the white guy refer to me as the nigger, it was him that she pointed to the door. The racist, white guy slowly got up and left, taking his crushed ego with him. Now, as for this racist white guy referring to me as the nigger and not him, the first thing that struck my mind was what was he basing it on? As for the young, white woman calling us both niggers, I thought it might have had something to do with her growing up with people of color living in her home. My guess is that her adopted brother and sister were under the influence and usage of the "N" word, and they allowed her to feel comfortable with its usage. But, it was in that small, private space confined in the universe that a white woman used the "N" word in front of two men of which one was black and the other white.

Even though she told him to leave, it was my asinine behavior that created the confrontation. Still, I have to admit that this was the first time I'd ever experienced a situation where a racist ass, white man called a black man a nigger right in front of his face, and the result turned out productive for the nigger.

Though, this young lady and I ended up in unfortunate and painful breakup, the one thing that still echoes in my mind after all this time is not her having used the "N" word, but her standing there, trembling in front of me, looking me sternly in the eyes while saying it would be better for her in getting over me if I turned out to be nothing. I just stood there and stared back, looking pitiful as the insides of my emotions screamed out, "how can I start becoming something that would somehow win her back?"

A few months after she'd uttered those fateful words, that winter, mid-term break when she graduated, I was barely able to scrape up enough money to buy her some roses. Afterwards, she gave me a little withdrawn smile and said that I had done the worse and best thing that a man had ever done in her life. She then went her final separate way. Regardless of how bad our relationship ended, I never saw anything racist about her. But, I do know this for sure, the use of the "N" word in an interracial relationship between blacks and whites is taboo if spoken outside of their private niche.

Before this incident occurred, I had just enrolled at this university as an art student, and the first day I walked into the main hallway of the art department, I observed this white female art student working on the display case. She was facing the display case, on both knees, and had art materials scattered about the floor. As I started to walk past her, I wasn't greeted with, "Welcome to the art department." Instead, I was greeted with her head snapping around, and her spewing, in the most venomous tone, "Watch where you are stepping, nigger!" The first thing I thought to myself was, this had to be some racist, crazed ass, white bitch. Her racist ass words echoed the attitudes of racism that I experienced in that art department, but I was finally able to obtain my degree. However, after having done so, I remember my track coach who was also a white professor at the university telling me that one of the reasons I had so much opposition was because he was not aware of any black students graduating from that art department. During my entire time there, I only saw one black student. After only a month, I never saw him there again.

I remember thinking how my journey began in that art department. As I stood, waiting my turn to step onto that ceremonial stage, I kept fighting back the anxiety of trying to convince myself that I was about to succeed at my goal of graduating college. There had been a time when I was barely able to attend school because of my family having to work on the rural southern plantations of Mississippi. There was a time when, as a sixth grade student, when I couldn't even read from a first grade book. But, now, here I was after an intense summer school of cramming college courses -- about to achieve one of my life-long goals. It was only after my name was finally called, that I breathed a big sigh of relief. The moment was so surreal that I was not able to absorb the entire experience even as I walked across that stage to receive the scroll of academic achievement. In fact, I didn't realize that I was the only nigger in my graduating class until the last name had been called.

There was one other glaring thing that immediately caught my attention after the commencement. I couldn't help but notice this white, female student that I had chatted with on occasion at the student union between class-time. I later learned through the campus newsletter that she had won the "Miss Minnesota Beauty Pageant," in her pursuit of becoming, "Miss America." There she was, standing about six feet tall and elegantly poised as a beauty queen. I didn't know if it was by coincidence or design that the proximity between us made it unavoidable not to speak to her. The white crowd gathered around her made me feel as though it was a small security detail, but I felt to not acknowledge her would've been somewhat of an insult.

I thought to myself, I have just obtained my college degree and by talking to her, no racist ass, white committee in that art department can take it from me. So, I gathered up the nerve and politely asked to be pardoned by the crowd as I made my way through. Once I arrived in her presence and seeing how we were already somewhat acquainted through conversation, she graciously acknowledged my greeting. I then, gently, lifted her left hand and endowed it with a subtle kiss and then congratulated her on winning the pageant. The most revealing part was that my gesture didn't seem to draw racist frowns from all of the onlookers. Still, I was not about to take any chances and wasted no time removing myself from her stage of fame.

Before graduating, I remember living off campus in a student rooming house. Out of about ten male students, I was the only black, but the racist problem didn't start with the white students that I roomed with. It was with the white man who owned the rooming house. I felt as though he was not aware that his property manager had rented out a room to a black student. I had been living there at least a couple of months before the owner came to meet with us and do an inspection of the property. I remember all of us assembling in the modest sized dining room to introduce ourselves. As those white students introduced themselves, everything seemed pleasant, but no sooner than I introduced myself, I felt as though I was under intense interrogation.

This racist ass, white landlord started giving me the third degree on why I had chosen to live in a rooming house and not on campus. The next thing he wanted to know was how long I was planning to stay at his rooming house. He didn't ask any of the white students the same kind of questions that I was being asked. After that meeting, he started showing up on a regular basis, and I never saw his property manager there again. I kept thinking to myself, did he fire his property manager for allowing me to rent there?

Each time this white landlord showed up, the encounter was negative. A short time later, his true feelings towards me finally came out into the open. Once again, he called a meeting in the dining room, but this meeting was called very hastily. All of us arrived uncertain about what this meeting would involve. I could look around the room and see that the expression on everyone's face was that of concern. Once this racist ass, white landlord finally showed up, it didn't take long for him to tell why he had called this abrupt meeting.

He started out by lecturing to us that he ran an above board and honest rooming house and that anything that didn't belong to us was not to be touched. And, to test us on this policy, he said that he had been setting out various foods in the dining room at different times and that it had been found missing once he returned. In other words, this racist ass white man had been setting out nigger rat traps. He then told all of those white male students that I was the rat who had been stealing the food and that my lease was being terminated immediately. On more than one occasion, I had walked through that dining room and seen food sitting out, and I never thought once that someone would disturb it knowing that it did not belong to them.

So when this racist ass, white bastard accused me as being the one taking the food he made it seem as though he had caught me in the act with his eyes or some sort of surveillance camera. But, if his racist, white ass was not blind as well as honest, and did have a surveillance camera, it would have proven my innocence. Fortunately for me, my white roommates stood up and didn't allow that White, racist ass landlord to wrongly accuse me. They told him they had thought he'd been bringing the food as a good gesture to help us out as college students and that they had been taking the liberty of enjoying it. If there had only been a camera to capture the mouth dropping, blank expression on this racist ass, white bastard's face. He was in utter shock that the dishonesty didn't fall on me. The dishonesty didn't fall on any of us. To be frank, it fell on that racist ass, white landlord. He went solely on the stereotype that if you put a nigger among whites and if something ended up missing it was no way possible for it to be anyone else but the nigger taking it.

For that moment, regardless of race, there was solidarity among us students. We all gradually walked away, leaving that racist ass, white bastard standing there with his empty ass, nigger, rat trap. Just one more, small example of racist, white, housing discrimination against people of color. Once I was able to find another place to stay, I moved out of that rooming house.

Even after moving, it didn't take long to run into another racist encounter in that small, white community. This particular experience began one afternoon when I was on my way to the university campus. It had gotten very cold outside, and when I met a woman whom I'll call, Nora, she had her four little daughters with her. They had just moved into the town. Nora stopped me and asked if I might be able to direct her to the business district. I could not help but notice how the baby and the little girl next to her in age were squeezed in the baby carriage together and that they both had no shoes on their feet. The other two, small girls did not appear to look that much older, tagged along while holding onto Nora's arms. Their shoes and clothes did not seem to be suitable for the cold weather, and neither did Nora's.

All I could see was a mother and her four little children in dire need of someone to help them. Despite how grieved it made me feel to see them in such a difficult situation, I sensed Nora's courage and the love she had for her family. Even though I had given her all the information about the town that I thought would be helpful, I still felt that there had to be more for someone to do to help that family. I decided I would offer to walk some of the way with her until she was more certain of her directions. But, I sensed that if I continued trying to help her, she might become even more withdrawn.

She explained to me that her husband, whom I'll call, Dan, was out trying to find a job and because he was somewhat prejudice he would not understand me trying to help them. This was enough to make me realize that I could be placing myself in a very awkward situation trying to help a white family in a small town where I was unsure of what all the attitudes might be. When Nora felt that she had to apologize for having to admit such a thing like this, it made me see how bad things were for her. Once she thanked me for the information, she started off down the sidewalk pushing the baby carriage with the two youngest girls still inside and the other two girls trying to keep up alongside her.

After seeing this, I could not let myself give up on trying to help them. So, instead of heading on over to the university, I turned around and walked back towards the direction where I lived. I thought of my next door neighbors a white couple, because of their Christian like attitude. I figured if I told them about what happened, they would be in a better position of helping Nora and her family than I could simply because of them being of her race.

When I made it to my neighbor's house and rang the doorbell, John had just left for work. I explained everything to JoAnn, and she felt just as moved as I had been. Once I let JoAnn know that the only reason Nora was afraid to let me help her was because her husband was prejudice, along with what the rest of that little white community might think, JoAnn thought this was very sad. It also upset her that attitudes like the one Nora feared had to exist.

JoAnn agreed that we should go out and look for Nora in her car. When we finally found Nora and those little girls, they were all tired and looked very weary from all the walking they had already done. Luckily enough, we found them when we did because Nora had lost her direction again and was walking mostly in circles. After spotting them, I asked JoAnn to pull the car over to the side of the street near them. I got out of the car, and could see that Nora had become somewhat frightened because she did not recognize me. JoAnn had gotten out of the car shortly behind me, and I could see that Nora had become less frightened. Still, it took a little while before JoAnn, and I could convince her to let JoAnn drive her and the children where they needed to go. Having known JoAnn and her husband for quite some time, I felt relieved when JoAnn explained to me that she would take care of things from that point. Even though I felt a bit saddened that it had caused so much difficulty just trying to help someone outside of my race, it did not overshadow the good I felt knowing this family was being helped by someone else who genuinely cared just as I had.

Later that day, when I made it back home, the first thing I did was to stop off by John and JoAnn to ask how everything turned out helping Nora. The way JoAnn described the situation to me was very hard to take after seeing someone in the condition that Nora and her family was in. But, despite how much JoAnn said her patience had been tested that day, she explained to me that she drove Nora everywhere she had to go, including to the county aid department, so Nora could get signed up to receive food stamps and other assistance her family would need. JoAnn let me know that she had been worn out, but not so much from all of the driving around town, but by seeing how those four little girls had been suffering. Because they had a little girl of their own, JoAnn told me it was even harder for her to ever imagine that someone could be this bad off the way

Nora and her family was.

I was surprised when JoAnn told me that when she drove them home, she discovered they lived only a block or so from us. JoAnn said that what disturbed her more than anything was that when she had been inside the house and the unkempt condition of the inside of the family's home. She could not bring it upon herself to tell Nora about her feelings. After JoAnn had gone by there several times that same week trying to see what else she could do to help Nora and her family, she explained to me that she was very unsure of what else could be done in such a difficult situation.

This was when I decided that maybe I should meet Dan myself. He did act somewhat distant at first, but when I began explaining to him that I lived just a block or so from where he and his family had just moved, and how a neighbor of mine had helped his wife out a few days before, I could see the distant expression disappearing from his face and he became more pleasant. He invited me inside his home and offered me a seat, then began telling me how Nora had spoken of JoAnn and me and how grateful he was to see how someone cared enough to do something like this for his family. When Nora walked into the room, I could see how relieved she was to see Dan and me talking the way we were after just having met. Dan had acted nothing like Nora thought he would once he had learned that I was a black person. But I always kept the faith and confidence in myself that sometimes, if people were allowed even half the chance to express themselves as individuals, there would not be so much bias and racist judgement passed against others simply because of their skin color.

After the three of us had talked a while longer, I could see that a great deal of Dan's frustration had to do with how parts of the community had scorned him and his family because of the impoverished conditions they had suffered from. Having grown up in a community myself where poverty was present and seeing some of the harsh realities and misfortunes people were facing I understood much of what Dan and his family were going through. What I believe made it even more difficult for him to take, was the fact that he was being made to feel more like an outcast by his community and not so much by someone outside of his race.

Dan later explained to me that the biggest factor in helping cure his prejudiced attitude occurred during one particular time when he had been very down on his luck. He said that as much as he had his pride, he felt he had no other choice but to go to a local parish for some help. But when he found himself being lectured to by the white man who was the overseer of the parish about how another white man like himself could have ever gotten in such a bad condition, it started to change his perspective on race. Dan said that he left that parish feeling more down on himself than he did before he had gone to that place.

After a couple of weeks or so, Dan and I started to become pretty good friends. But, little did I know, it was going to take a lot of courage for us to remain friends. I had a hard decision to make. Would I let the racist attitudes that Dan heard from parts of the white community get the best of me? It was just hard for me to take at first that some of the white people in the community would call me an "out of my place" nigger and put Dan and I down because of my effort to try and help him and his family. But I had finally made up my mind that I would not turn my back on them like so many others had done within that little, white community who decided to shut themselves behind doors and ridicule me instead of lifting up a hand to help make these people feel welcomed in the town.

I thought Dan and Nora were just starting to get a little bit back on their feet, but they told me they could not get settled in the town. Eventually, they moved back to the small town from where they had moved.

Before my family moved north, I remember growing up as a small boy in Mississippi, where racial problems were commonplace. One of the first racist incidents that comes to mind was when my family lived and worked at the place of a white landowner. The home of the white plantation owner was just up the dirt road from the farmhouse where we lived. Just out from the little house stood a huge shade tree where we had the rare time of playing when we weren't doing yard or field chores. I had to be about nine or ten years old. My younger brothers and sisters and I were playing under the big shade tree when the white landowner's grandson came walking down that dirt road carrying what appeared to be a rifle. The white boy was about my age and had been at his grandparent's house on many occasions. On some of those occasions, he had casually interacted with us. But unfortunately, on that particular day, it was not the case. That little, white boy was carrying an air rifle, BB gun.

He marched right up under that big shade tree with his BB gun, singled me out, and said, "Do you believe I will shoot you, nigger?" as he smirked. The strange part about him calling me a nigger is that he said it without any anger in his voice. He said it as though he was simply calling me by my name. I could only stand there in terror, and before I could utter a single word, he cocked the gun and pointed the barrel towards me. Before I could react, he had already shot me, right in the stomach, at point blank range. He still had the smirk on his face as I stood crouching over, grimacing in pain. But all of a sudden, a blur of anger and rage took hold of my emotions. At that moment, I forget all about the pain. I quickly stepped towards that little, white boy, snatched that BB gun from his hands, cocked it, and shot him back near the same spot where he shot me. I then tossed the BB gun at his feet as he jumped up and down from the same, intense pain that he had inflicted upon me.

Nothing had to be said at that point in order to know that it was one, little, racist ass, white boy against one little nigger boy. As soon as he settled down from the pain, he took off running up that dirt road, hollering and leaving behind a trail of dust. The only thing that frightened me worse than him taking off and leaving his BB gun, was him running to tell his grandparents that I had shot him. It didn't take long for the inevitable to happen. He showed back up with his grandmother by his side. Fortunately for me, my mother was already out in the yard trying to sort out what had happened. Not only did my mother slave in the white plantation owner's fields, she also worked in their home as a maid and cook.

In this case, that may have helped save me. Once the little, white boy's grandmother walked angrily up to my mother, she immediately demanded an explanation. My mother, not one bit shaken, told her that her grandson had first shot me with the BB gun. His grandmother then turned and looked at him with a stern face and asked him if this was true. The little white boy tightened up his shoulders and fists, and then turned red-faced and nodded to his grandmother that it was true. The grandmother without saying another word, made him pick the BB gun back up, grabbed him by his arm, and marched him back home without any apology from her or him. My mother didn't whip me, and to my relief, I never heard anything else about it.

A few years later, I had another racist encounter when we moved to a small, country town. It was during the mid-sixties around the time of the Civil Rights Movement when the fight to end school segregation was reaching a high point. Prior to moving, I remember that in the small town where we first lived after moving off of a rural plantation, Dr. Martin Luther King, Jr. led a civil rights rally dealing with many of the human rights issues involving African Americans which also included the one that I was about to embark upon. It would teach me as a small boy how the civil rights movement would change the course of my life. The main, little church in the town where Dr. King gave his speech was so crowded that me and my friends couldn't get anywhere near it. The people spilled out of the church and into the streets. Once I became an adult, I saw a documentary that captured that time and even showed Dr. King visiting the home of our neighbors who lived only about a mile from where we had lived in the same, little rural county.

In that little, country town that we had just moved into, during that summer, there was talk going around that, because of the fight by Dr. King and others to end segregation in schools, some of the black students would have to integrate into the white school system. It was being said that if some of the black parents wouldn't voluntarily send their children to the all-white school, the black school district would be forced to handle the selection process. Seven black boys voluntarily enrolled, and I was one of them.

It was a combined junior and senior high school. Our first day there was about the scariest and strangest thing I had ever experienced up to that point in my life. Once we arrived at the segregated, white school, we were immediately approached by members of the teaching staff. White kids gawked, stared, and frowned at us. We were walking so close together, you would have thought we were joined together at our hips. The white staff did very little to make us feel welcomed. At first, they acted as if they didn't know what to do with us. So, instead of inviting us out of the entrance hallway, they made us stand there for what seemed like forever, as they talked among themselves. We weren't sure if they were deciding whether or not to ask us to leave the building. I have to admit that it was terrifying to see all of those white kids pouring into that building and walking around us as if we were in a roped off area. The white students continued walking past us on both sides in an almost rounded pattern, with angry looks and scowls on their faces.

When that white staff finally ended their meeting and approached us again, I think all of us expected to be sent back home. But when they instructed us to follow them, we did it more out of fear and not relief. Once we started walking, it was very slow and deliberate. When we finally arrived at our appointed destination, we found ourselves on full display right down in the front rows of the school auditorium. The strangest part about it is there were no other students there. For most of the morning we just sat in that auditorium and answered questions about our grade levels. I do remember that the two older boys, who were considered as our leaders, had to be somewhere around the 10th grade level, while the rest of us were around the 7th and 8th grade level.

It took nearly the entire morning before they were able to figure out our grade levels and what classrooms we were to be assigned. But, before they led us to our classrooms, they made it clear to us that we would be picked up and brought back to the auditorium before school dismissal. I ended up being taken to a classroom with two of my closest friends, and that was a huge sigh of relief. I had no idea where the other boys were taken, but the white teacher in our classroom immediately seated the three of us together, and that was segregation inside of desegregation. But it was all fine with us, considering what we had just gotten ourselves into.

For that entire day, it felt as though we were on display as the white kids couldn't stop staring at us. I tried to do everything possible not to stare back at them. At the end of the school day, I was relieved to be out of that classroom. We ended up back in the school auditorium and was then released to go home. I can't recall how that eventual situation ended with having to report back to that school auditorium after school dismissal, but I still remember one thing very clear, and that is, we never left that racist, white school, not walking home together. Other than all the hateful stares and frowns we had to encounter, we survived our first day of school desegregation. The next few days of school, it was the same routine of reporting back to the school auditorium, but it didn't bother us because we were able to leave school together each day which was the only way we could feel safe.

The hostile frowns and stares didn't get any better, but at the end of that week a miracle experience took place, when we attended gym and found out that the gym teacher was black. He had to be God-sent to have been the only black teacher to desegregate into that school. Once he was able to get a handle on what was going on with us, he started taking all of us to the afterschool gymnasium. It was great at first, but the fun suddenly ended when we were getting ready to leave and found a mob of angry white students at the gym exit, brandishing bats, bottles, and sticks, and shouting, "Get out of our school, you niggers!" We were all trapped and afraid to attempt going past them and out of the door. But, no sooner than that black gym teacher became aware of what was going on, he courageously stepped up dispersed that racist, white, student mob with such a teacher-like, authoritative way of reason, we could not actually believe it ourselves. It allowed us to walk home without further incident. After that incident, things started changing fast for us.

The next thing I remember was the white football coaches had all of the Black kids in the equipment room being fitted for gear. We were then marched off to the football field to start practice with the white kids. After a few practices, those white coaches had already established where and what positions we would play. Among all the players, white and black, I had to be one of the smallest boys on that junior high school football team. But, those white coaches decided that I would be their starting nose tackle. As much as I wanted to play running back, they decided to place one of the other black kids at that position who was much bigger than I. It didn't take long for me to find out that I must have been a good tackler because during school lunch, some of those little white boys started sitting at the same table with me. They surprised me when they began offering me their chocolate milk if I would stop hitting them hard during football practice. At that very moment, I felt that those little white boys were about the best teammates that I could ever have.

During that difficult time of racial segregation, I believe that despite all of the racism, the fact that we were allowed to play sports in an all-white school helped us develop a team concept with those white kids. It also helped calm down some of the racial tension we were experiencing. However, off of that football field, the attitude of us being hated and resented niggers loomed each and every day we entered that school.

After that first racist mob incident, it didn't take long for racism to reveal itself again. It was after lunch had ended. All the kids were allowed to go outside for recess. One of the favorite spots for the students to hang out was on and around the football bleachers. The bleachers were very close to the school and the playground area. During recess, the small group of us black kids would always sit together on the lower part of the bleachers. This time we noticed this big white kid acting a bit odd around the bleachers and the playground area. We overheard some of the other white kids talk about the boy being mentally challenged or, as I later came to know it, having a special needs disability. It was obvious to see that when some of the white kids would either play with him or actually tease him, he became very aggressive. At other times, the boy would appear to wander aimlessly around the playground area and bleachers. Somehow, on this particular day, I ended up getting separated from the other black kids on my way out to recess. From the time we enrolled into that racist, white school, we never allowed ourselves to get separated. And, when it finally happened, those racist ass, white kids jumped at the chance to attack.

As I tried to get to those bleachers where the other black kids were sitting, I heard those white kids say, "get him! Get that nigger!" No sooner than this happened, this big, white kid with the disability seemed to have appeared out of nowhere and was now chasing after me. As that big, white kid bore down on me with one of the most menacing looks, those other white kids had locked arms, building a circle around us. As that big, white kid chased me, they kept pushing me back into that circle, while shouting racial slurs. All I could do was duck and dodge, and run in terror for my life. As I continued running around inside that circle, being surrounded by a mob of racist ass, white kids, they acted in a frenzy, like sharks having smelled blood. I wanted desperately to stop running and defend myself. But, I kept thinking that if I stopped and fought back, then all of those other white kids would join in the attack. It felt as though I had been running for what seemed like forever, when all of a sudden an angry, white lady with cook clothes on broke through the circle, waving a big frying skillet above her head. It turned out that it was the boy's mother who was employed in the school kitchen.

Now both of them was after me, and she was no small sized white woman, who kept trying to corner me, while screaming, "stop running, you nigger," as she kept swatting at my head with that big skillet. I kept running in that circle, ducking, dodging, and being pushed back in that circle by all those racist, white kids, as they jeered and laughed, shouting, "Get him, get him! Get that nigger!" I was about ready to collapse when, out of nowhere, this big, tall, white man broke through the circle and grabbed me. He was the school principal, and though he had this very hostile look on his face, it didn't matter because at that moment, nothing could have been more terrifying than what I had just experienced. Which is why I had such a hard time accepting what happened next.

That white principal pulled me by the arm and back into the school building and hastily walked me to his office. He then closed the door and grabbed a belt somewhere from the coat closet and gave me a severe ass whipping across my back and buttocks. As I grimaced in pain, I couldn't understand why I was getting an ass whipping for something that someone else had done to me. I supposed my color was at fault for provoking this racist incident. After being whipped, this racist ass, white principal made me sit in his office until recess ended then marched me back to class. I never told my parents about the incident, but I felt it was better that I took a belt whipping from that racist ass, white principal, rather than being murdered by having my skull bashed in by that white woman, along with her son while that racist ass mob of white kids cheered them on.

Even before I experienced this horrible, racist incident, I remember working in the cotton fields of Mississippi where buses carrying white kids to school would pass us by and the white kids would poke their heads out of the windows, stick up their middle fingers, lick out their tongues, and scream out the word, "niggers."

I remember being about 12, and my brother next to me being about 13 when my dad promised us that if we each picked 200 pounds of cotton by the end of the work day, he would buy us each a motorcycle. It took me and my brother before sun up until after sundown to finally pick that 200 pounds of cotton. One would have to understand the scale of which cotton is weighed to actually appreciate the feat of a 12 and 13 year old boy picking 200 pounds of cotton within a 12 hour span. Let me put it this way. If my brother and I, had been born during the time of physical slavery, the racist ass, white, slave-master would have labeled us as, "two, prized, young bucks."

My dad kept his word and bought us those motorcycles. It had to be about the greatest day of my life until I took that motorcycle into the little nearby country town, because on my way back home on that little, blacktop highway, a car filled with white teenagers pulled their car alongside my motorcycle and almost grazed me while shouting out the word "nigger." Once the back of their car became even with the front of my motorcycle, they stuck a bottle out of the passenger side window and started pouring what I thought to be soda in my face. They then threw the middle finger at me as they sped off. I never saw riding that motorcycle on that little blacktop road the same way again.

I also remember, shortly after having moved to Milwaukee at the age of fifteen, I had a couple of bad encounters with the police that I felt was part racism and harassment. The year was 1969, not too long after Dr. King was assassinated, and rioting was sweeping the nation. I have to admit that the first incident was caused by me having made a very callous remark. It happened when the young man I had just befriended invited me to go with him to the downtown mall. As I'd just moved from the rural south to what I thought to be big city life, I was determined to try and fit in by exhibiting some of the same negative behavior I had witnessed from other juveniles in my neighborhood. My new friend was somewhat of a jokester, and my wanting to impress him was what caused me to make such an ill comment.

Just as we were getting ready to leave the mall, I saw two uniformed, white police officers escorting an elderly white lady out of the mall. I had my friend take notice of it, and then said to him, "What are they doing, arresting her for prostitution?" We were nowhere near her or that exit when I made those disrespectful remarks. But, little did we know, there were two, white, plainclothes detectives walking just behind us, who could have been already monitoring our activities. They were so close that they were able to overhear my remarks and quickly stop us. My friend was a 6'6" tall, high school basketball player, and when they told him to get out of the mall in no uncertain terms, he used every step of those long strides to comply.

As for myself, those two white detectives snatched me up by the back of my coat collar, sandwiched me between them, and muttered a racist slur about me being a little, foul-mouthed nigger. Then they said that I was going to go over there and apologize to that elderly, white lady or else have my assed kicked. They held me, trapped between them, but once they started marching me towards her, one of them started walking just a little bit behind the other white detective, shielding his foot as he kicked me in the backs of my leg several times as they roughly walked me over to apologize. The elderly, white lady was too far away from us to have heard what I'd said. Still, those two, white detectives said that if she didn't accept my apology, things were about to get worse.

Before the other two, uniformed, white, police officers could assist the elderly, white lady into the cab waiting just outside the exit, the two, white detectives halted them and got the elderly, white lady's attention. One of the white detectives shoved me in the back just as the elderly, white lady began to turn in our direction. I couldn't help but notice that she had this gentle smile, though she had no idea why I was being brought before her. Her face was a bit puzzled as I uttered the words, "Ma'am, I apologize." She went on with her pleasant little smile as those two, white detectives quickly snatched me out of her presence. Then they marched me a short distance down the block and gave me a hard shove in the back and said I'd better never allow them to see me at that mall again. What really made me feel ashamed of what I'd done, was not how those white detectives had treated me, but seeing the polite expression on that little, old, elderly, white woman's face.

The next encounter could well have been more about police harassment seeing how it involved both a white and black cop. But, as I said earlier about the Freddie Gray case in Baltimore, MD, it's not impossible for a black cop to be involved in police brutality against another black person whereas the white cop's behavior could be racially motivated with the black cop's being driven by some other problem. I had not even gotten used to our new neighborhood before we ended up having to move to a different one. So, there I was, nowhere near adjusted to city life and returning home one night after visiting with my new friends in the neighborhood that I had just moved from when, all of a sudden, two uniformed police officers appeared behind me.

I was already feeling a bit fearful about police officers with the mall incident still fresh on my mind. The two officers were walking very close behind me. As I continued looking over my shoulder, my heart began to race. This went on for nearly an entire block, but for me, it seemed much longer. The next thing those officers did was make some sort of sudden, jumping motion towards me with loud sounds behind it. I took off running in sheer terror. I decided one thing for sure, after my first encounter with city police officers -- for a young, little nigger, having just moved from the deep-south -- they were certainly not role models or heroes.

As for the experience with that white officer, his behavior didn't come as a surprise seeing how racist white harassment and brutality was commonplace during the time I was growing up in the rural south. But, for that black officer, I kept thinking, "how could he do something like this to a black youth along with a white policeman." In that single moment, his actions shattered everything that I had come to believe about Dr. King's march regarding black people to be united.

As a small boy growing up in Mississippi and experiencing racism, I developed a mindset of trying to characterize whites by their attitudes and demeanor.

I remember an incident that occurred when my daughter and son were about six or seven years old. I had bought them training wheel bikes to practice riding. It was a warm, summer weekend when I put on a jogging suit and took them to an outdoor running track in a small, white, suburban township bordering the county of Milwaukee, WI - a track I had occasionally worked out on when I was a college football player. Once we arrived, I took my kid's bikes out of the trunk of my car as they looked on excitedly. No sooner than the bikes were on the pavement, they hopped on eagerly and headed for the track. They peddled just ahead of me, but I was quick to catch up with them. I immediately explained to them the rules for practicing their bike riding on the track. I made it very clear that they were to keep their bikes on the far outside lanes. As I stretched, I watched to make sure that they obeyed my instructions. But, just before I began my jog, I noticed three, middle-aged, white men walk onto the track. All three were somewhat stumpy built and appeared to be just above average height.

I had already jogged around the track several times before they'd finished their stretching and began their jog. They were about a half of a lap ahead of me when I looked across the track and saw my kids get off their bikes and jump into the sand box. The bikes were left on the two-inside lanes of the track. Even though the track had eight running lanes, the three white men had taken the three inside lanes. My kid's bikes were blocking the first lane and a small part of the second lane. I knew that I was not going to make it around there before the men arrived at those bikes. My first thought was that the men in the first and second lane would simply run around the bikes, and once I arrived, I'd move them onto the grass. But, what happened next came as a complete shock.

All three of those white men stopped at those bikes, and two of them picked the bikes up and threw them off the track and in the direction of my kids. My kids became startled, but in their childlike innocence, they went back to playing in the sandbox. Once I saw this, I sprinted the remaining distance as they all stood waiting. As I approached them, they were braced for an exchange of heated words. The first thing that I said to those three, white bastards, was that there was no need to toss my kid's bikes when they could've simply shown the courtesy of rolling them onto the grass. And, the first thing that one of those white men said to me was that my kids should not have had their bikes on the track. This could easily have stood as a legitimate argument, but that same argument could well have applied to white parents whom I'd seen do the same with their small kids. The three of them stood there, brandishing their words like three, bold, white authority figures who privately owned the track.

I felt a deep rush of emotional rage trying to take hold of me. Unless they were all trained in martial arts, I felt that I was still athletic enough to take on two of them in an all-out brawl. And, if I became too exhausted to handle the third one, my thoughts were to pick up one of my kid's bikes and slam it up against his skull. But, rational thinking quickly sunk in. It would either be my little kids watching their dad shot dead by racist ass, white cops or being handcuffed and taken to jail. In the midst of my anger, I rounded up my kid's bikes, and we left that track and those three, white bastards were all too happy to see us go. The most sacred thing to parenthood is being able to protect our children, but those three, white bastards left me feeling humiliated and powerless. Those three, white bastards made one thing clear to me - they were not part of a welcoming committee for niggers. It's an incident that will never be completely erased from my mind. It's just one more instance of how things can end up going wrong for a nigger out in a racist ass, white suburb trying to enjoy what's supposed to have been a public facility. As I said, just because racist whites were forced into taking down the Jim Crow signs, doesn't mean that Jim Crow, racist ass attitudes no longer exists.

When it comes to the ills of racism, I speak not only from a distance but from direct experience.

Chapter Fifteen

More on the "Nigger Identity" and the "Gatekeepers"

Our usage of the "nigger" word cannot be tied to the same brutal history of slavery that involved the racist ass, white man, nor to that of other races that have been influenced by racist ass, white supremacy ideology against the Black race.

Racist hate towards blacks is rarely ever fueled without the usage of the "nigger" word, and it has everything to do with slavery that was forced upon us by the racist ass, white man. It is vital for us to get to the very root of the "nigger identity" that became shaped under slavery, and we have to uncover the attitudes that it forced us into taking on.

Just as I said earlier, under the "nigger identity" we now have the "gatekeepers of the nigger word, niggers." These "gatekeepers of the nigger word, niggers" have created a subculture in which the "nigger" word has become rooted and accepted within the urban culture of black America. But, where the real problem and conflict arises is how the "gatekeepers of the nigger word, niggers'" attitudes and behavior is shaped under their "nigger identity."

Again, in order to truly find the answer, we have to begin our journey during our slave captivity, along with how the slave culture affected us. It is vitally important for black people to understand that the goal of the racist ass, white, slave-master was not only to enslave us, but a major part of his wicked scheme was to justify our enslavement. He was able to do this by portraying us as wild, uncivilized, savage niggers. He then forced and conditioned many of our African ancestors into actually behaving like subhuman, savage animals. It was these racist ass, white, slave-masters promoting all sorts of violent and savage perversion within the slave quarters, as well as forcing their own sick and perverted ass behavior upon our African ancestors. And yet, many of our ancestors fought and died before they would allow themselves to be broken under their "nigger identity." They are the ones who became the defiant and rebellious liberators.

To this very day, out of the slave culture, under their "nigger identity," they are the gatekeepers of the "nigger word niggers," who still hold fast to the same, rebellious attitude against the racist ass descendants of the racist ass, white, slave-master. They are the ones among the black masses who do not oppose the usage of the "nigger" word within our culture, but have no issue with other blacks within the mainstream of our culture who oppose and choose to distance themselves from any association with the "nigger identity." In fact, the most accepted and upheld position within the mainstream of black culture is to reform ourselves of any kind of usage of the "N" word because of all the horrors of slavery that will be forever attached to it.

Because of this upheld view against the usage of the "nigger'' word, it actually allows for the usage of the "nigger" word to exist within our Black subculture without having to deal with all of the backlash from whites and other races, believing that it would somehow become acceptable for them to use the "nigger" word against Black people. But regardless of any attempt, this kind of racist ass, point of view would never be allowed to stand in America as a whole. And, here is why. Unlike its void effect during the time of slavery, the Declaration of Independence and United States Constitution has gradually become the shining light on the dark deeds of racist ass, white America in which they have become snared within their own racist hypocrisy against humanity.

In order for white America to uphold any genuine integrity in fighting against racism, it becomes very intolerable for them to allow the party of racism to drive the white race into being seen as the only race on the planet in which racism defines their very attitudes, behaviors, and beliefs in relationship to the rest of humanity. Imagine for a moment, if all the other races started seeing the white race as their natural enemy. I don't think it would be in the best interest of white America or any race for that matter, to be defined and seen as the central hatemonger against all other races. But, in order for the racist ass, white man to lessen this perception, what he has slyly done is make the Black race the main target of hate and racism throughout the world. It is also a part of his evil ass scheme that all other races will line up against the Black race along with his dirty, racist, white ass. Tragically for niggers, this racist ass scheme is working.

The enslavement of our African ancestors served his racist ass wicked deeds to perfection because tragically, many of our African ancestors were broken and conditioned into behaving like subhuman, savage, "nigger" animals. In this day and age, this animal-like slavery conditioning still works in demonizing and dehumanizing us, so that hate and racism towards niggers will continue to remain alive and justified under the racist ass, white laws of this country.

As I stated before, slavery caused two distinct types of attitude under the "nigger identity," and from these two different attitudes came the "gatekeepers of the nigger word niggers." Once our African ancestors rebelled from the slave plantation, many of them continued to hold on to the "nigger identity" that was engraved in their minds from birth by the racist ass, white slave-master. As our ancestors passed on the "nigger identity" the "gatekeepers of the nigger word niggers" did not allow it to be uprooted from our culture. It will be these "gatekeepers of the nigger word niggers" who will determine how the "nigger" word will be defined within our black subculture. Will the "nigger identity" be defined by the descendants of the "gatekeepers of the nigger word niggers" who became defiant and rebellious against the racist ass, white slave-master, or will the "nigger identity" be defined by the descendants of the "gatekeepers of the nigger word niggers" within the slave quarters that caved into the animal-like conditioning of the racist ass, white slave-master? From slavery and out of the slave culture is where the conflict and struggle with the "nigger identity" and the "nigger" word begins.

Long before the Civil War had given black slaves their physical freedom they had to learn how to survive under their "nigger identity." They had no choice but to make it be something different than what it meant to their racist ass, white slave-masters. Even though many of them became broken under their "nigger identity," many more of them fought, rebelled, and died before they would allow themselves to be broken under their "nigger identity." They had to learn how to act submissive and yet not be submissive in their thinking. They had to learn how to acknowledge the racist ass, white, slave-master's authority while still despising it and not having any loyalty or respect for it.

Even though black women were brutally raped by these racist ass, white, slave-masters, in their minds, they could not be made to accept being violated by these perverted ass beasts. Even though the racist, white slave-master had the power and authority of beating and whipping black, male, slaves, and murdering and lynching them, they could not be broken from carrying out their defiant and rebellious behavior. But tragically, for those slaves who didn't think with this rebellious attitude under their "nigger identity," they became broken and caved in to the sub-human, savage, animal-like conditioning of the racist ass, white, slave-master.

We have held much debate about the "N" word, but have not addressed the "nigger identity" and the impact that it had on our African ancestors under slavery, or how it is still affecting us. There has not been a definitive answer as to why so many blacks have embraced the usage of the "N" word. We cannot go on simply saying it's a "black thing," or it's simply the way it is because of slavery, and never get to the root of the problem.

As I explained earlier, the racist ass, white slave-master forced black slave mothers into suckling their newborn slave babies under their "nigger identity." I also explained how during the Slave Rebellions and after the Civil War had finally ended physical slavery, many of our African ancestors didn't sever their ties with the "nigger identity," but instead, transported it from the slave culture. Our African Ancestors had to learn how to survive under their "nigger identity." During the time of slavery, they began rebelling against their racist ass, white slave-masters under their "nigger identity." In the minds of many of them, they became liberated from slavery under their "nigger identity." And while the "N" word will always remain a stigma within our culture, and even with the knowledge of knowing how it became a part of our culture, we still must get to the truth about why it still remains so deeply embedded within the fabric of our culture.

Tragically, after physical slavery had ended, many of our African ancestors found no grounds on which they were able to escape all of the psychological, ill effects of slavery. The damage had become too thorough and complete. Under the inhuman cruelty of slavery, our African ancestors were seen as no more than chattel. They were forced into a breeding cycle like animals, even before they had reached adulthood. Therefore, each generation from the birth of parents to their offspring began at a younger age. Instead of every 20-25 years, it could have been as low as every 12-14 years between some generations. Once these generations become broken down into nearly 246 years under slavery, we could be looking at nearly 17-20 generations of the institution of the black family torn apart under slavery. In fact, because of the racist ass, white, slave-master's demand for slave labor and financial gain, this heinous act of forced breeding children was more than likely far worse.

To this day, the cruel and inhumane residuals and ill effects of slavery still exist as the ongoing silent killer of how the institution of the black family is still being crippled and destroyed here in racist ass, white America. And not only in America but in all the other parts of the world where the Transatlantic Slave Trade took our African ancestors. Though there were some of our African Ancestors who were able to hold together their families on sheer will and determination to survive, many others were completely broken apart, both physically and mentally. And, it is this mental breakage under the "nigger identity" that is still at the root of producing much of this subhuman, savage behavior within our culture today.

Under extreme poverty and deprivation, the racist ass, white slave-master forced many of our African ancestors into behaving like subhuman, violent, savage beasts within the slave quarters. And now much of this same psychological conditioning is causing us to be victimized and preyed upon by other niggers within our own race. The racist ass, white, slave-master forced and conditioned niggers into despising themselves while worshipping him.

Today, under the "nigger identity," we have blacks who have become "stark raving, nigger-ill crazy." The ill effects of slavery have finally forced many of our people into behaving as though they have flown out of some giant ass, cuckoo's nest. This is comical shit to the racist ass, white man as he continues in his efforts to maintain and control the socio economic, and political seat of power, but it is, by far, one of the worst kinds of tragedies imaginable to see what slavery has actually done to niggers.

As a race of people, we should be deeply angered and should never allow ourselves to become desensitized to how slavery and the residuals of slavery have continually affected us generation after generation. To see ourselves being continually victimized by all the savagery of black-on-black crime, it cannot be dispelled as having a direct link to slavery. Just look at the sub-human savage-like conditioning of slavery still going on in our communities, schools, and our neighborhoods. You have niggers today in America under their "nigger identity" who vow to murder and destroy other blacks.

This is exactly how the racist ass, white, slave-master was able to condition many of us into destroying each other under slavery. We should become full of anguish to fully understand what this racist ass, white slave-master has done to us as a race. As a race, will we ever begin to truly understand the horror of this catastrophic loss and destruction of the institution of our families? Some research suggests that forty or fifty million Africans died during the middle passage of the Transatlantic Slave Trade. It could have been far worse according to some statistical accounts. And those who survived were small in comparison to those who did not. It defines who we are as a race when we are reduced to our sheer will to survive.

Will we ever fully grasp the depths of how far slavery has actually set us back on a socio, economic, and political level in this country? And, should this not give us a sobering perspective on the devastating impact slavery had upon our people? The evil attempt by the racist ass, white man to use and destroy the black race continues and by having many of our people conditioned into this violent and sub-human, savage-like behavior, they're able to speed up the systematic process of black genocide. The slaves that became conditioned into becoming the violent and savage niggers within the slave quarters are the same violent and savage ass niggers we are dealing with today. These are the niggers who are acting out like the slaves whose minds became psychologically broken under the "nigger identity." The racist ass, white man, could not have devised a more lethal way for niggers to assist in destroying their own race.

Even when racist ass, white politicians, and the racist ass, white, news media find themselves on the right side of an issue involving the black race, it's all for the wrong reasons. For example, I listened to a racist ass, White, news commentator, denounce Planned Parenthood founder, Margret Sanger, as a devout racist. Just look at the irony of one racist denouncing another racist. It's well documented that Sanger was a racist, but because she gained much of her notoriety for her work as a feminist activist, she is both revered and shunned.

Even though Sanger was a pioneer in the feminist movement, she should not be given a free pass regarding her racist ass views. The use of contraceptives is a universal practice. Sanger is credited for having founded the American Birth Control League which later evolved into the Planned Parenthood Federation of America. After forming the National Committee on Federal Legislation for Birth Control, it became a very important component in the legalization of contraception in the United States.

Sanger was the founder of the first birth control clinic in the state of New York and staffed it with all female doctors. She opened the first birth control center in Harlem, and it was said that she staffed it with mostly African Americans. But, despite Sanger's contribution to the feminist movement, the records still indicate that she was also a white supremacist. Part of her racist ass ideology of bigotry and discrimination was to eliminate what she deemed to be society's misfits. She targeted those who she deemed ignorant and poor, and she also believed in compulsory segregation and sterilization for the profoundly retarded.

Sanger supported the idea of coercion to stop those diagnosed as feeble minded from procreating. Sanger was said to have advocated sterilization and segregation for those with incurable and hereditary disabilities. Even in Sanger's racist ass, warped views there are still arguments that she was not being race selective and that her beliefs applied to all those who were deemed as society's misfits. But, the most critical thing that's being overlooked is that racist, white supremacy ideology has judged the entire Black race to be all of the things Sanger advocated on negative eugenics.

Sanger employed blacks no differently than a racist ass, white, slave-master who selects their good, obedient, responsible, hand-picked house niggers from among those deemed unfit for the master's household. It would be those niggers that would be spared to live and remain in the good submissive role of serving their superior, white, slave-master. It is so difficult for some black women to denounce Sanger's racist ass views and still practice their legal rights under Planned Parenthood no differently than other women. Making ourselves aware of Sanger's racist ass beliefs as the founder of Planned Parenthood doesn't mean Black women should live their lives shrouded in guilt.

Let's keep it real. About the rationale of human beings, for example: if a black person was somehow able to find the cure for cancer and the recipients for the cure were racist, 99.9% of them would most likely accept the cure. And, vice versa for blacks, if it were the racist white person who found the cure. Wouldn't it be amazing if a racist, white surgeon who'd operated on a person of color was asked, "Why did you save their life?" and the surgeon replied, "my commitment to being a skilled and successful surgeon is far greater than my desires of being a racist? If we were to put a little thought into this analysis, maybe it would cause us to think twice about so much of this race hatred.

Even though Planned Parenthood is notoriously connected to abortion and has divided this Nation on that moral issue, many women see it as a preventive clinic for health issues. Numerous young people, women and men, seek out its services for methods of birth control and prevention against sexually transmitted diseases.

However, when the racist ass, white, news media and racist ass, white politicians, criticizes the black abortion rate, it is not being done out of genuine concern for unborn black infants. It's all about stirring up white support and using any tactic within their grasp to denounce Planned Parenthood to gain white votes.

For white women, Sanger saw abortion as a woman's personal right to decide over her body. But, for black women, she saw it as a method to diminish and destroy the black race. Even though abortion is a woman's right, Black women should not go unaware of Sanger's racist ass agenda. Black leaders that collaborated with Sanger on Planned Parenthood clinics becoming established in their communities had to have been aware of her motives, yet they had their own agenda on contraceptives and abortion. Today a nigger would have to be a blind ass fool not to believe that Sanger's racist ass ideology on aborting Black babies is not still felt and supported by racist ass, whites.

Racist ass, white politicians and the racist ass, white, news media are not lobbying to defund Planned Parenthood because of the plight of unborn black babies. They are more concerned about protecting white lives and winning over white votes. They are not concerned one damn bit about the destruction of black lives.

Chapter Sixteen

Gangster Rap Music's Violent Influence

We now see generation after generation of our youth falling by the wayside with no education and little regard for obtaining it. This is the standard that slavery set for us, and continues to this very day because of having conditioned this slavery-time mentality into the minds of our people. Throughout this nation, we have black, urban youth with gang affiliations, hanging out on street corners, while vowing to be violent, savage, murdering niggers, hell-bent on helping the racist ass, white man destroy their own race. They boast and pride themselves on putting, or having already put, other black people in the grave as niggers.

Out of this slavery mentality, blacks have coined all sorts of twisted ways of associations with the "nigger" word. You will hear blacks say things like, "Don't make me show my nigger side," which means their bad side, and, "You're gonna find out what a real nigger is all about." What this means is a savage nigger who has no conscience about murdering other niggers. You will hear blacks say things like, "nigger, you have met your match," and things like, "nigger, I will show you who the craziest nigger is."

This persona of the "nigger identity" goes on and on. Need more proof of this sort of violent behavior associated with the "nigger" word? Look at the "nigger, gangster rap" music industry. The "nigger" word has become the symbol of violence and keynote word in a multi-billion dollar, gangster rap, music industry, mostly controlled by racist ass, white, Europeans. It doesn't matter if they are racist ass, white, Europeans, or racist ass, white, European Jews, they are the ones in control of much of the financial power produced by exploiting niggers in the music industry.

We now have these brainwashed ass niggers coming from the ghettos of poverty and getting rich as "house niggers" on the racist ass, white, slave-master's plantation. With the blessings of the racist ass, white man who puts millions of dollars in his own pockets while these brainwashed ass niggers exploit the poor, social and economic conditions of our urban black communities. How do you even begin to educate these "nigger ill-crazed ass niggers" to stop helping the racist ass, white man destroy the black race?

I am not against seeing any nigger gain power and wealth through the economic and political system of racist ass, white, America, but our rightful concern should be the methods we use in achieving our objective. Even when still being faced with the oppressed residuals of slavery, I feel it is treasonous to place our survival on exploiting the ill conditions of our race, for financial gain.

Even though rap music, as a unique and creative expression, has been able to positively capture and depict some aspects of our culture and struggle, the era of this gangster rap music has blatantly distorted and tainted it with this sub-human, nigger, slave mentality of helping the racist ass, white man destroy the black race. I support the true history of the black warrior spirit, but our goal should be to help wake these young, mentally dead minded ass niggers up so that they can see just how majestic they truly are as black men. We should teach them to stop failing the black man's identity of having been the first man created in God's own image. Because the real problem with many of our black warriors is that we have lost our true, Israelite identity within this warped maze that the racist ass, White, slave-master has trapped us.

Let me explain just how extraordinary blacks are. I am black, and I am in awe of the natural, God-given gifts that blacks have been endowed with.

The masses of the black Israelite nation here in America remains lost under their "nigger identity." What many of our moral and civic leaders fail to realize and understand is that within our modern day urban culture the majority of our black youth do not exist in what we appeal to as the mainstream values that were brought about during the Civil Rights movement. Unlike the call for unity during the turbulent times of the 1960's, the masses of our black youth do not identify with the brotherhood and sisterhood call to black unity as we once did during the civil rights movement. The majority of our black, urban youth exists within the sub culture of the "nigger identity," where the appeal for black brotherhood and sisterhood is seldom heard.

No matter how difficult it might be to accept, the masses of our black, urban youth cannot be appealed to unless it's being done under their "nigger identity." It is my belief that it will continue to be this way until we redirect them back onto the grounds of black brotherhood and sisterhood. For example, many of them will identify with one saying, "what's up, my nigger," before they will identify with someone saying, "what's up, my brother," or "what's up, my sister." In this regard, "nigger" is the only name that will quickly get their undivided attention, regardless of how it's being used. If one was to say, "Young brothers, stop murdering each other," or if one was to say, "Black men, stop degrading black women," or, "Black women, stop degrading yourselves," none would listen. But, if one stood up and said in the presence of other niggers, "niggers, wake up and realize how the racist ass, white man is destroying us from becoming united African brothers and sisters," and all of a sudden, some of them began to listen, do we then say that it doesn't matter because they did not listen when the cry was brotherhood and sisterhood? Which would be worse, them not responding at all to the evils of the racist ass, white man, or them responding under their "nigger identity" to the evils of the racist ass, white man?" For me, the greater of the two evils would be them not responding at all.

In the black, urban, subculture where the "nigger identity" exists, the problem has gone far beyond moral and political incorrectness. We have our moral leaders, educators, and politicians trying to appeal to our black, urban youth to stop the violence that's helping destroy our neighborhoods and communities. But, their efforts have fallen on deaf ears because of the ongoing widening of the generation gap and not understanding where the masses of our urban youth exists culturally.

Many of our black leaders have lost touch with the shift in the cultural sense of identity in the masses of our youth. The "nigger" word has gained more popularity than at any other time in history because of gangster rap music which continually propels it. First, I would like to make it clear that I am in no way against rap music itself. In fact, I think that within the creative ability of blacks, we have shown just one more unique expression in music. It is well deserving of the awards that it receives when the messages are positive. In fact, rap music, in its beginning, easily proved that it is an extraordinary platform for positive expression and messages of knowledge. But now that gangster rap music has taken center stage, much of the same can no longer be said.

I would be disingenuous not to say that I feel that some aspects of gangster rap music has an uncanny ability of appealing to the black man's warrior spirit. But, much of it is now misguided and destructive to black culture as well as society. It is in this respect that I find it excruciating and repulsive.

If one had to deal with the lesser of the two evils that takes place in gangster rap music that promotes the violent and warring attitude in niggers, the greater of the two evils is them actually acting it out on society, instead of just embracing the historical fact that black men have a legacy of being brave, conquering, warriors. Now, through the influence of gangster rap music, these ignorant, misguided, racist, white, slave-master, subhuman, savaged, brainwashed ass niggers are only interested in victimizing and destroying the black race. At worse, if these niggers are going to continue making millions of dollars by exploiting the ill conditions of their race, as well as degrading it, then the lesser of the two evils would be if these, mostly young, violent, insane ass niggers only did this in their music and these mostly young, insane, buck-wild ass niggers in urban ghettos only listened to it, and not actually carried out these violent, satanic messages in gangster rap music on society by violently beating, robbing, and murdering other niggers.

The black masses shouldn't support these gangster rap music artists hoisting up prestigious, Grammy awards when so many of our youth are gravitating towards the violent and debasing messages from which millions of dollars are being made. These gangster rappers are not getting the larger portion of the profits. Instead, it is these racist ass, white European devils who control it. Yet any argument against it will be rejected by their racist ass, white, slave-master and the gangster rap niggers who now eat from his table and live in his big, plantation houses.

The masses of our black, urban youth now have their ears flooded with gangster rap music. And now, these glorified gangster rap "slave plantation ass niggers" have become the pied pipers under the "nigger identity," leading many of our black youth over a cliff and off the path of positive values. We are now seeing more and more of urban, black America plagued with turmoil and violence, on top of physical poverty. The ills of slavery have created a psychological "nigger-ill" disease within the minds of many of our people, and as a race we have not been able to recover from this psychological, subhuman "nigger-ill" conditioning. Tell me, what kind of sellout, "nigger-ill," backwards-ass, cuckoo, insanity shit is this when "niggers" encourage and promote violence and destruction on their own race in order to sell records?

You have "niggers" helping the racist ass, white man destroy their own race and become honored with Grammys and other prestigious music awards. How can anyone in their right, Yahweh (God), common sense mind hold this sort of "nigger-ill" shit up as something positive for our children's future? Because the only kind of positive shit I know of is shit for fertilizer. Praising and glorifying these racist, white, slave-master, condition minded ass, "house niggers," is like giving a drug dealer the Nobel Peace Prize for serving drugs to our children. And, while I don't claim to be an authority on the struggle of the black masses, but I am confident enough to believe that these treacherous ass niggers are not the moral scholars and intellectual leaders of the black race. Again, what kind of insane ass shit is this to go out and rob, gang-bang, commit murder, sell dope, beat on, and degrade black women as bitches and whores, get shot multiple times, live behind it, and then come back and rap about it as a gangster rap star?

In the case where a "nigger" doesn't live behind gunshot wounds, the racist ass, white man sees it as just one more, dead, glorified, gangster rap, nigger who got what was coming to him. Allow me to try and put it this way. If "niggers" can go to these extravagant, gala events and support these so called "gangster rap niggers" who boast about destroying the black race while calling black people "niggers" along with every other type of degrading thing under the sun, and then hoist up prestigious awards, how can any of these same "niggers" get upset about my perspective of black people as "niggers?" I suppose some of these "gangster-rap ass niggers" will say, "You want to call me a so-called "gangster-rap, house nigger," because I will show you what a real "gangster rap nigger" is all about." I ask you, does this sound familiar, meaning like the lowlife, subhuman savage, murderous ass, animal "niggers" within the slave quarters of the racist ass, white, slave-master? Like I said earlier, this is some serious, insane, comical shit that the racist ass, white man has doped the black man's mind with.

We now have these subhuman, savage ass bastards against African brother and sisterhood, using gang violence and murder as their badge of honor. But, if one has to kill, it is not the same as this inhumane savagery. The cruelty of slavery should have already taught niggers how to be killers in self-defense of our lives from the racist ass, white man. But unfortunately during slavery, the racist ass, white, slave-master was very successful at conditioning many male slaves into becoming the bad and murderous nigger within the slave quarters. Tragically, while my family was still living in Mississippi, my father ended up having to kill a so-called "bad nigger" in defense of his own life. He had already been shot several times before he was able to return gun fire. As I recount this tragic incident, my father, by the mercy of God, lived past his 95th birthday. As a little boy, my dad even spoke about seeing the hanging tree in the small county where his family lived, and where the Ku Klux Klan actually hung blacks.

Back in his time and beyond, in the old south, even after slavery had ended, racist, white, plantation owners still felt they held some sort of power and ownership over niggers. If you were one of "Mr. Charlie's" prize niggers," you could get away with doing things to other niggers with his blessings. The man that my father had to kill was well known for having been one of "Mr. Charlie's bad niggers." I remember another incident that my father told me about. He said that it occurred some years before he had the fatal encounter with one of Mr. Charlie's "so-called bad niggers." But only this time, the encounter was with Mr. Charlie, himself.

I was already a young man when I first heard him tell about this incident. He said that in the small, Mississippi County, where we lived, the racist ass, white sheriff was known to have a bad reputation of beating, and pistol-whipping "niggers," and would not hesitate to murder them. He said, this old racist ass, white sheriff, was known for doing shakedowns and taking bribes from illegal bootlegging and gambling. My father told me that one night while he was out gambling at this country juke joint, the old, racist ass, white sheriff barged in to do one of his routine shakedowns.

My father said that he was sitting off in the corner of one of the gambling areas when he had an exchange of words with the racist ass sheriff about the shakedown. He said the sheriff didn't take kindly to it and immediately stepped towards him with his gun already drawn, pointed the barrel a few inches from his face, and told him that he was about to become a dead nigger. He said with the pistol pointed directly at his face, he never flinched or took his eyes off of it. He said that with his life on the line, he felt the trigger of that gun was only seconds away from being pulled, and with the least bit of hesitation from that racist ass, white, sheriff, he had to act. He said that no sooner than he thought it, the hesitation came, and he slapped the gun out of his face, grabbed the sheriff's wrist with his other hand and wrestled the gun away from him. He said the old, racist ass, white sheriff fell backwards on the floor, but quickly got to his knees and started begging not to be killed. He said the sheriff was pleading with him telling him that he had a wife and kids, but my dad said that he quickly refuted him by saying, "a moment ago, you tried to murder me and I have a wife and kids, too."

He said the tables had suddenly turned and it was now him pointing the gun at the sheriff and all the niggers were shouting to him, "Knox, kill him! Kill him, Knox!" He said part of him wanted to do it, but he quickly thought to himself that if he did go ahead and kill this racist ass, white sheriff, all of those niggers would be afraid to testify in his defense. But, he said that the very thing that helped him decide not to do it was the old, black madam who ran the joint. She shouted to him, "Knox, don't kill him, but kick his ass good!" The old, racist ass, white sheriff was spared of being killed as well as an ass-kicking. He was allowed to crawl up off his knees and made to leave without his gun.

As a little boy I was unaware of what had happened, but years later when my father told me about the incident he said that the following day the authorities came out to the plantation and arrested him. He said that the white man who owned the plantation that we lived on got him off the hook so that he could report back to work. It was situations like this that goes back to what I said earlier about being one of "Mr. Charlie's prized, niggers," good or bad.

Many of these "niggers" today can be coined as "Mr. Charlie's bad niggers." But the only difference now is Mr. Charlie has a different kind of plantation usage for niggers and not the same one he had for them during the time of physical slavery. So now, when one bad nigger murders another bad nigger, one goes to the graveyard and the other, to the prison yard. Also, when this happens, the racist ass, white man gets rid of two backwards ass niggers with one stone. In the eyes of the racist ass, white man, it has nothing to do with innocence or guilt because he feels that all niggers should be dealt the same fate. Instead of standing up as men, too many of us as black men allow ourselves to fall down like blind buffoons. Instead of wising up, many of us keep dumbing down under the racist ass, white man's control. Black women shouldn't have to be subjected to the kind of shame and disgrace of seeing black men this way.

When we mislead black women into admiring and looking up to us for behaving as women beaters, thugs, and murderers, it does great harm by psychologically leading many of them to raise their sons and daughters to accept this sort of cruel and dysfunctional behavior. It only serves in helping the racist ass, white man in his systematic destruction of the black family. It keeps the "slave mentality cycle" going just as the racist ass, white man planned it, during slavery. Many of our African ancestors would not allow slavery to rip away their moral sense of dignity and self-respect. Instead, they took the rebellious attitude of being willing to fight and die for their freedom and dignity as men and women, rather than be made to live as subhuman, savage, nigger animals. It was those attitudes that initially gave the "nigger identity" a notorious, defiant, and rebellious meaning under slavery.

Psychologically, the "nigger identity" is far too complex for us to dismiss it as only being a horrible, racist epithet without gaining a true understanding and perspective on how its usage has affected the black race. The "nigger" word will always face opposition within our race because of its ties to the cruel and wicked history of slavery and that same opposition will forever shout out why whites are forbidden to call us "niggers." As I explained earlier, the racist, ass, white man will never again be allowed to freely call black people niggers. All of the horrific things that happened to niggers under slavery and much of what is happening to us now is still because of the aftermath of slavery.

Why is it so difficult for us to face the truth that the ills of slavery is now causing the masses of our urban youth to connect more to their blackness, not through the mainstream of society, but within the sub-culture of the "nigger identity?" When our black, urban youth identify with the word African American on the surface, it's the exception and not the rule. Our true African identity was taken away from us during slavery, and now the masses of our people are lost in ghettos and poverty throughout the world under our "nigger identity."

What we have to come to grips with is the fact that, as long as there is one racist ass, white person and one black person in this world, the nigger word and hate for niggers will never cease to exist. And, as I've alluded to, our African ancestors rebelled and became liberated under their "nigger identity." Because of this, we are left to deal with two distinct kinds of gatekeepers of the nigger word niggers. On one hand, we have the liberated minded "gatekeepers of the nigger word niggers." On the other hand, we have these violent, subhuman, savage, conditioned minded, "gatekeepers of the nigger word niggers" who are hell-bent on helping the racist ass, white slave-master destroy the black race.

We cannot afford not to try and wake these mentally, dead minded ass niggers up. Because they are now rapidly spreading throughout the masses in violent, savage, wolf pack gangs willing to destroy any and everything in their path. How long do niggers think that we can keep producing the so-called exceptional niggers when the masses are being wiped out and destroyed? At such a self-destructive pace, we have no realistic chance of ever trying to stabilize our race. If we are content with being blind fools to keep thinking that we can, it is precisely what the racist ass, white power structure has designed and mapped out for our final exit from socioeconomic and political importance within mainstream society.

One of the core methods of the racist ass, white man for keeping niggers down and defeated is forcing us to defend ourselves from a position of weakness. If a nigger doesn't have an education, if a nigger doesn't understand the power of the voting process and doesn't vote, if a nigger doesn't have social, economic, and political power, the lack of all of these crucial things combined makes it impossible for niggers to defend themselves from a position of strength. Instead, as a race, niggers will continue falling further and further behind the rest of society with no ability to compete in the economic marketplace. Just look at the many niggers who have climbed their way out of the ghettos as ball players, singers, and actors, making multi-million dollar salaries, and then are somehow forced back into living from paycheck to paycheck just like the poor struggling niggers who never make it out of the hardships and impoverished conditions of ghetto life.

What kind of insane, financial management shit is this for a nigger, knowing full well what ghetto life is like and the racist ass, white man wanting to keep our Black asses there, would work to attain wealth and riches and then create an income to debt ratio that is above their means? The racist ass, white man knows full well that it's a hard sell to get a race full of broke ass niggers, barely getting by on a job from paycheck to paycheck, to strike in solidarity against his racist ass, white system of power and injustice.

What do niggers like this really accomplish but a swift kick in the ass by the racist ass, white man and a fast and hard fall back to the ghetto? If a nigger forgets where he or she comes from, that's a damn sure and convincing reminder. Therefore, niggers should never forget about all the masses of poor niggers left back in ghettos trapped and still struggling for a way out.

Instead of niggers having dreams of just becoming big time singers and actors, running out to Hollywood and onto Broadway stages, as well as dreams of becoming professional athletes, we need to sober up and see what is happening to the black masses. Unless we help educate the masses of our people, we will still be left trapped on urban, slave plantations and in the continually declining ghettos of racist ass, white America. It's already difficult enough dealing with the painful truth that slavery brainwashed and broke many of our people under their "nigger identity."

The nigger word has become the keynote word for gangster rap music in promoting gang violence and murder in order to keep selling records of which much of it is satanic. It has become a multi-billion dollar business and, just as I said earlier, the faces running this industry is mostly racist ass, white, European devils. It's no different than how these same, racist ass, white devils with their sell-out, house niggers within law enforcement confiscate, control, regulate and then redistribute illegal drugs in this country. Not only is the racist ass, white man a drug kingpin in this country; he is also the white collar crime kingpin. It's not called white collar crime because of being squeaky clean, it's called white collar crime in honor of his racist, white ass because of how underhanded, conniving, and dirty he is within the corporate world of pen and paper. The racist ass, white slave-master has caused much of this illness upon the black race, but has decided afterwards that there will be no diagnosis, treatment, nor cure. We are supposed to go onward as though no recovery process applies to all the devastation, suffrage and cruelty inflicted by slavery. Do we truly understand the magnitude of what is here for us to try and overcome?

We were shackled in chains and thrown into the cramped and filthy bowels of slave ships and brought to the Americas. Millions of slaves died during the Transatlantic, slave trade. Many of them died in the resistance while others died from sickness, disease and starvation. Once our African ancestors arrived in America they were brutally beaten and bred like live stock to work under some of the most harsh and extreme conditions ever to be place upon the backs of human beings. Our families were ripped apart. Female slaves were brutally raped. Children were brutally raped and molested. We were lynched and castrated. We have been left with the deep scars of all the perverse ills of slavery. We are a severely traumatized race. The diagnosis is post-traumatic stress disorder. We are a race suffering with very severe mood swings. The diagnosis is bi-polar disorder. We were an enslaved race severely deprived of essential prenatal care. The diagnosis is mental deficiency. And yet, the racist ass, white descendants of the racist ass, white, slave-master has the damned audacity to ask niggers why are there so many among us who're so quick to act out in anger and rage.

It is a divine miracle that we have been able to keep the strands of our sanity and temperament held together within our race. There is compelling, scientific evidence that supports the position that PTSD, post-traumatic stress disorder, is transgenerational. Tragically, we will never recover from all the residuals of slavery. But, the recovery process can begin within our race by forcing the racist ass, white man to take his wicked and devilish ass foot off of the back of our humanity. It is vital that we unify in defense and not allow this racist ass, white cancer to continue its rapid spread in debilitating and destroying both the mental and physical health of our race.

The cruelty of slavery was a long fuse to burn. But now the fuse has shortened to the point of exploding. And yet these racist ass, white, demonic bastards still want to keep pushing against the humanity of niggers. We are still being wrongly brutalized and racially mistreated in this country. Much of our explosive anger is a systemic problem rooted in the deep ills and inhumane cruelty of slavery. It is this foul and perverted history of slavery that the racist ass, white man would like to have permanently and conveniently swept under the rug of history while he continues carrying on with all of his racist ass, white, hypocrisy of saint hood.

Many of these gangster rap niggers are wising up and learning from their racist ass, white, slave-masters on how to scheme against their own race, and are going strictly commercial by exploiting the ills of urban ghettos while they themselves get rich and move far away from it. They have become content on stuffing their pockets with millions of dollars in blood money. Their hands are dirtied by all the violence of black-on-black crime and murder they're helping to influence niggers into committing. Many of these gangster rap niggers are finally getting a taste of eating and living the good life in the big plantation house of their racist ass, white slave-masters at the expense of helping destroy their own race. Many of these niggers are now more intent on faking this gangster rap shit because they know that dead niggers in real life don't get up from the coffin, eat good, smoke dope, and lay up with beautiful women, then go back and make more gangster rap videos.

What kind of insane ass, nigger ill shit is this for niggers to stand up in fancy attire and clap their hands and praise other niggers for using the racist ass, white man's methods of getting rich by exploiting and destroying the black race? Under the "nigger identity," masses of our black youth are being drawn under the influence of satanic, nigger gangster rap music. Sadly, gangster nigger rap music can be compared to drug dealing because no one is going to become completely effective in telling poor, ghetto, impoverished ass niggers not to hustle by creating this kind of music. The same way that one cannot be completely effective in telling them not to sell dope. Just like their racist ass, white, slave-masters, these niggers are not willing to take responsibility for the devastation that they help cause and continue to heap upon their own race.

Just as no one in their right mind would get up and give prestigious awards to niggers who become financially successful in drug dealing, the same should be said of these gangster, rap niggers who exploit the ill conditions of our communities for financial profit. Just as drug users become drug addicts, many of our youth are becoming addicted to the violent, satanic messages in gangster rap music. So now we have to stand up and show the courage to oppose this insane ass shit by making a critical effort to educate our youth to the danger and harm that it is causing them.

Because of the nigger word's ties to slavery, it will never be accepted within the mainstream of black culture. But, the fact remains that the nigger word will continue within the subculture of our race. The "nigger identity" was born out of the slave culture and was forced upon us by the racist ass, white, slave-master. In the end, it produced two types of "gate keepers of the nigger word" niggers.

For those who become offended by my having said this, many of them are willing to accept or tolerate how blacks in the music industry make millions of dollars using the nigger word. There are black critics who find the usage of the nigger word appalling and intolerable, and I doubt they would say that I am off base in how I have gone about explaining how I connect blacks to the "nigger identity." I believe that I have laid out a clear and compelling argument as to why it is utterly forbidden for whites to think that it would ever become acceptable for them to call us niggers. I have also attempted to explain the attitudes and behavior that became shaped under the "nigger identity."

Chapter Seventeen

Regaining Black Unity Over Disunity

In this day and age, most blacks have at least a basic sense of history and knowledge of how the nigger word became attached to us during slavery. Yet, this has done little to discourage our usage of the nigger word. We have well educated blacks who don't shy away from the usage of the nigger word, and it can't be because they are somehow totally blind and ignorant of its ties to slavery. The so-called moral and politically correct blacks should not try and hold up the disingenuous argument that the nigger word has never slipped off their tongues. It only leads back to my position on why we have these "gate keepers of the nigger word niggers." Again, I believe that many of our African ancestors became rebellious against the racist ass, white slave-master under their "nigger identity," but tragically, many became broken under it. Yet, both held onto the "nigger identity" after physical slavery had been finally abolished.

We now have a great divide among blacks within the subculture of the "nigger identity." Among the black masses under the "nigger identity," exists these violent, slavery conditioned-minded, subhuman, savage behaving niggers. Also among the black masses under the "nigger identity," are blacks who see themselves as liberated minded niggers. Just as Malcolm X stated about the field nigger and the house nigger, these rebellious minded niggers can be compared to the field niggers and not to the racist ass, white, slave-master's house broken niggers. On the surface, the nigger word carries the meaning of being a vile, racist slur against black people. But, below the surface, among blacks and because of slavery, it possesses an even deeper problem and meaning. It is vitally important that we finally understand what is going on here. We have to dissect and then examine the problem and stop attempting to only argue it.

Because of slavery, the "nigger identity" is rooted deeply in our culture and we have to begin dealing with the fact that it has taken a psychological effect on our attitude and behavior. During slavery, the racist ass, White, slave-master became aware of the fact that under the "nigger identity" the rebellious, defiant and revolutionary minded niggers began leading a charge against slavery. But, he was also well aware that under the "nigger identity" the blacks who became broken under slavery would help lead the charge in keeping blacks disunified and enslaved.

The urban ghettos of America are spilling over with generation after generation of the same kind of broken and mentally dead minded ass niggers that existed under slavery. And now the racist ass descendants of the racist ass, white, slave-master are the ones still masterminding the same demise of niggers in this day and age. The racist ass, white man, knows that just as long as we are not able to awaken these mentally, dead minded ass niggers, we have little to no chance of reforming the black race into becoming a united power in this country. The racist ass, white, power structure is well aware of the fact that unified niggers are a threat to the All-American, white, racist ass, way of life and that disunified and mentally dead minded ass niggers are not.

We also have the problem of having these so-called, intellectual, piece of shit minded ass, house niggers within the black race who have become brainwashed into believing that the only way of being accepted as human beings is by mimicking white people. These backward ass, delusional minded ass, house niggers see themselves as being the best alternative to the black masses that meets with the approval of their racist ass, white, slave-master.

Niggers of this sort will always be tame and dead set against unifying within the revolutionary struggle of the black masses. Like a modern-day Judas, these white-washed ass niggers have decided on treason and will remain satisfied and comfortable as house niggers on the racist ass, white, slave-master's plantation. We must call out these house niggers no matter which political party they reside under. We will know them by the fruits that they bare. They are dead set against any form of insurrection against the status quo of the racist elements within this government. These niggers, like the house niggers before them during slavery, have taken a vow to pledge their loyalty to their racist ass, white, slave-master. These treasonous ass niggers conscientiously support racist, white supremacy over the black race. Therefore, these token ass, house niggers are amongst the worst kind of illegitimate ass bastards against African brotherhood and sisterhood known to mankind.

As for the rest of the black masses and how the "nigger identity" affects our attitudes and behavior, the fight to define the "nigger identity" will be decided between the liberated minded "gatekeepers of the nigger word niggers" and these violent ass, slavery conditioned, unliberated minded gatekeepers of the nigger word niggers.

When I hear blacks sit in front of the racist ass, white, news media and say they are personally opposed to any use of the "nigger" word altogether, it sounds somewhat erroneous to me. For me it's like saying I like chocolate, but I hate eating it. And, it's not because I doubt their sincerity, but it's more about how racist ass, whites look at us when we say it -- something that will more than likely never change. So, why do so many of us feel the need to give the obvious answer that racist ass whites expect to hear knowing in their racist ass hearts and minds that they will always look at us as hated, inferior ass niggers regardless of how we decide about the usage of the nigger word? What an amazing psychological trap for us to actually believe that we are somehow able to convince racist ass, white people that we are no longer unreformed niggers and are now ready to take our rightful and equal place alongside them as human beings.

Just like my rebellious ancestors, I am a Nat Turner disciple. I am more bent on making this racist ass, white man understand the kind of nigger that I will not be. It doesn't bother me one bit for the racist ass, white man to perceive me as a dumb, submissive ass nigger. Because, if necessary, I am willing to burn the racist ass, White, slave-master's plantation down in a heartbeat, just as the rebellious field niggers did during slavery. I believe that dying for human justice and freedom is far better than living out your entire life doing nothing.

For the few who arrives at the level of being seen as the so-called exceptional niggers, it will not be enough to sustain the black masses. Do niggers of this sort go off to some newfound existence and not really understand where they came from? Seeing how the rise of the black race must start with unifying the masses, we must find measures that will put us on common ground. We have to learn how to live together, or continue dying as a fragmented race. Niggers have to understand that having been displaced in this land called America, only unity will produce power and power produces liberation, and true liberation will produce a powerful Black nation within this country. Organizing, organization, and structure are the basic fundamental building blocks that are necessary for race stability and nation building. Unfortunately, this fact has eluded niggers in this country for centuries.

Once the eyes of the black masses become open and we stop acting like violent, subhuman, savage minded ass, nigger animals hell-bent on destroying ourselves, the true journey back towards black power will finally begin. Because the racist ass, White, slave-master banks on the racist idea that if you keep a nigger ignorant, disconnected from race unity, uneducated, and broke with no ownership of anything that reflects real success and power, niggers will always be down in the dumps and at each other's throats.

There is nothing wrong with giving honor to true black achievement, but we are only disillusioning ourselves to think that one big hall full of niggers all dressed up in fancy attire at a gala event makes us the standard bearers for the entire black race. We cannot afford to allow ourselves to continue appearing as though we are trying to mirror the white, aristocratic elitist while being looked at by the black masses as no more than a bunch of aristocratic ass acting niggers who have forgotten their roots. No matter how many generations of which some of us became removed from the everyday struggles of ghetto life, let us not forget that the masses of our family's generations began in the cruel poverty of slavery where the majority of us are still trying to overcome.

The real standard bearers are the masses of everyday, common, struggling niggers from which the so-called exceptional niggers have sprung. These so-called common niggers are the ones we cannot afford to continually allow to keep falling through the cracks of society. The racist ass, white slave-master, knew that by fostering inferior attitudes and behaviors into our African ancestors under their "nigger identity" it would keep them ignorant and divided in conflict.

Today, the results are that nearly our entire race lives in impoverished urban ghettos and prison systems. On the surface, the racist ass, white man has made the nigger word a vile, racist slur against black people. Below the surface he knows all the vile, sick, and perverted things he did to us under our "nigger identity." But, again many of our ancestors had the backbone and willingness to fight and not give up under their "nigger identity." If it had not been for them, we would be far worse off than we are today.

All of their sacrifice and suffering exists as the ongoing lifeline and inspiration for our present and future generations to keep fighting and not give up our will and determination to survive as a race of people. Other than the racist ass, white man, one of the biggest problems hindering our fight for socio-economic and political progress and power is all of this internal, nigger ill, strife and insanity.

The "nigger identity" embodies all of the attitudes and behaviors of the slave culture. Blacks don't just simply use the nigger word; we actually act out many of the attitudes and behaviors associated with it. Therefore, among the black masses within the subculture of the "nigger identity," it becomes so important to be seen as a different kind of nigger. It holds a very profound meaning. It's the very thing that separates the "gatekeepers of the nigger word niggers" into two distinct attitudes. As I touched on earlier, the slave culture produced racist white slave-master, subhuman condition minded niggers, many of which are the niggers who descended from the same niggers who held no interest except committing savagery upon other niggers within the slave quarters.

They are also the same subhuman, racist ass, white, slave-master, conditioned minded ass niggers existing throughout the urban ghettos of this county, wreaking all sorts of violent havoc upon other niggers. No other ethnic group in America carries out more day to day brutal and internal crime against their own race than these savage, violent niggers. We must overcome existing like a third world, violent, savage, uncivilized race here in America -- again, much of which has to do with the ills of slavery and the aftermath that continues to plague our race.

Unlike the rebellious, liberated minded, “gatekeepers of the nigger word niggers,” who did not become broken by the vices of the racist ass, white, slave-master, these niggers would rather continue claiming themselves to be ruthless and treacherous ass, uncivilized, savage, subhuman thugs under the “nigger identity.” Therefore, both groups do not mirror each other. One group claims to be warring, street, savage ass niggers who hold no other interest but to take, rob and murder other niggers. But the other group who embraced the “nigger identity” are the “gatekeepers of the nigger word niggers” who claim defiance and rebellion against the racist ass, white, slave-master, and is not hell-bent on warring with other niggers.

These are the niggers who would rather exist in unity and peace and not become entangled in war, nor become victimized by these subhuman, savage ass, “gatekeepers of the nigger word niggers.” Out of the slave culture it gets right to the heart and conflict between the two groups. One group rebelled within the slave culture against the racist ass, white slave-master and then tried to influence the majority of the masses to following them. But the other group within the slave culture fell to the vices of the racist ass, white, slave-master and now they are the same violent, subhuman, savage ass, condition minded niggers of today.

It stands as the racist ass, white man’s blueprint of slavery that continually works to keep us divided and at war among ourselves. Even though the black masses are now forced into having to try and coexist with these violent ass, savage, subhuman behaving, “gatekeepers of the nigger word niggers,” the majority of us tries to avoid them like a plague. The racist ass, white man is at the core of having created these violently insane ass niggers, yet we are the ones being forced to live mostly in the same environment of ghettos with these treacherous and wicked, murderous ass niggers hell-bent on assisting the racist and demonic ass white man in destroying us. One of the worst things that could ever happen to a Black person, is to be born in the heart of the ghetto and be forced to grow up surrounded by these savage minded, wolf-pack ass niggers.

Until we unite as a powerful force, we have little to no power of changing it. We are the ones faced with having to walk or drive by these savage ass niggers, gathering in wolf pack gangs within our community while the racist ass, white man hides out in his suburban, safe-haven and blame the entire black race for this problem.

Please do not misunderstand me on what I am saying here, because young niggers who gather in lawful assembly to socialize within their community should never be profiled and stereotyped as thugs and hoodlums. But, sadly, whenever the situation is found to be gang related activity, then the racist ass, white news media turns and screams black-on-black crime as though this is somehow supposed to be only a black-on-black tragedy. But what if the situation was reversed and it was their racist white asses being taken out of the suburbs of white America and placed right into the midst of these subhuman, savage ass, nigger minded thugs that this racist ass, white system helped to create? And what if it was the majority of us living in the safe havens of suburbs? Let's see how the narrative would read then. Instead of the racist ass, white, news media screaming black-on-black crime, their racist, white asses would be screaming Black-on-White crime.

What doesn't these racist ass, white, news media bastards get? Can't these racist ass, white, news media bastards distinguish between gang-banging, thug ass, criminal niggers murdering their own race and racist ass, white cops murdering niggers? If not, then we might as well put badges on these gang-banging, thug ass, criminal niggers and call them cops.

The truth of the matter is, these racist ass, white, news media bastards are not willing to come into our communities and open their racist ass eyes and ears and hear our pain and outcry against these racist, white, slave-master, conditioned minded, thug ass, gang-banging, murdering niggers. The loss of black lives taken by these treacherous ass niggers are grievous to our hearts and our community. But these racist ass, white supremacist, news media bastards can't bring it to their racist ass hearts and minds to understand how helpless and vulnerable niggers are made to feel when the very peace officers hired and sworn to protect its citizens are no more than racist ass, white, thug criminals themselves using the racist ass, white, legal system in their defense as they go about their racist ass, white mission of murdering and violently beating niggers with no accountability. The brutal history of slavery, hate, and racism has always worked as the evil vice in marginalizing the human value of black lives.

As I said earlier, I will now address the problem that ignited the brutal attack on police in Dallas, TX, and Baton Rouge, LA.

July 5, 2016, Alton Sterling, a black man, was shot dead in Baton Rouge, LA, after having been subdued by two white cops. Not only did he receive bullet wounds to the front part of his body, but also to his back. Less than forty-eight hours later, another black man, Philando Castile, was shot dead by a white cop in Saint Paul, MN, in the Falcon Heights suburbs. He'd been pulled over for a minor, tail light violation, but the reason was later escalated to a police stop investigating a possible suspect. His fiancé set next to him in the front passenger seat while his four-year old daughter sat in the back. The white cop's dash cam recorder was conveniently turned off, but the man's fiancé showed incredible nerve in holding herself together as she captured much of the incident on her cellphone camera.

However, true to form, the racist ass, white, news media had the racist ass nerve to criticize the way this woman conducted herself during the shooting, saying, "She was being callous because she continued filming and not trying to aid her fiancé after his shooting." Of course, the masses of us niggers have no problem relating to her actions, because we know that when it comes to the word of a nigger against a racist ass, white cop, our voice will never be heard. As this woman was obviously aware, the camera is the most powerful tool in gathering evidence in support of the truth that has any chance of aiding us. So, to continue filming this heinous act with a gun pointed at the window of the car in which her fiancé lay dying was very courageous.

The following evening, more violence erupted. A black civilian brutally murdered five police officers in Dallas, Texas. His target? White cops. It happened during a march protesting the shooting death of the two African American males. As usual, the first thing the racist ass, white, news media and racist ass, white, criminal justice system did was utter their favorite words, "Wait until the investigation is over, before we rush to judgement - their sworn mantra when racist white cops brutally murder niggers." They say it so piously, as though we should have faith in this racist ass, criminal justice system that has repeatedly shown a miscarriage of justice by failing the black community over and over again.

When racist ass, white cops wrongfully murder black people in cold blood, should they not be held accountable for helping destroy our trust along with the credibility of a predominantly white police system in this country? But, just as the racist ass, white, news media and their piece of shit, house niggers would have it, they readily pinned the violent massacre on the *Black Lives Matter* movement because the killer expressed sympathy towards it.

Less than two weeks later, in Baton Rouge, LA., another violent shooting and murder of three cops by a black assailant took place.

While it's tragic for any innocent human being to be murdered, as brutal as it might sound, if racist, white cops want to continually open up this country's violent and racist history of a race war by cold bloodedly beating and murdering innocent, black people, it's difficult to see the shooters in each incident, Micah Xavier Johnson's, and Gavin Eugene Long's, actions as any different than that of Nat Turner -- a martyr during his time of a violent revolution in a race war against the murdering and lynching of niggers during slavery? I will not demonize these brothers, nor others who follow in their path, any more than this racist ass, white system is willing to demonize this system of racist ass, white, police brutality and violent history of beating and murdering niggers. If this racist ass, hypocritical, white, news media, and political system wants to portray Micah Xavier Johnson and Gavin Eugene Long in such a negative and inhumane light, doesn't it stand that racist ass, white police brutality and cold blooded murder of blacks bear the same demonizing judgment?

After the horrific tragedy that happened in Dallas, TX, and Baton Rouge, LA, does anyone in their right mind believe that nigger's fear of racist ass, white cops will not grow even deeper in this country? With their racist ass, white, legal authority to exist as cold blooded, licensed murderers by a racist ass, white, police system, they will now double down on their racist ass, white hate, and brutal means of terrorizing the black community. The racist ass, white, political and judicial system built this racist ass war against black America from the time of slavery. Yet, we are the ones held solely accountable by this racist ass, illegitimate, legal system of having to bear the responsibility for this white and black race war.

This is the real tragedy of our racial divide in this country. Sadly, it is no more than the racist ass doctrine of slavery that's repeated itself throughout this country's racist ass history. If the police system is the last line of civilization, as one racist ass, white, Republican put it, what happens when that last line of defense is racist and uncivilized when it comes to protecting all of its citizens regardless of race? Thus far, there has been no empathy for niggers each time that we've been wrongfully and brutally murdered by racist ass, white cops. So, we now live in the worse conditions in regards to our safety, well-being, and the full-fledged terror of what has happened, and is liable to happen to us, at the hands of these racist ass, white, demonic cops.

This racist ass, white, news media and the racist ass, white, political system has bent themselves on throwing a racist ass, shit fit about President Obama choosing to not use the term, "radical, Islamic terrorist." Yet, their racist, white, hypocritical asses are not willing to call it out the same way by saying, "racist, white, police, terrorist system." Try telling niggers that this is not how the majority of the masses feels about the police systems of white America policing our communities. These racist ass, white bastards in the news media and politics make it a point to view the murder of blacks through the narrow lens of isolated incidents carried out only by a few, bad, racist ass cops. In their racist ass eyes, they refuse to look through the broader lens and see the harsh reality of the cultural and racist atmosphere in the system of white, law enforcement in this country, propelling the brutal violence and injustice targeting the human rights of blacks to co-exist equally with whites under the same laws. No way can these heinous acts be considered mere, isolated incidents.

Having continually been victimized, blacks are in fear of gang-banging, thug ass, murderous, criminal niggers. So, why is it that these racist ass, white, news media bastards refuse to understand how much terror and fear niggers live in each and every day of our lives because of black-on-black crime, compounded by the fear of knowing racist ass, white cops have the legal power to act as brutal and vicious criminals in murdering niggers? If they understood the reality that niggers have to live through each and every day of our lives within our communities, maybe then these racist ass, white, news media bastards would stop using the racist excuse of black-on-black crime to offset this brutal horror and racial injustice inflicted by racist ass, white cops with the blessings of the racist ass, white, criminal justice system.

Their racist, white, news media, reporting asses need to quickly learn, the hard way, that these violent, racist ass, white, slave-master, conditioned minded ass niggers have no respect of person when they commit crimes. I am sure they've heard the old saying about the vicious dog that turns on his master. Well, the reality is that African American citizens are being held hostage in inner-city ghettos by these subhuman, racist ass, white slave-master, conditioned, savage minded ass, criminal niggers. The ill effect of slavery and poverty has now caused niggers to behave like cannibals amongst ourselves. The slavery mentality has now forced niggers into behaving like some of the most ignorant ass, disrespectful, rudest, savage human beings on the face of the earth. In inner-city ghettos, niggers are rapidly becoming more and more socially dysfunctional. If you find yourself walking past violent, savage minded, ass niggers and glance the wrong way, you might get jumped or have your brains splattered on the sidewalk.

These crazy, backward ass niggers will deliberately stand out in the middle of neighborhood streets and not allow cars to pass safely while taking their gang-banging ass posture. Along with violently murdering each other, these ignorant, wild ass, savage niggers carry out reckless, gun violence with total disregard for innocent lives. These crazy ass niggers will get behind the wheel of cars and speed up and down neighborhood streets, swerving their cars all over the road with no regard for the safety of children. These crazy ass, road raging ass niggers will create an accident and then be willing to commit murder behind it. These crazy ass niggers will stop their cars in the middle of the street, blocking traffic, while having conversations with other crazy, piece of shit ass niggers in cars or on foot. As much as it might bother some niggers to have it said, because of the slavery mentality, in many instances, whites who stand together against racism, show far more courtesy towards niggers than niggers show towards themselves.

I remember an incident while I was out jogging when I had to sidestep to avoid getting deliberately hit by a car full of young, thug ass niggers. I had to use both of my arms to brace against the impact of their front bumper. And as it was happening, they were laughing at the panic and fear on my face. In another incident, while jogging, a different group of young, thug ass niggers drove recklessly past me in their car while one of them opened the front passenger side door and leaned out, shouting obscenities at me and making a gesture as though a gun was in his hand while pointing it towards me. There was yet another incident when I was returning home from a night job when a car full of young, thug ass niggers were blocking the road. When I cautiously passed them, they sped up alongside me, scraping the side of my car and knocking my driver side mirror off. To avoid further harassment and intimidation, I quickly turned onto a side street.

When juvenile niggers do this kind of violent and wicked ass shit to their own community, it's hard to argue in their defense of not getting their fucking brains blown out. Sadly, this has become the violent behavior of many of our youth, having no respect for their community as well as society itself. These mostly young, crazy ass, ignorant niggers carry out this same disrespectful and animal like violent behavior all across America. And the racist ass, white slave-master, because of slavery and the residuals of slavery, is as much at fault for helping foster an environment of failing education, poverty, and despair that helps to produce these kinds of subhuman minded ass niggers.

Just as it existed in the slave culture, these niggers want to project the image of being the "violent ass, bad niggers" within the slave quarters. They make "mean mugging" other niggers a daily part of their ritual. One of their main purposes for this sort of hostile behavior is because they do not want to project a sense of peace and brotherhood with someone who they have already targeted as their next potential victim. But, unlike these racist, white, slave-master, savage, conditioned minded ass niggers, the majority of us, as African Americans, try to struggle against the racist ass, white, power structure without being caught in a vacuum of constant friction and violence amongst ourselves. Despite what the racist ass, white man thinks of us as a race, the masses of us niggers are not this filthy, sick breed of violently wicked, murderous ass niggers. The masses of us are everyday struggling niggers, frustrated with this racist ass, white system of oppression forcing us into becoming victimized.

When we are not able to avoid these savage and violent behaving ass niggers, we are left trying to project a false sense of peace and brotherhood with them to try and avoid being attacked. Generation after generation we have been forced into trying to make social, economic, and political progress under some of the most oppressed, crime ridden and rapidly declining conditions in America. Be it in extreme poverty or surrounded by it, it has forced us to become psychologically segregated amongst ourselves. Those of us who have made marginal progress within this vast landscape of poverty and oppression, live in constant fear of being envied, despised and resented by other niggers who have made very little or no progress at all.

A nigger can easily become harassed, hated, envied, or actually lose his or her life for owning just a little more than the next nigger. Slavery conditioned niggers to be pitted against each other, and the same attitude and behavior still exist today. As much as niggers will hate to admit, such attitudes are all part of the house nigger syndrome. Just like the house nigger being only concerned about gaining their own, individual status in the master's house (system), the slavery attitude that exists among niggers is to be more content on seeing the next nigger with nothing. With this slavery-time minded attitude, we are full of contradiction in complaining about whites and other ethnic groups always getting ahead of us by owning businesses in our communities while we remain deprived. Far too many of us would rather spend our money with whites and other ethnic groups, than with legitimate businesses owned by other blacks. This ideological, brainwashing manner of loving and worshipping the racist ass, white slave-master exists as the central, racist, white-washing recipe designed to keep niggers from nation building in this country. It keeps us growing in constant fear, and farther and farther apart with segregated attitudes in our neighborhoods and communities. All this does is foster even more hate, mistrust, resentment, and suspicion among ourselves as a race. Instead of further unifying, we are becoming more and more of a fragmented race, still living and existing like an enslaved and conquered people.

As I said earlier, the racist ass, white slave-master taught and conditioned niggers to hate their own race while worshipping his. With our identity and great, African heritage severed by slavery, we have only inspired two profound movements that we are now able to look towards in our effort to regain our human rights and desire to unite ourselves as proud brothers and sisters of the black race. These two movements are the abolitionist's movement to end slavery and the civil rights movement. Other than these two extraordinary movements, slavery and the residuals of slavery have kept the link to race, respect, and unity broken for niggers. Now, tragically, generation after generation, niggers have been moving farther and farther away from showing respect for ourselves as a race. Slavery taught and conditioned niggers into psychologically believing that our existence is connected to a worthless race that counts for literally nothing beyond our individual selves with no race pride. It is the very reason why it is so easy for niggers to murder and destroy each other.

Chapter Eighteen

The Absence of Strong, Black Leadership

Race unity and race value for African Americans seemed to have mostly deteriorated after the fifties and sixties of the civil rights movement. And, the black race will have to take up the fight against the racist, white, discriminatory opposition by nurturing our children with moral leadership and education in order to start taking back our communities from this vicious cycle of producing violent ass, uneducated, juvenile criminals who carry this behavior into their adult lives.

The days of the civil rights movement has long passed when blacks were able to be united under the same common struggle as black brothers and sisters. I believe that if we were able to do it then, we are still capable of doing it now, and it is essential to the survival of the black race that it be done again. But before such a revival like the civil rights movement can happen, a very powerful revolutionary type movement must be inspired in which we can awaken these mentally dead, racist ass, white, slave-master, subhuman minded, savage conditioned niggers.

As noted earlier, once slavery was abolished, the black reformers set their mission on trying to lead the masses of ex-slaves onto a higher moral, social, economic, and political ground. They actually pioneered the leadership that led us to the civil rights movement. It was their efforts and the civil rights movement that worked in putting us on a course towards gaining our human rights in this country. Beginning with the black reformers after slavery, and later with the civil rights movement, it worked in providing leadership and keeping niggers off of a head on collision course that had been set in motion from the time of our enslavement. But once some of our most important black leaders were slain, our black, militant, revolutionary movements along with the civil rights movement was weakened. Having being infiltrated and destroyed by the racist ass, white power forces within this government, they were only able to push so far in the decades to follow.

It was at this critical point that the strides we had made would begin a backwards slide. Yet, the momentum and power of the civil rights movement will forever speak to when the first Black president became elected in this country. But now, the powerful forces of racism have worked with all of its political power to under-mind this great achievement, and are regaining their grip by trying to keep the old guard of racist politics intact and in control of this government.

During the height of the civil rights movement, we were on the verge of reforming the minds of many of these subhuman, savage, racist white slave-master conditioned minded ass niggers. And then, with the loss of some of our most influential leaders, the bottom began to fall out. Now, for this generation and onward, we desperately need leadership that will be effective in appealing to the minds of the Black masses. We need leadership that can appeal to the minds of these subhuman, racist, white slave-master conditioned minded ass, niggers to stop the gang violence of murdering and destroying their own race.

We need black leaders who have the inborn willingness to reach out with a voice that touches the entire heart and soul of black America and brings them back to the united, revolutionary fight against racist ass, white oppression in this country. But, if these violent and savage, subhuman minded ass niggers are hell-bent on not reforming, then right along with the racist ass, white man, into the pits of hell their illegitimate, treasonous asses should go. These violent, savage, racist ass, white, slave-master condition minded ass niggers are helping to harm our race and we have to face the difficult truth that the black race is responsible for their birth. Therefore, as a race, it is our responsibility for how we raise and nurture our children and not keep producing this sort of savage minded ass nigger who only exists to help the racist ass descendants of the racist ass, white, slave-master devour the black race.

As for those who are willing to receive the message of black brotherhood and sisterhood and let go of this racist ass, white, slave-master, brainwashed, condition minded, savage behavior, we should not fix our minds on totally condemning them because of their past transgressions. Instead, we should do everything within our power to help these niggers rehabilitate themselves back into the black, revolutionary fight and struggle against racist ass, white supremacy and oppression in this country.

The masses of niggers have to wake up from this mentally dead state of mind and become 100% dissatisfied with this racist ass, white system of power. Only then will we be able to gain back race unity and force a revolutionary change that will give us social, economic, and political power that we have been denied from the very beginning of slavery.

Let us not be fooled by all the condemnation we received from racist ass, white politicians and the racist ass, white news media about black-on-black crime in America. The racist ass, white man is very content to see niggers destroy themselves. And, the racist ass, white, news media exploits it in order to keep justifying the racist ass view existing within the white race that niggers exist only as an inferior minded, dependent race of savage criminals, living off of the honest, hard earned, economic achievements of the so-called, upstanding, white, all-American way of life.

At one point in the early stages of my adult life, I held this naïve and false notion that the only problem with racist ass, white people was their ignorance and lack of education on race relations. But, no black person should allow themselves to believe that the overwhelming, majority of racist ass, white people will ever change the racist ass attitudes that exist at the core of racist, white supremacy ideology. And, while it might hold true that most of these ignorant, back woods dwelling, racist ass, whites base their racism solely on the racial make-up of black people, we have to stop allowing ourselves to believe that intellectual, racist ass, whites are basing their racism solely on the same racist ass attitude.

Intellectual, racist ass whites are not failing at race relations because they somehow lack the infinite wisdom of not being able to see other human beings as individuals. They do not need niggers trying to tell them about their racist ass attitudes, beliefs, and behavior and, to continue doing so is just a waste of humanity's energy. They know exactly what they are doing and when black leaders try to point out human rights issues as if they don't know what they are doing, it insults their racist ass, white intellect. You see intellectual, racist ass, whites see racism not only as an attitude but an ideology. It's the method they use to gain and remain in power. It's the blueprint of how they built this institutionalized system of racist, white supremacy in this country.

It is this establishment of institutionalized racism that will continue keeping the doors of opportunity shut for African Americans. House nigger or not, I cannot respect the view of any black politician, civic leader, or news spokesperson who supports the position that institutionalized racism no longer exists in America. Just because the racist ass, white power structure was forced to take the signs of Jim Crow laws off of their exterior doors of white establishments, it didn't tear down its inner walls.

To continue preserving their all-American, white, racist ass way of life, they have to keep that inner wall firmly intact. They know this is vital for them to keep niggers out of the doors of opportunity, divided, and at war amongst ourselves. They still practice and rely on the same methods of slavery which kept blacks divided under their "nigger identity." But, in the end, which is more important for us, to continually be more concerned about our use of the "N" word within our black subculture, or be more concerned with how the racist ass, white man is trying to destroy us outside of it?

As for these gangbanging ass, nigger thugs helping the racist ass, white man destroy the black race, not one of these niggers throughout the urban ghettos of America is able to step out on center stage as a single leader of a powerful gang organization and command its followers to accept any nationwide code of truce among themselves. If these niggers were this well organized in defacto power as a credible threat to racist ass, white America, then, if not the Federal government, the State governments would seriously have to consider diplomatic discussions with them. All this racist ass, white man's system of law enforcement is concerned about is keeping these violent ass, subhuman, savage minded ass niggers contained in urban ghettos, for the purpose of helping destroy the black race. In reality, these gang banging, illegitimate ass, thug bastards against African unity and brotherhood are no more than a bunch of rogue niggers with gang affiliations, holding no loyalty outside of their own circles. These niggers are vicious predators preying upon their own community, while outside of their miniscule circles, everyone is prey.

For example, two groups of niggers with the same gang affiliation can be living in the same neighborhood on different blocks and could well be enemies. You see, these niggers do not live by some complex code that has the racist ass, white man fooled. The only thing that these niggers have the racist white man sold on is that we are a race full of criminal ass niggers with their mugshots exploited as the face that represents the entire black race. Tragically, some of our youngest and brightest minds are being lost and destroyed because of gangs and gang violence. The promise of our future generations cry out, demanding solutions in solving this grave problem. But, because of the ongoing gang violence of black-on-black crime and the rebellious and out of control behavior problems spilling over into both our communities, and urban, black schools, educating our youth has become one of the most difficult jobs in America, and finding qualified teachers willing to risk safety and sanity continues to be equally challenging.

I watched Chuck Todd, of Meet the Press, interview Spike Lee about the movie "Chi Raq." He asked Lee if he had an answer for all of the violent Black-on-black crime taking place in Chicago. Lee paused and then said he had no definitive answer for the senseless violence. But, Lee is not alone in this regard because these gang banging, subhuman behaving ass, violent niggers are so impressionable from day to day.

Many of these violent, juveniles, and young adult males committing violent crimes need to be committed for psychiatric treatment in a juvenile or an adult, prison, mental institution. It would not come as a surprise to find out that a very alarming percentage of them suffer with some type of special needs disability. Much of it being brought on before birth and the trauma of the environment that they have been birthed into. They exist as some of the most violent and cold-blooded murderers roaming our communities, but what makes them so dangerous along with the rest of these violent and murderous ass criminals, is that, with their deep mental imbalance, they have gained a very keen sense of how to exploit ways of fulfilling their own self-gratification under criminal influence. Apart from it, they are severely mentally detached from any real sense of accountability for their actions.

In this respect, their minds are so mentally deranged and under-developed in adult maturity that if even a penny was the mere obstacle standing between them and their own self-gratification, they would have no problem committing cold blooded murder to obtain that penny. After having lived most of my life in inner-city ghettos, regardless of what mental state of mind any of these violent ass niggers are in, one time is one too many of having had the eerie experience of crossing the path of these niggers without becoming a casualty.

It takes very little to influence or set these violent ass niggers off. These niggers are vicious, territorial predators and the masses of us niggers, who are not these violent, treacherous ass niggers, have become no more than prey on their feeding ground. The value of our lives literally means nothing to these wicked, hateful, envious, and violent niggers. They have no conscience and will not think twice about robbing and murdering for what they do not possess, regardless of whether it's out of poverty or greed. Slavery is at the root of having helped create this deeply disturbing problem along with continually devaluing black lives, is causing much of the violence and destruction being acted out by niggers. During slavery, the racist ass, white, slave-master was able to impose his barbaric will upon niggers within the slave quarters. He forced and conditioned them to act and breed like subhuman, savage animals. To this day, it has accelerated into these niggers imposing the same, barbaric behavior upon their race. These wild and psychopathic, insane, murderous ass, gang banging niggers have become no more than violent and vicious, roaming, wolf-pack predators seeking to devour their own race with the help and support of their racist ass, white slave-master.

These treacherous ass niggers not only beat and murder, they also seek a warped sense of recognition in doing so. Even though a movie like Lee's was made to shed more light and awareness on black-on-black violence and not from the lack of Lee's genuine effort, sadly and tragically it becomes counter-productive in reaching these violent, savage ass, niggers who strive on living up to the negatives of society and not the positives. These treacherous ass niggers would rather be perceived as "Chi Raq" or in the political sense, being compared to terrorist groups. These ignorant ass, savage niggers would rather live up to the image of terrorists within their own communities rather than denouncing it.

Slavery and the residuals of slavery are at the root of having created the negative, cultural atmosphere existing in urban, black ghettos. And, these racist, white, slave-master, brainwashed ass, savage niggers are a core product of it.

Slavery didn't allow for niggers to read books. In fact, slavery taught and conditioned niggers to despise education. Many of these niggers cannot read and comprehend at an elementary grade level and have no interest in reading literature. Therefore, it becomes very difficult to reach and educate these niggers by exposing them to book knowledge. Many of these violent, insane ass niggers are uneducated and mentally deficient derelicts constantly being exposed to the black market of illegal drugs and deadly firearms. Slavery and the residuals of slavery are at the root of having caused impoverished, socio-economic conditions that has left many among the Black masses without self-determination and the desire to pursue moral family values.

From the time of slavery in this country, the Black family has been the target of oppression, exploitation, denigration and destruction - all of which are overwhelming in causing the psychological problems for niggers that quickly leads to a lack of self-worth, despair, and hopelessness. I cannot stress enough the truth that the continual erosion of the black family is due mainly from slavery and the residuals of slavery. Poor socio-economic conditions has always been the main driving force behind the vicious and reoccurring cycle of crime and violence among niggers throughout the ghettos of urban America.

Slavery and the residuals of slavery are at the root of having produced this sick and dysfunctional cultural atmosphere in which niggers are continually becoming mentally dead to family values and the richness of their African heritage.

But, in spite of all the poverty and racist injustice, we are faced with on a daily basis, the masses of our race producing families must still learn how to build and hold onto family values. We have to fight like our African ancestors who were forced to America under slavery and under some of the worse conditions ever to be inflicted upon any race of people. They were willing to die before allowing slavery to rip apart their families and their family values. The masses of the Black race living in inner-city ghettos today must break free of being pulled down the same destructive path of these racist ass, white, slave-master condition minded ass niggers, who are abandoning their families both mentally and physically.

Slavery and poverty have so badly deprived niggers that it has caused us to become selfish with the little material things that we are somehow able to attain. We have become so obsessed with trying to obtain the little material gratification for ourselves that we do not understand the value of producing privilege for our children no matter how small.

When disciplining our children to manage privilege with responsibility, it becomes a very valuable tool in giving them a sense of self-importance and reassurance. This is exactly how whites use financial wealth and power to produce privilege for their children. But because of the history of slaver, poverty, and discrimination, this has become a value that's supposed to remain foreign for niggers and their children. It's one of the very reasons that niggers as a race have such a difficult time trying to sell our children on the value of education.

The white race, in control of the vast wealth of this country, tells their children to get an education by showing them the great empires of white America that they will be privileged to inherit. They tell them to look out across the nation and see the great empires that have been built for them to own and manage. This is what helps inspire white children to become educated. But, what empires do niggers own in this country as a race that will help inspire their children to become educated and then obtain privilege of ownership and management? Instead, the majority of our children look out across the nation from the desolation of inner-city ghettos and see only more ghettos of poverty and despair with dope dealers, pimps, hustlers, and gang leaders as their role models.

I ask you then, where are there any empires that niggers have built in this country for our youth to become inspired to become educated so that they might inherit and have the privilege of investment and ownership? What good is it for us to try and inspire our children to obtain an education when we, as a race, don't have a damn thing to show for it ourselves, but to offer them more inherited poverty and debt owed to the racist ass, white man? When our children look at us as though we are speaking a foreign language to them about obtaining an education, now we should know and understand why.

It's undoubtedly true that racism and poverty have the odds firmly stacked against us in prevailing over its evil forces. But, if we are to have any real chance at race stability, we must gain the mental strength and self-determination to overcome and overpower the odds. We must empower ourselves with family values and not allow the deprivation of material things to continue causing us to falter and lose faith in what we have within our own power to control. No matter how difficult poverty and racism makes the task of building our family values, we still have it within our power to do it. We owe it to our children to strive for change with the hope, faith and belief that by doing so they will have a fighting chance to survive and maintain their self-respect and dignity. We must unite together and make it happen if our children are to have a real chance at a bright and productive future. We must continue teaching them to not falter nor fall prey to all the evil temptation of committing violence and treachery because of continually being deprived of the greater portion of the material things within this racist ass, white society of America.

As I said, the only thing the racist element in this government is concerned about is keeping niggers contained in ghettos while we destroy ourselves. The racist ass, white man, sitting in the seat of political power, is only concerned about keeping niggers divided and at war amongst ourselves. The only thing that would ever concern the racist ass, white, political establishment is seeing niggers become unified and on a path of gaining real power in this country.

But, when ignorant ass niggers violently murder other niggers, then holler out, "kill the police," and "fuck the police," they are no more than a bunch of Judas ass, thug niggers with misguided attitudes and off the point messages on how to deal with the alarming, racist problem within the white police system of law enforcement. Take for example the release of the movie, "Straight Outta Compton," about NWA. In my opinion all a movie like this does is further mislead our urban, Black youth into destroying themselves as well as becoming victims of racist, white, police brutality. Because lawless ass niggers not willing to abide by any reasonable amount of lawful authority, are not the kind of niggers that should be allowed to guide or influence other niggers. We are not a race of niggers bent on anarchy.

We are a race bent on bringing order by rooting out racist ass, white politics within this system of government in order to gain the fullness of our freedom in America.

Even though the NWA movie at the end will have made millions of dollars, it should not be overlooked that the era surrounding the NWA 'gangsta rap' group was about a culture of gang banging ass, thug niggers committing violent crimes within their own communities while protesting racist, white, police brutality. It's all hypocrisy when these same gangsta rap niggers encourage, promote, and glorify the overwhelming and disturbing problem of black-on-black crime. In truth, the NWA movie is no more than an old, brushed off, rerun about the gang culture of the mid-eighties and nineties that unfortunately continues to spread decade after decade throughout urban, black America.

The making of the movie only exploits for financial gain, the deep racial divide of what has been occurring with racist ass, white, police brutality against niggers in this country. Movies of this sort do nothing to help find real solutions to the race problem between black America and white America. The movie only further promotes negative messages on how not to deal with the racist ass elements within law enforcement. As for the movie itself, you can be certain that white European power brokers at Universal Studios put a spin on the movie by promoting these niggers as being a socially conscience, radical, gangsta rap group striking out against a racist white system of injustice. It should not be surprising to find out that the making of the movie places white Europeans as the front-end financial benefactors and niggers as the back end financial benefactors, regardless of the amount of money that both will receive.

If anyone were to look at the real history of NWA, they would quickly learn that the group labeled themselves as violent, gangsta rap, thug ass niggers with no regard for their community nor society itself. Niggers have to understand that, in the end, this sort of violent rhetoric shit does nothing to help niggers overcome this racist ass, white system. First, it takes an immense effort in building moral family values along with education and the knowledge to formulate a plan to fight a system with a system. In the grand scheme of things, the racist ass, white man in the seat of economic and political power, thinks to himself that, at worst, as a threat, he only has to deal with a small pocket of unified and knowledgeable, informed, un-brainwashed, intellectual niggers. But, at best, he thinks confidently to himself that the masses of us are either mostly sellouts, uneducated, dumb, ignorant, destitute ass niggers, and pose no real threat to anyone but ourselves. Tragically, it is so difficult for African American leadership to persuade the black masses to invest their minds into education. The problem is due mainly because niggers have been ideologically brainwashed into believing that education and knowledge is not African inspired and is solely the creation of the white man's mind.

If you take stock in biblical history, go to Genesis, chapter 10, verse 8 and follow the exploits of Nimrod, a great, black ruler. Even the black Shemetic family of Abraham is from a region that was once a part of this great, black king's vast empire. The very root of Genesis unfolds with the creation and exploit of niggers. Follow the path of Noah's three sons, Ham, Shem, and Japheth, and you will discover that Japheth is the only one of these three niggers given credit for having been the progenitor of the white race. Whites certainly could not have been responsible for the diversity of the human race, seeing how whites do not have the necessary melanin in their skin for pigmentation. However, melanin is abundant within the genetic makeup of niggers.

Instead of just rejecting this racist ass ideology of white supremacy, the slave mentality has conditioned niggers into rejecting education and knowledge itself. But if the masses of us Western civilization ass niggers were to become fully aware of our great African heritage and history, we would have an easier time understanding that when Africans with knowledge of our rich heritage stress the value of education, it is because they know how important it is as we were the first ones to inspire it. In fact, it was the path of the black man that the white man followed to civilization.

They followed it to ancient Egypt in ancient Mesopotamia of the Babylonian and Sumerian Empire. They followed Black Moors' civilization in Spain from about 710AD and lasting nearly 800 years. They followed Black Moors' rule in Timbuktu, in West Africa, which became the center of world civilization and learning when the Renaissance in Europe was just starting and Europe was trying to pull itself out of medieval existence. Niggers have to un-brainwash themselves from rejecting education and knowledge because of their misguided attitudes of having been deceived into not wanting anything to do with it because of the false representation of racist ass white's claim of having been the first to own it.

So, when a nigger hears an African, who knows his history stress education and knowledge, just remember that we are the authors of it. Niggers have to get rid of this racist ass, white supremacy ideology, brainwashing idea of believing that the foundation of education and knowledge was laid by whites. And while it holds true that racist, white supremacy, ideology has masterfully whitewashed nearly the entire world through history books and mass media technology, the cause and effect shouldn't be that niggers become brainwashed into taking on an inferior complex. Aside from music, sports, comedy, and some exceptions within the movie industry, be it from lack of choice or conditioning, niggers gravitate towards white entertainment.

While bringing this out into the open, I see nothing wrong with any culture gravitating towards the enrichment of other cultures. The racist ass, white man certainly did it at the beginning of our culture and without openly acknowledging it are still greatly influenced by the creativity of our culture. But, as for this racist, white, supremacy, ideology brainwashing, niggers should tell the racist ass, white man to take his racist, white, supremacy ego and shove it up his racist, white, unappreciative, snake ass, and not forget that black civilization played a vital role in helping shape and build his culture.

What niggers have to do is: organize, mobilize, and then have the ultimate revival that connects us to the very root of our great African heritage. We have to have the kind of black, revolutionary revival that picks up the way the abolitionist movement and the civil rights movement began in the 50s and the 60s. We need the kind of revival that will transform us into becoming a great and powerful, black nation and force to be reckoned with and not just a movement that forces gradual progress or change and then loses its momentum no sooner than the racist ass, white, power structure establishes ploys to undermine it. So, unlike these savage ass, mentally dead minded, racist ass, white, slave-master condition minded ass niggers, we must decide if we are to be destroyed or if we will prevail.

In defense of the black reformers of the post slave era and for those of us who continue to support their position, I firmly believe that the gap dividing our position on the uses of the "N" word should never be bridged. By keeping a moral objection to the "N" word to never be accepted within the mainstream of society, means that there will never be any tolerance or acceptance of racist ass whites to think that they can openly label us as niggers.

Even so, the reality is we will never change the racist ass, white man's mind about seeing us as a bunch of worthless, ignorant ass, niggers, falsely blaming him for all of the ills that we are facing in this society. But again, as for our usage of the "N" word, you have to remember that our African ancestors became defiant and rebellious under their "nigger identity."

Chapter Nineteen

Summation

Not only have I explained from my own perspective, why we have the nigger word so embedded in our culture, I have also used the nigger word to help lay out the ongoing history of white racism against African Americans.

I feel that the black reformers, during the post slavery era, was on the right path in trying to reform blacks to sever any ties to the slave culture. But, if those same, Black reformers during that time could have lived to the present they would see that the "nigger identity" still has the same racial divide among blacks that it held during slavery. They would also see that the nigger word has taken root within our culture like an irresistible force.

But, regardless of what interpretation blacks have about the usage of the "N" word, it will be blacks alone who will forever remain set apart by the racist ass, white man as niggers to be despised more than any other race of people in the world. It is important that I note here that, during the writing of this essay it was never my purpose or effort to try and argue for the acceptance of the 'N' word within our culture. It's a far gone conclusion that the 'N' word will not be uprooted from our black sub-culture. And, therefore, I have neither tried to argue for or against its usage.

Part of my effort has been to explain why we have not abandoned its usage from the beginning of slavery until the present. It has also been my effort to explain why whites are forever forbidden to call us niggers.

I have also tried to give my own social, economic, and political perspective as to where I stand on the issue of our historical and racial struggle in this country under the "nigger identity." I have made a clear and conscious effort to take the race conflict between black America and white America off the politically correct platform. But, hopefully, not in the same shallow and biased way that it has been used to justify racist hate in politics. I have not wasted my energy and effort by attempting to carry out some race appeasing ass effort of trying to find acceptance from blacks or whites on how I have chosen to handle this issue. I have made a conscious effort not to put some sort of superficial, cosmetic affect or spin on this issue dealing with the racial conflict between white America and black America. The central body of this work is about the ongoing history of slavery and racism in this country against African Americans.

I have also tried to clear up much of the controversy surrounding our usage of the "N" word in support of how I use it between these pages. And, just as I stated during my introduction, I have made a conscious effort to use the "N" word in such a way as to allow white America to look into the shadows and see the hidden ways in which we look at ourselves seeing racist ass, white America see us as niggers with the deep, historical, racial divide and conflict behind it. Even though our usage of the "N" word will continue to be debated and seen as a contradiction to our moral stance against racism, it is my belief that it is not a contradiction as to why whites are forbidden to use it. Again, our use of the "N" word could be seen as a paradox that reveals even more truths about the cruel and evil history of slavery.

Racist ass, white, hypocritical devils should never be allowed to misconstrue our usage of the "N" word as condoning their racist, white asses for all their evil and wicked deeds of slavery. The entire problem and racial conflict is not about some standoffish argument and simple amusement by the racist ass descendants of the racist ass, white, slave-master questioning us as to why they are no longer allowed to call us niggers while the descendants of ex-slaves continue to hold to their own expression and meaning of its usage. These racist ass, white supremacist bastards refuse to understand any of the devastation of how slavery affected us. The "nigger identity" is a much deeper and complex problem stemming from and dealing with the history of slavery and racism in this country. And the racist ass, white descendants of the racist ass, white, slave-master needs to be made fully aware of it.

By getting to the root of the "N" word and how it became connected to our African ancestors under slavery, our usage of it is not a contradiction when we tell whites that they are forbidden to use it.

I find it very difficult to believe that any white person in their right, non-racist, common sense mind would dare take our usage of the "N" word as grounds for racial discord between blacks and whites - something which must be internally resolved if we are to continue our efforts in launching an effective attack against racism and racist ass, white supremacy in this country. Regardless of any forthcoming criticism and argument on how I have handled this subject, I stand firmly on the position that I have not been partial on my attack on both, the external, racist problems with white America, or the internal, destructive problems of black America.

In conclusion, it has been my attempt to put together an effective and compelling argument on why blacks use the "N" word and whites are forbidden. I have used both positions to dig deeper into the ongoing, historical, racial divide and conflict between both races. I hope that my explanation will help close this ongoing debate over why we use the "N" word while whites are forbidden. In earnest, I have tried to have an honest conversation about race in such a way that is both taboo and extremely politically incorrect. But, just as I said earlier, not being done to try and justify the use of racist ass language or race denigration in politics. So, my hope is that it brings out many of our real and hidden attitudes, feelings and behaviors about race so that we might in the same vein of honesty, start dealing with these issues as well as finding ways to finally start resolving them.

The black and white race, in spite of all our racial differences, find ourselves in a unique position of having the racial makeup of all the other races between us. Even though we are mankind's two polar opposite races in regards to our own racial make-up, if we would work to bridge the gap and end our race war within this world, I believe that it would also work in leading us onto a more stable course of co existence with all of humanity.

There exists one undeniable and unchallenged power of truth about mankind. We are all born into physical life. But, unlike the divine transformation of Enoch into heaven, we cannot escape physical death. It's what we do in-between - as human beings - that makes the quality of life sustainable for all planetary existence.

Only time and further examination by my critics will tell if I am on the mark or have strayed further off of it concerning the indifferent attitudes and behavior still facing both races of which we are struggling to overcome.

* * * * * * *

References

Article One of the United States Constitution. (n.d.). Retrieved September 24, 2016, from https://en.wikipedia.org/wiki/Article_One_of_the_United_States_Constitution#Slave_trade.

Battle of Black Jack. (n.d.). Retrieved September 24, 2016, from https://en.wikipedia.org/wiki/Battle_of_Black_Jack.

Battle of Osawatomie. (n.d.). Retrieved September 24, 2016, from https://en.wikipedia.org/wiki/Battle_of_Osawatomie.

Fernandez, M., PÉrez-peÑa, R., & Bromwich, J. E. (2016, July 08). Five Dallas Officers Were Killed as Payback, Police Chief Says. Retrieved September 25, 2016, from http://www.nytimes.com/2016/07/09/us/dallas-police-shooting.html?_r=0.

Consummation of the Ages vol I. (n.d.). 155. Retrieved from https://books.google.com/books?id=H63oAwAAQBAJ.

Epps, H., Jr. (n.d.). Consummation of the Ages vol I. Retrieved September 24, 2016, from https://books.google.com/books?id=H63oAwAAQBAJ.

John Brown (abolitionist). (n.d.). Retrieved September 24, 2016, from en.wikipedia.org/wiki/John_Brown.

John Brown | HistoryNet. (n.d.). Retrieved September 25, 2016, from http://www.historynet.com/john-brown.

John Punch (slave). (n.d.). Retrieved from https://en.wikipedia.org/wiki/John_Punch_(slave).

Latest on the Alton Sterling shooting investigation. (2016, July 11). Retrieved September 25, 2016, from http://www.cbsnews.com/news/the-latest-on-the-alton-sterling-shooting-investigation-baton-rouge/.

Nigger. (n.d.). Retrieved August 17, 2016, from https://en.wikipedia.org/wiki/Nigger.

Race and ethnicity in the United States. (n.d.). Retrieved September 25, 2016, from https://en.wikipedia.org/wiki/Race_and_ethnicity_in_the_United_States#White_Americans.

References (cont'd)

Shapiro, R. T., Bever, L., Lowery, W., & Miller, M. E. (2016, July 9). Police group: Minn. governor 'exploited what was already a horrible and tragic situation'. Retrieved September 25, 2016, from https://www.washingtonpost.com/news/morning-mix/wp/2016/07/07/minn-cop-fatally-shoots-man-during-traffic-stop-aftermath-broadcast-on-facebook/.

Slavery in the United States. (n.d.). Retrieved from https://en.wikipedia.org/wiki/Slavery_in_the_United_States#The_end_of_slavery.

Vesser, S. (2016, July 18). 3 officers killed; 3 injured in Baton Rouge. Retrieved September 25, 2016, from http://www.cnn.com/2016/07/17/us/baton-route-police-shooting/.

Williams, C. (2012, February 29). [OPINION] Nigger: 500 Years and Counting. Retrieved September 24, 2016, from http://www.ebony.com/news-views/n-word#axzz4LC7MVHQS.

www.tribalnationisrael.com

www.ingramcontent.com/pod-product-compliance
Lightning Source LLC
LaVergne TN
LVHW051515080426
835509LV00017B/2068